Danes in North America

Danes
in North America

❖

Edited by Frederick Hale

UNIVERSITY OF WASHINGTON PRESS

Seattle and London

Library of Congress Cataloging in Publication Data
Hale, Frederick.
  Danes in North America.

  Bibliography: p.
  Includes index.
  1. Danish Americans—History—Sources.   2. Danish
Americans—History.   I. Title.
E184.S19H24 1984   973'.043981   83-17077
ISBN 0-295-96089-2 (alk. paper)

This book was published with the assistance of grants from the National Endowment for the Humanities and the Andrew W. Mellon
Foundation.

Contents

Preface

The history of Danish immigrants in North America is an almost virgin field of research. It has received scant scholarly attention from modest beginnings at the turn of the century until the 1970s when the reawakening of ethnic consciousness belatedly stimulated the founding of the Danish American Heritage Society. Professional interest in Danish-Americans lags far behind that in other Scandinavians in the New World. The reputable Norwegian-American Historical Association, for instance, came into being in 1925; during its more than half-century existence, it has published several dozen books and hundreds of articles analyzing the history of Norwegian immigrants in the United States and Canada. Similarly, the Swedish Pioneer Historical Society, born in the 1950s, publishes a respectable quarterly journal and at least one book annually. Finnish-American history, for linguistic reasons formidable to most scholars, has made great strides in recent years, owing to the goundbreaking efforts of historians in North America as well as Finland.

In contrast to these achievements, study of the Danish immigrants has progressed at a glacial pace until very recently. Beginning in the 1890s a handful of amateur historians dabbled in it, but, usually lacking methodological competence and a grasp of the wider context of American history, they produced a small corpus of works almost invariably too narrowly focused to attract or be of value to either a scholarly or a general readership. Moreover, inauspicious choices of provincial publishers have relegated nearly all of their studies to obscurity. Relatively few scholars with doctoral training, such as Marion Marzolf, William Mulder, Paul Nyholm, and Donald Watkins, have managed to avoid these pitfalls, and even they have found it challenging to work in a field that has lain fallow so long, because pertinent materials are so widely scattered. In the late 1970s the Danish American Heritage Society began to publish a modest journal, The Bridge, *which may eventually become a significant vehicle for historical articles. The same organization has undertaken a project to catalog relevant archival material. Nevertheless, it*

*will unquestionably be many years before research on Danes in North America
yields an abundant harvest of mature findings.*

*Several related factors have severely retarded and continue to hinder the
development of Danish-American studies. The most important is perhaps the
geographical and cultural diffusion of Danes in the United States. While the
Norwegians, to use the most appropriate comparison, settled heavily in Minnesota and the surrounding states and founded several thriving colleges that
today serve as archival centers for that immigrant group's history, the Danes
spread relatively evenly throughout the northern United States. Only a few
areas, such as Racine County, Wisconsin, and certain communities in western
Iowa and eastern Nebraska, have ever been distinctively Danish. A small
number of tiny colleges and theological seminaries were founded, but most
soon closed their doors and the remaining two, Dana College in Blair, Nebraska, and Grand View College in Des Moines, Iowa, have demonstrated
only meager interest in preserving their ethnic heritage. Furthermore, the broad
settlement pattern of Danish immigrants helped to erode their ethnic identity.
This was another reason why they failed to found a historical society or open
an archive. Consequently, much of the existing material necessary for serious
research is scattered in scores of repositories from Denmark to Hawaii.*

*In another sense, however, Danes who emigrated to North America un-
knowingly eased the historian's task by writing millions of letters to friends,
relatives, and newspapers in their native land. The vast majority of these
documents were soon destroyed, but a surprisingly large number still exist,
although many of them have been squirreled away, unintentionally shrouded
from the researcher's inquisitive eye. When disinterred from such repositories
as the Royal Library in Copenhagen and the Danes Worldwide Archives in
Ålborg, or retrieved from the musty back files of the Danish press, these accounts testify vividly to a new life in the New World. They tell of immigrants'
aspirations and apprehensions, successes and joys, homesickness and American patriotism, disillusionment and defeat.*

*In the present volume, I have sought to further professional study of and
awaken popular interest in the history of Danish-Americans by presenting a
representative cross-section of these "America letters." It is intended to parallel
to a considerable degree H. Arnold Barton's* Letters from the Promised
Land: Swedes in America, 1840–1914, *and Theodore C. Blegen's collection of Norwegian-American correspondence,* Land of Their Choice:
The Immigrants Write Home. *Most of the letters I have selected are mun-
dane, relating the misery of transatlantic passage in steerage, the workaday
life of a packing plant employee in Omaha, the infatuation of a teenage girl*

in New Jersey, or the entrepreneurship of a farmboy on the threshold of man-hood in western Canada. Others, however, convey the sudden death of a lum-berjack, near-starvation in Arizona, and disdain for certain other ethnic groups. Yet none are sensationalistic. Admittedly, few immigrants were capable of relating their experiences in a consistently objective manner, and some could not resist the temptation to exaggerate their exploits and either the opportu-nities or the hardships of life in North America. Throughout, I have considered plausibility when selecting a wide spectrum of letters that reflect the immigrant experience from the Atlantic crossing to eventual assimilation or disenchant-ment with life in the New World.

In translating these documents I have generally followed precedents estab-lished in the parallel volumes edited by Blegen, Barton, and other historians of immigration. Rendering nineteenth-century Danish into modern idiomatic English poses few if any insurmountable problems. In some instances, how-ever, difficulties arise from archaic units of measure; wherever possible these have been converted into meaningful ones, though this has occasionally ne-cessitated approximations. Throughout I have sought to retain the tone and degree of formality or informality of the original letters. Many words were not necessary to translate, for Danish-Americans, like other immigrants, quickly picked up the habit of sprinkling their letters with English terms. All of these have been italicized.

This project could not have been completed without the support and assis-tance of several individuals and organizations during a period of four years. I began my research in Danish immigrant history as a Marshall Fellow at the University of Copenhagen in 1975 and 1976. A fellowship from the National Endowment for the Humanities and a summer grant from the American Philosophical Society allowed me to complete it in 1979. I wish to thank the personnel at the Royal Library in Copenhagen, the libraries of the Universities of Århus, Copenhagen, and Oslo, and the Danes Worldwide Ar-chives in Ålborg for their unfailing courtesy and assistance. Jens N. Nielsen of Brabrand, Denmark, rendered invaluable aid in locating immigrant letters printed in provincial newspapers. Professors Timothy Smith of The Johns Hopkins University, H. Arnold Barton of Southern Illinois University, and Marion Marzolf of the University of Michigan, as well as the Danish par-liamentary librarian Kristian Hvidt and Kenneth O. Bjork of the Norwegian-American Historical Association encouraged the undertaking and advised me at several stages. To all I owe a profound debt of gratitude.

Introduction

Between the middle of the nineteenth century and the outbreak of World War I in 1914, approximately three hundred thousand Danes emigrated to the United States and Canada. By Scandinavian standards Denmark lost relatively few of her native sons and daughters. Norway, whose population in absolute figures and rate of increase was similar, sent about seven hundred fifty thousand people to the New World during the same period, while more than 1.1 million Swedes left their considerably larger fatherland. But the intensity of emigration from Denmark—the percentage of the national population that departed—was greater than from Germany or Russia, for example, or even from Italy before the 1890s. On the other hand, the exodus of Danes was miniscule compared to that of the Irish; the Emerald Isle's population of roughly 8 million in 1840 was halved by the turn of the century. Perhaps Norway, whose intensity of emigration was the highest in continental Europe and approximately twice that of Denmark's, offers a more meaningful comparison. The percentage of Swedes who departed lay about midway between that of Danes and Norwegians.[1]

The prime mover in Denmark was rapid population growth, a phenomenon common to nearly all European countries in the nineteenth century. Improvements in health care, coupled with a not fully explained increase in fertility, lifted the number of Danes from fewer than a million in 1800 to over 2.8 million by World War I. The rural economy was unable to accommodate such an explosion, especially during that era of rising economic expectations. Consequently, several hundred thousand landless peasants were compelled to leave their agrarian life and seek to improve their status elsewhere. The majority drifted into the cities. Copenhagen, for ex-

---

1. The most convenient study of Danish emigration in English is Kristian Hvidt, *Flight to America: The Social Background of 300,000 Danish Emigrants* (New York: Academic Press, 1975). For an even more detailed study, see Hvidt's *Flugten til Amerika eller Drivkræfter i masseudvandringen fra Danmark 1868–1914* (Århus: Universitetsforlaget, 1971).

ample, grew from two hundred thousand in 1870 to nearly five hundred thousand by the end of the century. Both Århus and Ålborg trebled between 1860 and 1900.

For many, however, the flight to the city proved to be only the first leg of a journey to North America. Indeed, the intensity of emigration from Danish cities was approximately twice as high as that from rural areas. The Industrial Revolution came to Denmark chiefly in the 1860s and 1870s, slightly later than to Germany, but a decade or two earlier than to Sweden or Norway. Copenhagen and some of the larger provincial towns became important centers of light industry, but the generally small factories that became fixtures on the urban landscape proved incapable of employing the vast influx of peasants. Emigration consequently served as a safety valve, both for the natural increase of the urban population and for rural migrants whose hopes of prosperity in the burgeoning cities were disappointed. The urban experience of many Danish-Americans in their native country may have eased somewhat their transition to city life in the United States.

Another noteworthy characteristic of emigration from Denmark and many other countries was the numerical dominance of men. Female Danes were relatively scarce in the United States, especially before the fourth quarter of the nineteenth century. Between 1868 and 1900 slightly over 60 percent of all emigrating Danes were males.[2] This disproportion became a matter of concern to many of these immigrants, who expressed their longing for Danish girls in countless letters. In the "old country," concomitantly, the resulting surplus of women lasted well into the twentieth century.

Closely related to sexual distribution was the familial structure of Danish emigration. While the records usually do not indicate the marital status of those who left Denmark, passenger lists often reveal families migrating together, especially before the flight to America crested in 1882. After that time, though, family emigration became the exception; between 1868 and 1900 unmarried adults outnumbered married adults by almost three to one. During the same period children constituted 18 percent of all Danish emigrants.[3] One factor that lowered the percentage of married couples in the exodus was the steadily declining average age of people leaving Denmark. Those in their early twenties were always a plurality, and they stead-

---

2. Hvidt, *Flight to America*, p. 83.
3. Ibid., p. 92.

ily widened their lead over older emigrants, while teenagers became the second largest group after 1882.[4]

Because they came from the cities as well as rural districts, Danish emigrants spanned much of the professional spectrum. The largest group of men, not surprisingly, were farmhands; during the last thirty-two years of the nineteenth century 43.2 percent fell into that category. Fewer than a tenth of that number (3.4 percent), on the other hand, had been smallholders. Most of the rest were either unskilled laborers unable to find work in Danish factories or craftsmen who could not compete with mass production methods.[5]

Not all who left Denmark were economically dislocated, however. An incalculable but undoubtedly small number sought adventure, of which there was little in this docile Scandinavian country. Perhaps education played a role in stimulating such people's imaginations; during the nineteenth century Denmark changed from a relatively illiterate society into a land where nearly everyone could at least minimally read and write. Adventuresomeness is difficult to measure, though, so one of the few ways to begin to understand why some Danes traded secure homes for the uncertainties of the New World is to read the letters and accounts, such as those written by Torben Lange, Alfred Bjørnbak, and Cathrine Møller, included in this volume.

Religion was not a factor in most Danes' decision to emigrate. The Danish constitution of 1849 preserved the Lutheran state church while granting dissenting bodies a considerable degree of toleration, if not complete freedom. During the next generation evangelistic "returned emigrants" and others from the United States and Britain planted Methodist, Baptist, Irvingite, Adventist, and other Anglo-American denominations on the spiritual landscape of Denmark, while revivalistic Lutheran communions sprang up from within and separated from the established church.[6] Many Lutheran pastors and lay leaders resented the incursions of free evangelists, but their attacks were hardly strong enough to drive Protestant nonconformists to America.

For Danish converts to the Church of Jesus Christ of Latter-day Saints,

4. Ibid., p. 78.
5. Ibid., pp. 112–16.
6. No satisfactory study of religious pluralism in Denmark exists. The best treatment, although not fully reliable, is Michael Neiiendam, *Frikirker og Sekter*, 4th ed. (Copenhagen: G.E.C. Gads Forlag, 1958).

or Mormonism, however, the situation was much different. Mormon missionaries began to proselytize in Denmark in the early 1850s and baptized
more than twenty thousand people there by the end of the century. The vast
majority of these converts had been members of the state church, although
a significant number of proselytes came from Baptist congregations.[7] The
Mormon practice of polygamy as well as several of its theological doctrines
soon came under heavy attack, and a barrage of vituperative anti-Mormon
literature was circulated in Denmark to counter the embarrassing success
of the missionary effort. Social ostracization no doubt pressured some of
the Danish converts to emigrate, but the Mormon teaching of a gathering
in the "Zion" of Utah was clearly a stronger factor in drawing more than
half of them to the American West.

The Danish conflict with Germany played a clearer role in fostering
emigration. Until 1864 the provinces of Holstein and Schleswig were linked
with Denmark through a personal union with the Danish crown. In that
year, however, a joint military venture by Prussia and Austria wrested
away those ethnically and linguistically mixed areas. The defeat caused
widespread national pessimism and engendered a lingering fear of further
Bismarckian encroachment among the Danes. Moreover, it exacerbated the
anti-German strain that had been evident in Danish nationalism for many
years. In the conquered provinces a program of Germanization was initiated as part of Bismarck's consolidation of the newly assembled Reich.
No doubt owing to this, approximately sixty thousand Danish-speaking people left North Schleswig during the first forty years after the annexation.[8]

Emigration was big business. Long before the tide of America-bound
Danes crested, many of their nonemigrating countrymen as well as foreigners had begun to profit from the mass exodus, which they encouraged
through various means of enveiglement. Most obviously, of course, the
shipping companies profited from the tremendous increase in transatlantic
passenger traffic. By the 1870s, when the transition from sails to steam
was nearly complete, several foreign steamship companies vied for the prospective Danish emigrants. They included, among many others, German
concerns such as HAPAG and North German Lloyd, and the major British
Cunard, Inman, and White Star lines. In 1879, immediately before emigra-

7. William Mulder, Homeward to Zion: The Mormon Migration from Scandinavia (Minneapolis: University of Minnesota Press, 1957), is an excellent study of the topic that
gives the Danes extensive coverage.

8. Hvidt, Flight to America, p. 39.

tion from Scandinavia peaked, the Danish Thingvalla Line was founded, providing an alternative for nationalists who preferred not to travel on foreign vessels.

Most of the actual recruiting was done by emigration agents who represented these firms and, occasionally, American railroads, land companies, and state governments seeking to attract immigrants. Stationed not only in Copenhagen but also in most of the important provincial towns, these agents tempted prospective emigrants with a steady stream of propaganda that described the New World in roseate terms. They established a vast network of subagents who served a similar function in smaller communities. Some, such as the notorious Mogens Abraham Sommer, made several transatlantic voyages accompanying the emigrants whom they had recruited. Depending on such factors as honesty and the degree of personal service rendered, the agents earned either praises or curses from the new Americans.

For many the transatlantic voyage was the most traumatic phase of the emigration experience. The minority who booked passage on the Thingvalla Line sailed directly from Copenhagen to New York. Most migrating Danes, however, had to travel by rail to Hamburg or Bremen, if they were to travel on a German vessel, or sail first to northeastern England (usually to Hull), take the train to Liverpool, and sail to America from there. Occasionally Danes booked with Norwegian or Swedish ships and thereby gained the opportunity to see a bit of Oslo (before 1925 called Christiania) or Göteborg, but most found it more convenient and economical to use Danish, English, or German lines. The crossing itself lasted from ten days to two weeks after the advent of steam power, but normally three or four times that long in the days of sailing vessels. The vast majority who emigrated could afford nothing better than steerage accommodations. The ticket, which cost approximately thirty dollars,[9] usually ensured crowded conditions and often meant unpleasant food, seasickness, mistreated baggage, and bad relations with surly, exploitative crew members as well.

After landing in the United States, usually in New York City, Danish immigrants scattered more widely than other Scandinavian-Americans or, for that matter, most other ethnic groups. A relatively large number remained in New York or found employment in nearby northern New Jersey. The terra cotta works in Perth Amboy, for example, were partly owned and managed by Danes who hired several thousand of their countrymen.

9. Hvidt, *Flugten til Amerika*, p. 457.

Many more, however, settled in the Midwest. To the extent that a Danish center existed in the United States, it was a belt reaching from eastern Wisconsin and Chicago across the southern counties of Wisconsin and Minnesota and much of Iowa into Nebraska. Important settlements began at Racine, Neenah, and New Denmark, Wisconsin, as early as the 1840s, as did the Danish community in Chicago. From these focal points Danes gradually drifted westward, founding such colonies as those in Shelby County, Iowa, in the mid-1860s and Dannebrog, Nebraska, during the following decade. Along the way they concentrated in Minneapolis, St. Paul, Omaha, and Council Bluffs. The names of several smaller towns in the belt, such as West Denmark, Wisconsin, or Ringsted and St. Ansgar, Iowa, betray the part Danes played in their origins.

Statistically, Iowa was for some time the most Danish state. According to the census of 1910, 10.4 percent of all Danish-Americans lived there, while 9.6 percent were in Wisconsin and 9.4 percent in Minnesota. These small percentages are themselves evidence of the dispersed nature of the group. By contrast, 28.6 percent of the Norwegian immigrants and 19.6 percent of the Swedes lived in Minnesota at that time.[10]

Outside this Midwestern zone there were several Danish pockets of varying size. Clearly the most important of these was Utah, which attracted most of the Mormon proselytes who left Denmark. In Michigan, the area around Greenville became a gathering point, as did the lumber town of Manistee on the eastern shore of Lake Michigan. Some Danes caught "Washington fever" in the 1880s and 1890s and moved to the Pacific Northwest, especially to Puget Sound, but the Danes in that area numbered far fewer than the Norwegians and Swedes there. California attracted far more, and today more Americans of Danish ancestry live there than in any other state. North and South Dakota, on the other hand, drew few Danes, although both states already had rapidly growing Norwegian populations when admitted to the Union in 1889.

Because they were a small minority group in almost every American community where they settled, and owing to the sexual imbalance, male Danish immigrants often chose non-Danish wives. Most frequently they turned to the large German-American group for their spouses. The census of 1910 revealed that more than ten thousand of the Americans with Danish immigrant fathers had German mothers. Swedish-Danish offspring were the secondmost frequent

10. Hvidt, *Flight to America*, p. 167.

combination, with Norwegian-Danish a close third. Apparently romantic at-
traction meant more to many newcomers from Denmark than did their native
land's suspicion of Bismarck's Reich. *Only 57 percent of the children with*
at least one Danish immigrant parent were of purely Danish descent.[11] In-
termarriage probably further weakened the Danes' sense of ethnic identity and
accelerated the process of assimilation that their settlement pattern had begun.

As was the case in most immigrant communities, some Danes resisted the
cultural transition and sought to preserve a measure of their Old World iden-
tity. One of the first efforts was the formation of the Dania Society, a self-
help organization founded in Chicago during the Civil War. Initially pan-
Scandinavian, it soon became exlusively Danish when the Norwegian and
Swedish members seceded to form their own clubs. In addition to purely social
programs, Dania administered a health insurance scheme, collected funds for
assisting Denmark after the defeat of 1864, helped newcomers secure em-
ployment in the Windy City, and rendered other services to ease the transition
of Danes to life in a booming American metropolis. Similar organizations
were spawned within a few years in Racine, New York, Minneapolis, and
several other cities.[12] On the national level, an immigrant insurance company
in Omaha was reconstituted as the Danish Brotherhood in America in 1882.
It soon became the largest secular society for Danish immigrants and is still
thriving today. Smaller local and regional associations were founded to serve
musical, athletic, literary, and other interests.

The churches also served as rallying points for a minority of these immi-
grants, although their role in preserving ethnic heritage was ambiguous. The
first congregations that American Danes formed were neither exclusively Dan-
ish nor related to the established Lutheran church in Denmark. Beginning
in the 1850s Christian Willerup and a Norwegian, Ole Petersen, gathered
several Scandinavian Methodist congregations, chiefly in the Midwest. These
local bodies coalesced in 1880 to form what was later called the Norwegian-
Danish Conference, which enjoyed close ties with English-speaking Meth-
odists until the ethnic unit was absorbed in the 1960s.[13] Only slightly later
Danish immigrants began to organize Baptist congregations, especially in
Wisconsin and Minnesota. These bodies also included many Norwegians. Like

11. Hvidt, *Flugten til Amerika,* pp. 314–15.
12. Philip Friedman, "The Danish Community of Chicago, 1860–1920" (Master's thesis, Northwestern University, 1976), chap. IV.
13. Arlow W. Andersen, *The Salt of the Earth: A History of Norwegian-Danish Meth-odism in America* (Nashville, Tenn.: Parthenon Press, 1962).

the Scandinavian Methodists, the Baptists relied on the existing American denomination for financial assistance and ministerial education for several decades. The same can be said of Danish Seventh-day Adventists and scattered independent congregations, which became one root of the Evangelical Free Church of America. Some Danish converts to all of these denominations returned to their native country to proclaim their new faiths, strengthening religious pluralism there.

By the 1870s Danes who desired to preserve their native Lutheran heritage began to form churches in North America. Several factors made this task relatively difficult. First, the settlement pattern of these immigrants had scattered the few Danes who were spiritually active. Consequently, congregations often had to include members from several communities, often quite far from one another. Moreover, many pastors had to minister to a number of scattered flocks. Second, the state church of Denmark, although repeatedly expressing interest in supporting missionary work among Danes abroad, had neither the funds nor the clergymen to do so effectively. Finally, a de facto schism that had existed within the established church in Denmark since the 1860s was soon reflected among the Danish pastors in America, cleaving their limited resources and making it impossible for them to launch and maintain a united evangelistic effort. Since the 1870s, therefore, the Danish Lutheran tradition in the United States has always been divided into two denominations.

The first of these to exist as an autonomous organization was the Danish Evangelical Lutheran Church in America, founded in 1872. Several of its early pastors had been active in the wing of the Danish state church inspired by the views of Nikolai Frederik Severin Grundtvig (1783–1872), the distinguished theologian, forklorist, and psalmist. Like their mentor, they were liturgically formal and tended to subordinate the Bible to the Apostles' Creed and the sacraments. The "Danish Church," as the denomination was popularly called, opened a theological seminary at West Denmark, Wisconsin, in 1887 and Grand View College in Des Moines, Iowa, nine years later. Several of its leaders were instrumental in transplanting to America the "folk high school" movement that Grundtvig had initiated. In these schools young Danes were taught several traditional academic subjects as well as the Danish language in a Christian environment. Through these schools the Danish Church sought to preserve the best of its national heritage while educating the children of immigrants in the New World. In 1962 the denomination, which had nearly twenty-four thousand members and had changed its name to the American Evangelical Luthern Church, merged with several synods of immigrant

German, Swedish, and Finnish ancestry to form the Lutheran Church in America.[14]

Many pietistic Danish immigrants opposed the Danish Church. Temporarily united with like-minded Norwegians in the Conference for the Norwegian-Danish Evangelical Lutheran Church in America, they seceded in 1884 to form what was eventually called the United Evangelical Lutheran Church. The same year they opened Trinity Seminary and Dana College at Blair, Nebraska. This denomination, popularly known as the "Blair Church," emphasized Biblical authority, revivalism, the necessity of conversion, and strict personal morals. Somewhat larger than the quasi-Grundtvigian Danish Church, it was absorbed in the merger of 1960 that formed the American Lutheran Church.[15]

The Danish immigrant press, like the group's religious organizations, was partly intertwined with that of Norwegian newcomers. The similarity of their written languages in the nineteenth century made it easy for immigrants of either nationality to read the other's newspapers and periodicals. Initially some of the larger Nordic immigrant newspapers, such as Skandinaven *of Chicago, consciously served both groups, although Norwegians dominated it. Before the 1870s, when the number of Danes in North America was still very small, practically no specifically Danish immigrant press existed. In 1872, however,* Den danske Pioneer *was first published in Omaha. It is still printed in a suburb of Chicago. In its wake followed approximately fifty other newspapers, many of which appeared weekly in Chicago, Racine, Minneapolis, and several other cities and smaller settlements. At first, a chief purpose of the Danish-language press was to present general news to immigrants who could not yet read English, although a number of the periodicals were more narrowly focused and were directed at specific groups within the Danish community, such as women or the members of a particular denomination. Many of these were short-lived, however; apparently there were too few Danes in most places to support a newspaper for more than a few years. The relatively rapid assimilation of the group, especially in terms of linguistic transition, undercut the need for newspapers in Danish. After the turn of the century the number of periodicals declined steadily; today only three are published in*

14. Enok Mortensen, *The Danish Lutheran Church in America* (Philadelphia: Lutheran Church in America, 1967), is the standard history of the synod.

15. The standard but woefully inadequate history of the "Blair Church" is John M. Jensen, *The United Evangelical Lutheran Church* (Minneapolis: Augsburg Publishing House, 1964).

the old language. Their primary function is no longer to convey general news, but to provide a means of communication for Danish heritage groups.[16]

For a minority of the Danes who sought new lives in North America the final phase of their immigrant experience was return emigration, sometimes called re-emigration. It is exceedingly difficult, though, to gauge the extent or significance of this phenomenon. That an immigrant chose to return to the Old World does not necessarily mean that his dream of settling in the New ran awry. Many newcomers had no such dream, but simply hoped to make enough money in America to return to the "old country" on a higher rung of the economic ladder. Even some immigrants who seemingly desired to sink permanent roots in American soil by claiming homesteads admitted that they merely intended to sell the deeds acquired by fulfilling the five-year residence requirement and return to Europe in style. Conversely, lifelong residence in the New World is not proof of success or fulfillment of immigrants' hopes. In a few cases, newcomers were simply too indigent to afford return passage. More frequently, though, immigrants who did not prosper in North America probably believed that they were in the less economically constrained of two worlds; the hardships of the 1890s, for example, undoubtedly cast dark shadows on the hopes of a large number of "hyphenated" Americans, but to many there was no viable alternative to remaining.

Precise statistics of Danish return emigration do not exist. It is known, however, that as early as 1875 more than two hundred people returned from America to Denmark. The following year some of these repatriates organized the "United States Club" in Copenhagen. Between 1908 and 1914 more than five hundred citizens of the United States emigrated annually to Denmark. No doubt nearly all of these people were in fact returning to their, or their parents', native country. The leading historian of Danish emigration regards the American statistics on which this average rests "with some skepticism," however, and suggests that the real figures were probably somewhat higher.[17]

---

16. A fine study is Marion Tuttle Marzolf, *The Danish-language Press in America* (New York: Arno Press, 1979).

17. Hvidt, *Flight to America*, p. 181.

Danes in North America

·I·

The Atlantic Crossing

One common feature of European immigrants' experiences was a long and usually strenuous Atlantic crossing. Before the transition to steam power during the third quarter of the nineteenth century, the journey generally lasted a month or two—for those fortunate enough to survive the ordeal. Many did not. Shoehorned into steerage without fresh food or appropriate medical care, countless emigrants fell victim to typhoid fever, smallpox, cholera, measles, and other communicable diseases. One German immigrant exaggerated, of course, when he observed that "if crosses and tombstones could be erected on the water as on the western deserts, where they indicate the resting-places of white men killed by savages or by the elements, the routes of the emigrant vessels from Europe to America would long since have assumed the appearance of crowded cemeteries."[1] Yet the few Danes who crossed the Atlantic on sailing ships—about one-tenth of all who emigrated from Denmark to North America—frequently told of widespread disease, unexpected deaths, and burials at sea. Those whose only malady was an extended period of seasickness could number themselves among the fortunate.

The use of steam power on the Atlantic shipping lanes slashed the journey to about ten days but failed to eliminate the miseries caused by inhumane treatment on board. Emigrants still had to undertake arduous journeys by rail or other means of travel to the ports of embarkation, where they were often forced to spend several days before sailing in quarters unfit for human inhabitation. Their lot did not necessarily improve when allowed on board, where crowded conditions prevailed until well into the twentieth century. Moreover, many were soon parted from their meager savings by crew members who monopolized the sale of food and other essentials. Luggage was frequently stolen or otherwise mishandled. The thousands of Danes who booked passage

---

1. Quoted in Theodore C. Blegen, *Norwegian Migration to America: The American Transition* (Northfield, Minn.: Norwegian-American Historical Association, 1940), p. 21.

on German or English vessels were vastly outnumbered by emigrants of other nationalities whose drinking, raucous behavior, and lower standards of personal hygiene were described vividly in many America letters. Culture shock thus began for many Danes long before they reached the shores of the New World.

Letters depicting the crossing exist in abundance. Immigrants typically recounted the experience in their first greetings from New York or elsewhere to concerned relatives in Denmark. Many newcomers sent Danish newspapers detailed caveats against certain shipping lines or routes to North America. They also warned those who would follow against booking passage with certain emigration agents. Beginning in Denmark around the middle of the nineteenth century, the number of these professional agents grew to vast proportions as it became profitable to encourage the exodus of Danes. Emigrants purchased hundreds of thousands of transatlantic and overland tickets from these agents and in general placed much of their fate into their hands.

It must be acknowledged that these agents rendered a number of indispensible services for emigrants and undoubtedly facilitated the way of many to the New World. They informed Danes from Copenhagen to the smallest villages of transportation possibilities through a sprawling network of subagents and extensive advertising in the press. Moreover, many served as barometers of business trends in North America, promoting emigration most heavily during periods of prosperity and, conversely, often warning prospective clients to postpone departures when recessions struck the American economy. Working with railroads and other large companies, agents also secured jobs for many Danes who may otherwise have experienced difficulty finding work in the United States. Finally, some agents accompanied groups of emigrants to North America, thereby perhaps easing the transition to a new land.

On the other hand, the agents were not essentially philanthropists, but businessmen with a vested interest in increasing the flow of Danes from the Old World to the New. At times they used unscrupulous tactics to raise the "body count." Their bag of tricks included misrepresenting the length of the Atlantic crossing and conditions on board crowded steamers, exaggerating the wages that laborers and artisans could expect in American cities, accepting fees for wedding prospective emigrants to nonexistent jobs, bribing Danish-Americans to write glowing descriptions of conditions in the New World and praises of certain agents or shipping lines, and even resorting to such semantic legerdemain as quoting American temperatures verbatim without bothering to mention that the Fahrenheit scale differed greatly from the Celsius and Reaumur systems to which Danes were accustomed.

❖

*In 1847 a young wheelwright, Andreas Frederiksen Herslev, emigrated
with his brother Casper. He eventually became a farmer in Wisconsin. In his
first letter home he described their voyage on a sailing ship and prospects of
employment in the New World. (Source: Danes Worldwide Archives, uncatalogued materials.)*

New York
5 October 1847

Dear Parents and Brother,

No doubt you want to know how we are doing on our long trip.
I shall begin by telling you that we are in good health and feeling
fine after arriving in New York on 5 October. I wanted to
mention that right at the beginning so that it would not hurt you
so much to hear about the less pleasant aspects of the journey.

We sailed from Hamburg on Saturday, 7 August, but not until
two days later did we reach the mouth of the Elbe. I reckon that
day as the real beginning of our voyage to America. There was a
headwind from the southwest, so we had to sail north of Scotland
toward Iceland, which is considerably farther than through the
English Channel.

Both of us became sick, especially me, although it wasn't real
seasickness that struck me. But after it had gone away, I picked it
up from others who were sick. It was unpleasant. I didn't have
any pain, but because I could hardly eat I began to look rather
gaunt. It was especially bad because about eight days earlier I had
had diarrhea from the first illness. Many people were hit by both
illnesses, but Casper has hardly been sick at all. The wind was
against us for most of the trip, but we had only one storm of any
significance.

We arrived here yesterday evening,[2] and today at six o'clock we
leave for Albany by steamboat. You should be happy to learn that
while on the ship we arranged to work for a man, but first he has

---

2. Frederiksen contradicts himself. His letter is dated 5 October, and he states in
his first paragraph that he and his brother arrived that day, but here he remarks that
they arrived the previous evening.

to buy some land. It wasn't a sure deal, but today we had a better offer. The German Society had to hire three or four fellows for a farm near Buffalo. Even though there were plenty of men available among the immigrants, I think most of them were either handworkers (although only one wheelwright) or belonged to families who didn't want to be sent up there. So we got the following offer: (1) free transportation to Buffalo, where we would be passing through anyway; (2) twelve dollars a month plus room and board, and when he heard I was a wheelwright he said I could take care of the farm machinery, for which I would probably be paid sixteen to eighteen dollars; (3) finally, we can begin work whenever we want, and we can either accept the deal or turn it down, but if we don't take it we'll have to pay for our own transportation, of course. The contract can be as long or as short as we want.

If we don't like the work, we'll go to Wisconsin as we originally planned and get jobs with the man who talked to us first. Besides, we can find carpentry work out there. We don't have time to write any more now because it is almost four o'clock. I constantly pray that God will bless you just as much as you have blessed us.

Andreas Frederiksen Herslev

P.S.: We will write again as soon as we have found permanent jobs.

Torben Lange (1818–51) was a member of a middle-class family in Frederikssund, northwest of Copenhagen. Educated as an agriculturalist, this young adventurer emigrated at twenty-three on board a German vessel that sailed from Hamburg. (Source: Torben Lange, *Fra Roskildefjord til Mississippi. En Udvandrers Breve til Hjemmet 1841–1851* [Copenhagen: H. Hagerup, 1945], pp. 39–41.)

New York
17 August 1841

Dear Parents,

   . . . I have to tell you a little about my voyage across the Atlantic. It went very well. We had only one storm, on 10 and 11

July. As soon as we reached the North Sea the wind shifted to the southwest, so we had to sail north of Scotland around the Orkney and Shetland Islands, which we passed on 5 July.

In the evening there was the usual concert. A choir of about fifty of us men sang the German song "À dieu Europa, à dieu o Vaterland." It was a song worth hearing, sung with unparalelled enthusiasm.

The steerage passengers were not so bad as I initially thought they were. Their faces were generally somber, but on close examination they were characterized less by evil than by worry and melancholy. Dissension reigned on board. Even among us cabin-class passengers there were two factions, the ladies with their patrons, and the rest of us. We managed to stay harmonious, however, except for some cutting remarks. In steerage, on the other hand, the Bavarian Jews and the Hessian farmers were pitted against each other. Among the Hessians there were two real devils. Several times there were fights down there, and the Jews were constantly getting a drubbing. Several of the Jews had lice; this was the cause of the constant commotion. It was really hilarious to see how one Jew after the other would be chased up through the hatch whenever they were beaten up. It was terribly filthy below decks, so I don't blame the farmers for forcing the Jews to wash themselves. The man whom the passengers respected most was the cook, a Jew. He had a lot of work to do, as you can imagine, and was never able to keep the passengers out of the galley. They were constantly trying to steal food until the cook caught one of those saints, a big fellow whom he probably would have killed had not the second mate appeared in the nick of time. Then somebody complained to the captain. I don't know what he said to the cook, only that one of the other saints went to the galley to inform the cook that he had acted incorrectly. He came a bit too close, however, and the cook knocked three teeth out of his mouth. From then on there was respect for the cook, and nobody complained to the captain. Captain Flor is quite a man. We never heard him growling or scolding anyone. From morning to evening he walked up and down the deck singing softly and seldom speaking to anyone without being addressed first.

There were five deaths and three births during the voyage, so I had the opportunity to see how a burial at sea is done. I was never seasick, although the last few days at sea I had terrible diarrhea.

After visiting his family in Denmark, Lange sailed again to America, this time on the Washington *from Cuxhaven, Germany, as a steerage passenger.* (Source: Lange, *Fra Roskildefjord til Mississippi*, pp. 176–78.)

New York
27 May 1846

Dear Father,

After a long and boring voyage we finally arrived here the day before yesterday. The first fourteen days we had a strong tailwind and everyone thought we could count on a short voyage. Then things changed. During the past month stormy and calm days alternated almost without interruption. . . .

This was the most unpleasant journey I have ever made. The sea was almost always rough, and it wasn't safe to go up on the deck. I fell down only once, but some of the other passengers fell about three times a day. It was impossible to stay down below very long because of the lice and stench, but it was also impossible to stand on the deck without being drenched in an hour.

Holm and I were the only ones who were never seasick, and during the past three weeks I had a strong appetite. I was never full and still am not! In order to get extra helpings of food I had to slip the cook some tips. I was afraid I might get sick, but am still completely healthy and today I took a strong laxative. This afternoon I took a hot bath and now feel as though I have been created anew. It's amazing how much dirt accumulates during a voyage in steerage.

The most unpleasant thing about the voyage were the villainous passengers. You would have to search long and hard to find such a blasphemous brood of vipers. I've never seen a gang like them. With the exception of four or five families from Holstein and a couple of families from southern Germany, they were all rejects— foul language and cheating all day long. Especially pitiful were twelve or fourteen fellows from Bavaria, Prussia, Hamburg, and southern Holstein—obdurate sinners without a spark of virtue left in them. Most of them were well educated.

Steerage became a regular brothel. People gambled their clothes away and fistfights ensued. We had four prostitutes and at least five thieves. One of the latter was searched, and it was discovered that he had stolen thirty-one different items, including one of my handkerchiefs. One thief stole from the next. One of them wanted to jump overboard but was held back. When finally released he decided not to jump.

A large sausage, two glasses, and the old knife and fork I received from Grethe were stolen from me. I got the fork back again. I told the thief, who came from Holstein, that I knew he had stolen it. I said that if he gave it back I would keep my mouth shut, but if not I would report him to the police in New York.

Many of the passengers gambled away their bedding. When we arrived here I bought five blankets for 25¢ and six mattresses for 10¢ each from one of the winners. That was about one-tenth of their value. I also bought a brand-new coat and trousers for $1.75 but sold them for the same price to one of the deaf-mutes, a very decent but extremely poor person.

After completing his apprenticeship as a cabinetmaker, Julius Petersen left the southern Danish island of Lolland in 1887 at nineteen. He recorded his initial impressions of Copenhagen and New York in a letter to one of his younger brothers. (Source: Danes Worldwide Archives, Julius Petersen MSS.)

[Undated, but 1887]

Dear Brother,

I left you at the railroad station on 11 April. There were many of us on the train. In Nykøbing we had to change to the train from Berlin. At the ferry crossing there were so many people that an extra steamer had to be used. When we arrived in Copenhagen we took a cab to Hotel Carl the Fifteenth in Nyhavn.[3] The next morning we went to the railroad station and hired a porter to take

3. Nyhavn is a well-known sailors' district in central Copenhagen, known for sleazy entertainment and cheap hotels.

our baggage down to Larsen Square.[4] Then we walked the streets all day and saw a good deal. We went up into the Round Tower,[5] looked at the Art Exhibition, saw the castle ruins, visited the Marble Church, and looked at several other things.

As you know, we sailed from Copenhagen at noon on Wednesday, 13 April. In Kristiania[6] I saw Carl Johan Street, the Royal Palace, the Parliament building, the university, and many attractive private buildings. Up at the palace a soldier armed with a halberd, or battle axe, was standing guard. I also saw an equestrian statue of King Carl the Fifteenth that bore his motto, "The Love of the People Is My Reward."[7] It is similar to that of Frederik VII.[8] He was loved by the people of Sweden and Norway just as Frederik was by us Danes. In Kristiansand[9] I also went ashore. The whole town was built of wood.

Here in America we sailed right past the Statue of Liberty, which looks magnificent. We disembarked in Jersey City and sailed to Castle Garden in a steamboat. This building was a fort, but the Swedish singer Jenny Lind bought it and presented it to the immigrants. Its granite walls are nearly five meters thick, and it is more than one hundred meters wide. Over in New York I rode on the elevated railroad, went across the Brooklyn Bridge, and saw several sights. In Castle Park there were electric lights. They are one of the most beautiful things I have ever seen. Compared to an electric light a gas flame looks like a dismal tallow candle.

American railroad cars are very comfortable. You can read about them in my letter to our parents. I took the train through the state of New York, which is very swampy and hilly, over a suspension bridge across the river that has the Niagara Falls, and

4. Larsen Square (Larsens Plads), near Amalienborg Palace, was a quay that served as the departure point for thousands of Danish emigrants. Ships of the Danish Thingvalla Line later docked there.

5. The Round Tower is an observatory constructed in 1642 in central Copenhagen.

6. The Norwegian capital, Oslo, was called Christiania or Kristiania from 1624 until 1925.

7. Carl XV (1826–1872) became King of Sweden and Norway in 1859. He supported Denmark against Prussia and Austria in the 1860s.

8. Frederik VII became King of Denmark in 1848. He was the country's last absolutist monarch, reigning when the first constitution in Denmark's history was adopted in 1849.

9. Kristiansand is a harbor city in southern Norway.

through a corner of Ontario. So I've been in the dominion of
Queen Victoria! We continued north of Lake Erie, across a little
bay in that lake, into Michigan, and from there to Illinois. These
two states appear to be very fertile. The crops were coming up.
Wheat, clover, and grass were tall and thriving. It was a pleasure
to see them.

Best regards from Rasmus and your brother,

Julius Petersen

*A satisfied immigrant reported on his journey on the Danish Thingvalla
Line and on working conditions in New York. (Source: Aarhus Amtstidende,
26 April 1882.)*

Brooklyn
7 April 1882

Dear Editor,

When I left you asked me to send you a report of my trip
across the Atlantic. I am happy to do so, because I feel I must
express my satisfaction with the Thingvalla Line.

We left Copenhagen at 1 P.M. on 7 March, accompanied by a
brass band and various emigration agents, who disembarked at
Helsingør. The agents were very friendly to the passengers and
did all they could for them. We stopped in Kristiansand for two
hours and used the time to see the church, the bank, and the
observation post up on the hill. Everything went fine until we got
out into the Atlantic. Then most of us became seasick. There were
rough days when we were not allowed on the deck, and at night
we had to put up rails along our berths to prevent ourselves from
falling out. Two of the waiters fell down while doing their duties;
one of them hit the floor rather hard. The weather was awful at
times, and the last Sunday night we almost rammed a schooner,
although it was saved by the conduct of our capable captain. When
the weather was good a waiter named Peter Sørensen, whose stage
name was "P. S. Geyser," put on a show with jokes, songs, and
dancing. A Norwegian played the fiddle very well, and a couple
others played horns, flutes, and so on. A Norwegian woman gave
birth to a child on board, but it was stillborn.

The passengers were very friendly and helpful to one another.

The officers and crew were very able. I wish especially to mention Captain Thomsen, who, along with First Mate Nielsen and the boatswain, looked after our needs exceptionally well. The food was excellent, which must be attributed to Steward Petersen and the way he did his responsible, difficult job, as well as to the cook and the baker. This is a part of the menu: 7 A.M., coffee with bread and sugar; 9 A.M., breakfast with a hot side dish and tea; 1 P.M., a two-course lunch with fresh cakes (we had apples only once; that was on a stormy day); 4 P.M., coffee; 6 P.M., dinner including lobster, sardines, aquavit, anchovies, tea, and so on. Everything was served in generous, well-prepared portions. The service was also good and beverage prices were low: a half-bottle of Bavarian beer for thirty øre, a bottle of port wine for three crowns, a bottle of soda pop for fifteen øre, and so on.

Regarding work, I can remark that there is not much to be had in Chicago, but there is in Wisconsin and here. The best daily wages are paid to masons (three to four dollars), carpenters (two or three dollars), and painters (two to four dollars). Gardeners cannot find work unless they know the language. Office clerks cannot do business here. A final word of advice before I close: Avoid using hotels, if at all possible. They are far more expensive than living elsewhere, even for only eight days. One can arrange to get *board* and everything else, such as bath privileges, for five dollars a week.

I am fully satisfied with the place where I live. It seemed a bit strange at first, but now I am far more satisfied with my situation than I was with the oppressive one back home.

I hope you will be kind enough to print my letter in your esteemed newspaper and join me in recommending the Thingvalla in the strongest terms. I also hope you will send me a bit of news *from our old country;* as you might imagine, we get little news directly from home, even though we have Scandinavian newspapers.

C. Ravn

An anonymous immigrant regretted booking passage on the Inman Line. (Source: *Holbæk Amts Avis,* 7 November 1882.)

Cedar Falls, Iowa
1 June 1882

Dear Friends,

   Since we now have some peace and quiet after the long voyage,
I shall fulfill my promise to tell you what we have experienced
since leaving Denmark.

   We sailed from Copenhagen at noon on 21 April and reached
England three days later. Because the big ship could not sail
directly to the pier, our baggage was taken in on one smaller ship
while we were transported on another into Hull. We were there
for four hours getting tickets for the journey through England. At
ten o'clock we steamed away and reached Liverpool at four in the
morning. We did not see anything, because the trip was at night.
In Liverpool we were received by "a lady" who led us to a spartan
hotel where we were given a little food and coffee. Our stay there
was far from comfortable. At night mattresses were placed along
the walls of several rooms, and we all slept together, husbands and
wives, boys and girls, and children. After two nights of that we
were taken to another hotel, where we at least had beds to sleep
in. We were there two days and two nights. Finally, more than a
week after leaving Denmark, we boarded our big emigrant ship.

   We believed conditions on board would be better than those we
had hitherto experienced, but we were certainly disappointed.
Indeed, our misery had only begun. We were hungry when we
boarded, but the food was almost inedible. It was partly rotten and
tasted old. The food we had brought along from Copenhagen was
inaccessibly stowed in the hold. We did not see it before our
arrival in New York.

   After we were shown our berths all of us, large and small, were
herded up on the deck to be counted. We had to show our
contracts, something which took several hours. I felt sorry for the
many families with small children. The smallest ones had to be
carried and the others held by the hand. However hard they tried,
they could not avoid being squeezed, stepped on, and knocked
down. It was really a lamentable scene. The children cried, and
the adults cried, too. Many began to regret leaving their homes in
Denmark. It is not as easy to travel to America as is claimed back
home. If parents with small children knew what they had to

endure, I believe many of them would think twice before leaving. Many also lost some of their baggage. Some found the locks on their trunks broken, while others were not able to find their trunks at all. Still others lost their bed linen. I lost only some canned goods I had bought in Copenhagen, a jug of liquor, and a carpet worth seven crowns. We believed the sailors had used the opportunity to pilfer.

On Sunday we docked in an Irish harbor, Queenstown, where 450 Irishmen embarked. I don't know exactly how many we were in all then, but I heard between 1,450 and 1,750. Our quarters were cramped, in any case. There were seventeen of us in a cabin meant for ten, and the bad food did not improve our spirits. Even if we had been given enough it would have been bad, but we received only half of what we could have eaten. On Sunday morning, 7 May, we did not get any bread in our cabin, even though we were four families with children. It was pitiful to hear the children cry for food, but we were told that none had been baked. All of the stewards were Englishmen who did not try to take care of anyone but their countrymen and a few Germans who gave them rum, which could be bought for one crown a bottle on the ship. It was also possible to buy some food from the sailors, but it was very expensive and of low quality. We had to buy it anyway, because for several days we didn't get any bread and were ready to die of hunger. The soup we had at dinner every day was very thin and contained nothing but potatoes. We had to add soup stock and pepper.

You can imagine what condition the passengers were in when we arrived in America. I advise you in the strongest terms to avoid the ships of the Inman Line. If you believe you absolutely must try your luck over here, I can recommend unconditionally that you travel on the Thingvalla Line. The *Gejser* arrived here the day after we did, and everyone praised both the food and the way they were treated on board.

On Sunday, 14 May, we reached America's coast, a little seaport that was also a fortress. All of us who could still walk were ordered up to the deck to be inspected by a doctor who came out in a little steamboat. Then we sailed farther down the coast to New York. It was interesting to sail down there. We saw many parks and attractive towns and met hundreds of ships, too many to count. Some had railroad cars with passengers in them, nine cars per ship, and much larger than in Denmark.

On the evening of 16 May we boarded a train and traveled all night. At daybreak I was surprised to see that we were winding between high cliffs. We saw nothing else all day. Later the landscape became flat, indeed so flat that in places it was under water. We traveled through that for half a day, then entered higher country with fertile soil and large forests. Everywhere we noticed thousands of trees, large and small mixed together.

Here in Iowa, where I now live, there is not much forest but a great deal of fertile soil. Fuel is therefore just as expensive as it is in Denmark. Everything is very expensive and it is almost impossible to get accommodations. Here in this small town a hundred fit men are unemployed.

I have to cut this off here, or else the letter will be too heavy.

Anonymous

An immigrant from Morsing in western Denmark, who sailed from Bremerhaven in 1892, found eastern Europeans especially unpleasant. (Source: Ringkøbings Amts Avis, 1 July 1892.)

Chicago

On Saturday, 5 March, my family and I boarded a southbound train to start our journey to the "promised land," where we would try our luck. After saying goodbye to friends and acquaintances in Skjern, where we had lived for four and a half years, and to my brother-in-law in Varde, we rolled along to Esbjerg. There we were met by the agent, H. N. Friis, who helped us in every respect, and accompanied us to the German border the next day. After crossing the border we said goodbye to the agent and to Denmark for a long time—perhaps forever. Then we continued on to Hamburg, Bremen, and Bremerhaven, where we were to board the *Darmstadt.* At all of these stations we were met by emigration agents who treated us well. The food we were served was good.

Actually, we were supposed to sail on the *Spree,* but it was already overbooked, so we had to be content with the *Darmstadt.* It was not known as a fast ship. The *Spree* made the Atlantic crossing in eight days; the *Darmstadt* took ten.

Nevertheless, it appeared that we would be a large group of passengers, fifteen or sixteen hundred in all, including two hundred Danes. The rest were Swedes, Germans, Jews, Russians, Hungarians, and a large number of Poles. The Poles shuffled in with large bundles on their backs; some also carried their children that way. It was the most motley assembly I have ever seen: young and old, large and small, cripples and thieves, whom I shall discuss later.

We were taken out to the *Darmstadt* in a little steam boat. What a commotion when we got on board! Some of us Danes avoided the crush by staying back, and we were shown to quarters astern. That way we avoided being put together with Poles and Hungarians, which would have made the crossing even less pleasant. They are not especially clean. Nevertheless, we were not able to avoid them completely. The ship weighed anchor, and we sailed full steam ahead out into the Atlantic.

The food we were served on board was more like pig slop than fare fit for human beings. It was impossible for my wife and me to eat the soup. Fortunately, we had provisioned ourselves so well that we did not have to eat their slop during the entire voyage. The Poles, on the other hand, ate so voraciously it seemed they had not had any food for a month.

When so many different people are put together, it is not surprising that some have little respect for others' belongings. Hence, we had to keep an eye on every finger, especially when these sticky-fingered individuals sniffed around us. Whenever any of them seemed to be getting too bold, we took them by the collar and sent them on their way.

There was little variety in the life on board, except when a stillborn baby was committed to Davy Jones's locker and a sailor suddenly collapsed on the deck and died.

We had been promised a speedy passage on the Bremen Line, but I cannot imagine why this line is recommended so strongly above other lines, especially since the food is so unappetizing. For my part, I shall never advise any emigrant to travel on this line for the sake of speed. A fourteen-day journey from Bremerhaven to New York can hardly be called fast.

Finally we were able to see the New World, and of course all of us got up on deck to enjoy the magnificent view. As we stood there, many thoughts crossed our minds. We wondered whether we would be able to lead better lives here than in the old country.

In New York we changed from the uncomfortable ship to a well-appointed American railroad train. After two days we arrived in Chicago, where our friends and acquaintances welcomed us heartily.

With that I shall conclude this brief description with a [unintelligible word] greeting to all of my friends in Denmark who happen to read these lines.

Mikkel Kirk Pedersen

An agent in New York offered his services to the readers of a newspaper in Jutland. (Source: *Vejle Amts Avis,* 15 February 1882.)

Utica, New York

Those of my countrymen who intend to come over here this spring but who can neither speak nor understand a word of English should not lose courage. There is plenty of work of every kind in America for people who are willing to work. Even those who do not know any English can earn a good wage, provided they are willing to take whatever kind of work is offered until they have learned the language. Personally, I was an artisan, but I had to plant hops for a farmer. I did not like it, and as a result I did not think very highly of America at first. But now I would not return to Denmark. I would not be satisfied with the long workday back home or with the niggardly wages there. Nevertheless, I worked for the hops farmer for only ten days. Then I left with a Dane from Kolding. It was six kilometers to the nearest railroad station, and we had to carry more than fifty kilograms on our backs. We were not paid a cent for the ten days we had worked.

After arriving at the place where I presently am, things went much better. I earn a good salary and live as comfortably as a lord in Denmark. Many people who come to America without connections or a knowledge of the language will have similar experiences.

I ask all of the Danes who intend to come here this spring to write to me before they buy their tickets. I want to tell them about the best shipping companies for Danes to use as well as the best places in America for farmers and professional people. I also have information about the climate, and I can answer any questions as soon as I receive their letters. I want to send papers and books in Danish free of charge to all who request them and who intend to emigrate. Those who do not know anyone in America can come to me and I will find them work immediately, although I cannot promise them employment in their own fields right away. It will be good work, though, and the wages will be just as good as those paid to Americans. Write my name clearly in your address books.

P. S. N. Petersen

An immigrant told how an unscrupulous agent tricked him and others into booking transatlantic passage. (Source: *Aarhus Amtstidende*, 2 November 1882.)

When I decided to emigrate to America in January of this year, I read in the newspapers of a man named Smith who was the manager of a large farm in America. He was then in Hamburg and wanted thirty-two Danish workers. I wrote a letter to him, which he answered immediately. He offered me six crowns a day plus room and board. That was more than I could earn in Denmark, so I decided to go with him. The trip cost 150 crowns, but I knew I could earn the money quickly in America, where I would have such a large salary.

I arrived in Hamburg on 1 February, and the ship we were supposed to take was to sail the next day. Smith was able to get only twelve men, whom he sent on this ship. He himself wanted to remain in Hamburg in order to recruit the rest of the men, with whom he decided to travel by way of England.

All twelve of us were in good humor because we believed we were going to live like kings in America. In reality, though, we were on our way into slavery. We arrived in Havre on Saturday, 5 February, and that afternoon we went ashore to see the city. It is a large, attractive city, heavily fortified on the sea side. The next day we sailed from Havre out into the Atlantic, into a storm that lasted four days. Many were afraid that we would end up in Davy Jones's locker. On 20 February we arrived at Castle Garden in New York. We were taken immediately to the Scandinavia Hotel. Our boss, Smith, had sent a letter to the manager of the hotel, whose name was also Smith, asking him to give us good room and board, which he did. He also wrote that he would arrive on the next ship and pay our bill. One day went after the other, however, and we began to wonder whether we had been tricked. We waited there for ten days, but Smith did not come. On the eleventh day the train came with twenty-three men who had landed in Philadelphia, but Smith was not with them. They said Smith had given them coffee and bread in England and told them his wife had fallen ill, and that he had to stay there another day in case his wife would improve. They could sail on to New York confidently, and he would arrive about the same time. Perhaps he had taken the wrong way.

Among those who had come in this second group were several from Fyn. Some of them had three to four hundred crowns more than they needed for the trip, and had given this money as well as their conduct books and other securities to Smith. He had warned them about pickpockets and assured them that he would take care of their valuables. It had not occurred to them that Smith himself was the lowest of scoundrels.

Thirty-four of us were there without employment. We were sent north to work on a railroad and earn eleven dollars to send to Smith in New York for our room and board. That did not last long. After two days four of us agreed to turn back, even though we did not have a cent. We began to walk, begging along the way, and, after tramping for fourteen days through snow-covered hills, we reached Castle Garden. We stayed there for eight days and received free board. Then two of us began to work for a farmer outside the city for ten dollars a month. It became intolerable there. We were given only potatoes, pork, and *turnips* to eat, and anything we left on our plates was thrown to the pigs. We may as well have eaten with them. After we had been there a month we were each given a dollar, so we left.

We heard about a town where many Danes live, and decided to go there. We were fortunate enough to find work the next day. The daily wage here is $1.25 to $1.75. Room and board can be had for twelve to sixteen dollars a month. If a man is fortunate enough to find a steady job he can earn a living more easily here than in Denmark. Back in Denmark one can toil from early in the morning until late in the evening for only fifty øre a day, and in many places the food is bad, too.

These lines can perhaps serve as a little warning to my countrymen who wish to emigrate to America. They should not let themselves be duped into traveling with such dastardly persons, or be fooled into emigrating in such a shameful way. It is no fun to arrive empty-handed in a foreign country. This is especially important for married people; they can take care of their own money and should not turn it over to a thief who offers to accompany them. I had to learn that the hard way, and have often regretted that I did not listen to Mr. Alfred Bjørnbak when he advised me not to put my faith into Smith's promises. I advise anyone who intends to come to America to use the steamship line "Thingvalla." Mr. Bjørnbak is its agent.[10]

Søren Petersen, Fløjstrup

10. This is hardly a neutral evaluation since Bjørnbak, a prominent emigration agent and adventurer in the United States, worked as a journalist for *Aarhus Amtstidende*.

·II·

Farmers and Farmhands

The majority of the approximately three hundred thousand Danes who emi-
grated to the United States and Canada found homes on farms and in small
towns. They dispersed more widely than nearly every other ethnic group. A
vague "Danish belt" soon stretched from Chicago and Racine, Wisconsin,
across much of the Midwest into eastern Nebraska, but even within this area
the Danes were a small minority and did not cluster heavily in any one state.
While Iowa, Wisconsin, and Minnesota led the nation in the number of Dan-
ish-born residents in 1910, more than 70 percent of the American Danes
lived elsewhere at that time. By 1900 Danish immigrants could be found in
every county of California, Connecticut, Idaho, Iowa, Maine, Montana, Ne-
vada, New Jersey, South Dakota, Utah, and Wyoming, and in all but one
county in Massachusetts, Minnesota, Nebraska, New York, North Dakota,
Oregon, and Washington.[1]

This diverse settlement pattern reveals, among other things, the Danes' quest
for land and its availability through the renowned Homestead Act of 1862.
That landmark piece of legislation caused repercussions throughout much of
Europe and was undoubtedly one of the strongest factors luring immigrants
to the United States. Under its provisions any adult who did not own land
elsewhere could claim 160 acres of government property. The homesteader
had only to promise not to use it for speculation (a requirement that proved
difficult to enforce) and live on the claim for five years. At the end of this
minimum residency the settler was given the deed to the claim. A similar law
was enacted in Canada a few years later.

The Homestead Act was a godsend to the land-starved peasantry of Den-
mark. Emigration agents soon brought it to their attention and used free land
as bait to sell tickets to the supposed Shangri-la across the waters. Despite
their poverty, Danish farmers were not disenchanted with agriculture, as were
many other European peasants. Farming, especially dairying, underwent a

1. A. M. Andersen, *Hvor Danskerne i Amerika findes* (Blair, Nebr.: Danish Lutheran
Publishing House, 1903), pp. 4–5.

21

technological revolution during the nineteenth century, bringing some mea-
sure of prosperity to many landowners. Hence, many young Danes eagerly
leaped at the opportunity to get farms merely by emigrating to North America
and asking for them.

Not all acquired land under the provisions of the Homestead Act. Those
few Danes who arrived before it was enacted could purchase farmland from
the federal government at the bargain price of $1.25 per acre. Later, after
the railroad companies were granted wide swaths of real estate as rewards
for extending their lines to the Pacific, many immigrants bought "railroad
land" at varying prices. Others, especially those who arrived after the most
favorable acreages had been claimed, turned to real estate agents or bought
land from farmers eager to sell their homesteads at a profit. Another method
of acquiring land was for a group of immigrants to purchase collectively a
large tract, either from the government or from a private owner, and establish
a colony.

Once in possession of farmland, immigrants often became quite prosperous
while world demand for their produce remained strong. An entrepreneurial
spirit became evident among these newcomers, many of whom quickly acquired
a keen sense for American business methods. For others, however, the dream
of land ownership proved less than idyllic. Latecomers discovered that fertile
land close to towns or railroad lines already belonged to others. Others com-
plained about the seemingly endless toil required to transform the virgin prai-
rie into productive farms complete with houses and outbuildings. Many young
men had to labor for several years as farmhands before acquiring sufficient
funds to purchase land of their own. And the depression of the 1890s, which
led to the rise of populism, sounded the death knell for countless farmers who
found themselves caught in a squeeze between the disastrous grain prices of
a flooded market and the demands of creditors during that deflationary era.

The present chapter is appropriately the longest in this volume. It includes
letters written between the 1840s and World War I, from New Brunswick to
Washington and from Saskatchewan to Texas. The bulk of the correspon-
dence, though, comes from the American Midwest during the fourth quarter
of the nineteenth century. The letters tell of the quest for land, grueling work
in the fields, hopes of prosperity, the solitude—but also the feeling of group
cohesiveness—of life on the prairie, and hardships of farming in an often
harsh environment where the weather, predators, and business trends could
spell disaster.

❖

Andreas Frederiksen Herslev, whose account of his Atlantic voyage appears in Chapter I, dropped his last name and claimed land in eastern Wisconsin. (Source: Danes Worldwide Archives, uncatalogued materials.)

Milwaukee, Wisconsin
24 November 1849

Dear Parents and Brother,

I haven't received any mail since I answered your letter in September. Since then several changes have taken place in my life. I was on board the ship *Cleveland* until 9 November. In fact, I was on board for six months and sixteen days and managed to save eighteen dollars. I deposited five dollars in the bank and used the rest to buy clothes and other things I needed. When I quit I was paid eighty-four dollars.

I traveled to Milwaukee to take care of affairs with the Danes who were keeping my bedding and street clothes, which I didn't want to use on the ship, and to put my money into the bank. Mossin, who knows the bank director and has helped me before, was willing to help me again. He told me, though, that I should take my money out of the bank, where I get only 5 percent interest, and buy a "land warrant" instead—and make 100 percent.

I'll have to explain what a land warrant is. Over here soldiers are not conscripted from among the people and forced to go to war or be flogged by barbarian sergeants as in Denmark. Here they are all volunteers who serve for five years. They earn nine dollars a month and get free meals. Recently, however, the United States had a war with the Republic of Mexico and needed far more soldiers than usual. In order to get them the government issued posters stating that soldiers would get seven dollars a month and 160 *acres* of land, which could be selected from anywhere in the United States where there was unsold public land. That was just about the time Casper and I came over here. A recruit had to serve as long as the war lasted. If he was killed, his relatives would receive his land and salary. The war ended this year, so the soldiers were issued vouchers that were as good as payment for the 160 *acres*. Many of the soldiers didn't have any use for their land, but they had the right to sell the voucher to anyone. The government was willing to pay one hundred dollars for them. But

there are advantages in selling them privately, of course, and now
there is a lot of speculating with these vouchers, or land warrants,
as they are called. Last summer when so many immigrants were
arriving they cost as much as 190 dollars. Now the demand is not
so great, so the speculators either have to sell them for less or
have their money tied up in warrants until next spring. Now the
price is down to 118 dollars, so I bought two. It's the safest
investment I know. Frederik Lenche also bought one. Together
with a ship's carpenter from Lolland, Rasmus Rasmussen, and a
Norwegian, Peder Pedersen, we sailed a little over one hundred
kilometers north of here to a little trading center called Manitowoc
where there are quite a few Norwegians. Then we walked about
thirty kilometers northwest. Our companions claimed land there.
Besides them there are [unintelligible word] Danish immigrants,
Niels Hansen Gotfriedsen and Frederik Hjorth, and two Norwegian brothers named Andersen. Their land is all together
and is right next to some unclaimed land. It didn't take us long to
decide to claim land there, because it was the best I have ever
seen. It is slightly hilly. The topsoil is about thirty centimeters
deep, and underneath is a layer of clay. Most of it is wooded, but
it is not thick with trees, and most of them are small. There is a
swamp in one corner of my property with fir trees by the
hundreds. Most of them are about twenty meters high and thirty
centimeters in diameter. But the most important kind of tree is
the sugar maple, which you know about since you bought Fribert's
book. I have enough trees to make two to three thousand
[unintelligible word giving unit of measure] of sugar a year. A
little stream runs through my land. On its banks grow hops with
buds larger and stronger than any I have ever seen in Denmark.
Some springs flow out of the rocks, so I have the best water I've
ever tasted. That's an advantage over here where water is the
usual drink. (People drink tea or coffee twice a day everywhere,
though.)

Not far from my land there is a waterfall on the same stream. It
will probably be used to drive a mill. There is a windmill a little
farther away.

My neighbors' wheat crop was very good this year, so there is no
doubt that this is excellent land. We don't plow the soil here the

first year after the trees have been cut down and their leaves burned because it is so dry that one can plant five or six grains in it and harvest only enough to have seed for next year.

The settlement is new and difficult to reach by wagon, even though a main road leads here. Nevertheless, the ground is being cultivated everywhere. The post office is not far away, and the trade centers of Green Bay, Twin Rivers, and Manitowoc are all within twenty-five kilometers. We have discussed naming our town "Denmark." I am considering living on half of my land and giving the rest to Casper. I'll let you know. If I make enough money I'll come home and visit you before I make any long-range plans. I'm not as afraid to travel as I was when I left home. I am thinking about taking a trip south on the Mississippi River, possibly tomorrow morning.

Now that I have overcome the homesickness I had at first, I think better and better about America. I can always come home, of course, but I don't want to be a burden to you, and you should not have to do anything for my sake in your older days. I don't want to lure anyone over here, but I am grateful to those who encouraged me to carry out my plan to emigrate.

Give my regards to Christian Thobiassen and my other friends and acquaintances. I have been in good health all the time, and the climate here seems to be just as comfortable as back in Denmark. I hope you will write to me often, because I find it especially refreshing to hear from you. Keep addressing the letters in the same way.

Casper is doing well, working on a farm. He has managed to save a hundred dollars, and earlier this year commissioned Rasmus Rasmussen to claim a piece of land for him. When I offered him half of mine he preferred that, of course. I don't know if Rasmussen will buy him some land before Casper can write to him. If that happens, I'll be able to make a lot of money selling my land, because it is worth two hundred dollars on the open market.

I won't write again until I have found work. In case working on a steamboat down there doesn't please me, I'll find another job. God bless you.

Andreas Frederiksen

Frederiksen later commented on the Civil War and his success as a farmer in Wisconsin. (Source: Danes Worldwide Archives, uncatalogued materials.)

New Denmark, Brown County
11 December 1861

Dear Parents and Brother,

It has been a very long time since I heard from you, and perhaps just as long since you heard from us. I want to write, therefore, even though I don't have much to report other than that we are still doing fine and are in good health. Our children are growing fast. The crops and our cattle breeding are quite successful. We live in peace and have to thank God for protecting us from evil and bestowing His blessings on us.

I was down in Wilmington recently and returned a few weeks ago. On the way back I visited some acquaintances in Racine, where I was told that a fellow who fits the description of Hendrik Stedsøn from Herslev has come to America and is currently in the army. Since then I've learned that both Christen and Lars from Margrethehaab volunteered for a Scandinavian infantry regiment that is being formed here in Wisconsin. Both sons of the gardener from Bistrup are cavalrymen in the regular army. They get twelve dollars a month. The volunteers, on the other hand, are paid thirteen dollars a month. All of them get free meals and clothes from the government. I won't report on the other news regarding the war, because you can read about it in the Danish newspapers. As you probably know, it went badly for us in the beginning, but during the past few months it has been going better.

As you know, we intend to move farther inland and settle on a piece of land that I bought a year ago. I haven't been able to sell the farm we have now, but we cannot complain about our life here. There is enough pasture for our cattle, regardless of how many we have, and that will not be the case on the new farm for quite a while. On the other hand, we now live seven kilometers from town, but there it will be only two. Here all of our neighbors are Danes, but out there most will be Americans, and I prefer them. The soil is good in both places. About twenty-five of the forty *acres* I want to sell are cultivated and fenced. The buildings are quite good, and I believe I can get about five hundred dollars for it. I will still have 114 *acres* left here, of which ten are cultivated and fenced, but there aren't any buildings on that land. There is no rush in selling it, though, since there aren't any buildings to be maintained on it.

Last year I planted six bushels of wheat, one and a half of rye, two and a half of barley, ten of oats, four of peas and a little over an acre of millet. I let part of my land lie fallow with timothy grass because grain prices are low and it is more profitable to raise cattle. Besides, I have no desire to plant more grain than Johanne and I can harvest. We have butchered and sold two pigs that weighed two hundred kilograms together and have eight left, which we intend to butcher during the course of the winter. Pork is cheap, though, so we got only about six dollars per one hundred kilograms. We also have ten cattle. They are cheap, too; a good cow is worth fifteen to twenty dollars. But horses are expensive because of the war. I have thought about buying a mare, but will wait until prices go down.

Right now is a good time to emigrate to America. Those who have families will be able to buy food cheaply until they can grow enough to support themselves. Single men will be able to make good money next summer, because the government has drafted most of the men into the army.

Here in the settlement there is a society that subscribes to *Berlingske Avis*, so we stay well informed about everything back home.

Andrew Frederickson

Remember that my address is:

> Denmark, Brown County
> Wisconsin
> North America

Write soon because I long to hear from you.

Several years later Frederickson reported that eastern Wisconsin was still booming and offered a bright future for his children (Source: Danes Worldwide Archives, uncatalogued materials.)

Neenah, Winnebago County
Wisconsin
29 September 1872

Dear Brother,

We received your letter a month ago and were happy to learn
that all of you are in tolerable health and good circumstances, and
especially that Kirsten is happily married.

Here there haven't been any great changes, or perhaps I should
have written, no sudden changes. Nothing looks the same as it did
thirteen years ago when Casper and I came here on foot from
New Denmark. But things have changed only gradually, so we
haven't noticed it. Nevertheless, it seems to me that Johanne and I
are about the same. Perhaps I look a little older than the last time
you saw us, but age hasn't changed Johanne's appearance.
Caroline is now sixteen and a half years old and five centimeters
taller than her mother. Last February she began to take piano
lessons at a convent that the Catholics built a few years ago. The
same nun who teaches music also has a small private school, so
Caroline began to go to school regularly about six weeks ago. I
pay four dollars every three months for her schooling and five
dollars for her music lessions. Andrew is now fourteen years old
and rather big and strong for his age. He helps me on the farm in
the summer and goes to school in the winter.

As a rule I have one or two hired men, who are very expensive
at the moment. Last summer I had one man from 8 May for
sixteen dollars a month for the first month and a half, then a
dollar a day for three months. He was a bad worker. I hired a
very capable man for eighteen days during the harvest and paid
him two dollars a day. At the moment I don't have anyone, but in
a month we have to make hay and spread manure, so I'll need
one or two men. Last winter I hired Lars Kjeldsen's hired man
Christen from Gjerninge. He is not very energetic, but at least he
behaved himself and I made sure he didn't get his hands on any
alcohol, which is not used as food over here.

The reason wages have gone up so much is undoubtedly the
fact that so many railroads are being built. No fewer than five are
close enough to attract laborers from this area. Four of them
already pass through or will soon pass through Neenah and
Menasha, which are so close to each other that I don't know where

one ends and the other begins. And I can tell you that twenty-five
years ago those towns were a large forest where the Indians went
hunting. Workers on the railroad section gangs earn two to two
and a quarter dollars a day, but practically none of them work
close to home, so they have to pay from three to five dollars a
week for room and board. That reduces their wages. Despite the
high wages there is a shortage of workers. From time to time
there have been posters hanging all summer in the towns
announcing in both German and English that a thousand workers
and three hundred wagons and teams of horses are needed by the
Milwaukee Northern Railroad. They promise two dollars a day,
which shows how desperate they are because the previous summer
the same railroad offered only a dollar and a half a day, as far as
I know.

Because of the high value of labor I am careful that the
children get as much ability as possible in everything that will be
useful in the future. Even though Caroline is now learning music
and studying subjects about which I know very little, she first had
to learn how to cook and bake, milk cows, and use a sewing
machine. She has sewed her own clothes since she was fourteen
years old.

We are all happy and in good health, and hope that God's peace
and blessing be with you. Greet your brother-in-law.

Your brother,
Andrew Frederickson

*An immigrant in Wisconsin found the valley of the Wisconsin flooded, but
not with Danish girls.* (Source: *Langelands Avis,* 1 September 1876.)

Last spring and right up to the present we have had a lot of
rain. Three times the water in the stream that flows through my
forest has risen five or six meters over its normal level. I have
heard that between twenty and thirty bridges have been washed
out here in Jackson County. The bridge and mill at Muscoda [*sic*]
had to be lashed to old tree trunks with thick ropes; otherwise the
water would have taken away both the bridge and the mill. There
is room for a mill in my forest, and I have thought about writing
to Denmark concerning plans, but have given up the idea after

seeing the flood. The nearest mills are about twenty kilometers from here: the steam mill in Holten and the water mill in Muscoda. They cost twenty thousand and twenty-four thousand dollars to build, but their owners get one-sixth and one-fifth of the grain as payment, so both millers are rich men.

Genuine Danish girls are just as scarce as mills here. The few who come get married immediately. Wages are a dollar or a dollar and a half per day during the harvest season, but otherwise usually sixteen to twenty dollars a month.

There aren't any poor people here, nor is there a poor tax. If anyone is in need he gets help from private charities. Even though there is a great deal of evil in America, there is also a great deal of good. People could lead a good life here, but selfishness and financial greed are considerable. I believe corruption is worse here, and there are far more criminals than in Denmark.

The forthcoming presidential election will show whether the people are awake and understand how to use their rights. I do not have much faith in this republic, and even though things are generally going well for me here I still long for Denmark. We get only about half of the retail price for agricultural products, and farm implements and other machinery are high priced. It is also expensive to maintain a hired hand. Farming is certainly not a get-rich-quick venture, but cattle breeding is the most profitable form of it.

A bitter farmhand in Iowa believed he was being exploited. (Source: *Langelands Avis,* 7 November 1872.)

25 August 1872

At the moment I am in the state of Iowa, two miles west of Sabula and the Mississippi. The work itself is said to be easier than at home, but in reality it is far more difficult because our only rest periods are at the most necessary mealtimes and at night. Considering that we also have to work hard and practically never get anything but water to drink, you can understand that it is not easy to survive among these slaves.

The summer heat is far more intense here than in Denmark; in fact, at times it is unbearable. On certain days it is so intense that the air around here smells like the anteroom of a Roman bath. As a rule, though, the heat waves last only a few days and sometimes only one.

I earn a wage of about 260 Danish *rigsdaler* where I am now and expect to be for a year. In all respects I am as content as one can be in America.

Usually a farmer has one hired man for every 90 to 100 *acres* of cultivated land, but the one I work for has 120 *acres* and gets along with me alone. Usually a farmer who has only one hired man in the summer has none at all during the winter. All kinds of work are limited in the winter, so the people who are let go have no choice but to become lumberjacks up in the northern forests or else live on their savings, if they have any. Generally speaking, the demand for labor is decreasing because the grain is harvested by machine, threshed by machine, and cleaned by machine. Each machine has its own district and goes around from farm to farm within it. At harvest time the rule of thumb is that one man can bind and shock thirty *acres* of grain, so we really have to work hard with all our strength, almost harder than we can without breaking down. In the meantime the good *farmer* sits up on his harvesting machine and laughs at his workers who are stupid enough to allow themselves to be exploited. Believe me, immigrants become hollow-cheeked and often sick after they have been here a while.

Wages vary considerably. The best positions pay 160 to 200 dollars a year, or 18 to 20 dollars a month, occasionally more. Very few can earn that much, though, because this area is full of people. Besides, not all farmers can pay large wages, especially this year when the market is worse than it has been for a long time. Pork and beef cost three dollars per hundred pounds. That is the largest source of income the farmers have. Good work clothes and boots cost the same here as in Denmark, but a pair of wooden shoes cost a dollar and a half here. Machines, farm implements, and household items—in short, everything that is needed to run a farm—are ridiculously expensive. A factory owner, unlike a farmer, cannot keep going with only a few employees. Everything he uses in manufacturing—metals and wood or coal—is expensive, because it has to pass through so many hands before he gets it. In order to recover his investment he is forced to charge high prices, and it is the farmer who must pay them.

Despite the late summer heat, a farm worker in Iowa thought conditions were better there than in Denmark. (Source: Danes Worldwide Archives, Ole Andersen MSS.)

Atlantic, Iowa

2 September 1889

Dear Brother-in-law,

Today I want to write a few lines to you and tell you a little from this side of the Atlantic. First, it's very warm over here. In fact, the temperature has been 116 degrees, but I understand there are two English degrees for every Danish one. It's easy to start sweating, and my shirt is so wet it looks like it was just pulled out of a well.

We just finished the harvest. It was hard to work in this heat. We had to drink a lot of water, since they don't brew beer here. Other than that I don't have much news. I'm healthy and things are going all right, but English is damned hard to learn. I've begun to speak a little, but I can understand it better than I can speak.

I'm working for an American now about five kilometers from town. There aren't as many small towns here as there are back home. The farmers drive quite a way to the larger towns to sell their wares.

Over here it's not at all like back home. Nobody has to hire himself out for a year at a time, only for a month. If a worker wants to quit, he doesn't have to tell his employer in advance. He can just leave when his time is over, and the farmer can't come into town after him. This is a free country. Nobody is bound like back home.

It's hard to find a job in town, but always easy to get work on the farms. It isn't so risky now for a man who doesn't have a wife and children to come over here. He can quickly earn enough to go back to Denmark again. But it's worse for a man with a family because he can't travel around looking for work. I think things can work out over here. Everyone should bring along his sense of humor. It doesn't help to go around with a long face. The only thing I really miss is a good bottle of beer, but I just can't get one here.

Now I'll close for this time.

Best regards from your brother-in-law,

Ole Andersen

An anonymous farm laborer expressed his thorough disenchantment and regretted not listening to his returned emigrant brothers. (Source: *Holbæk-Posten*, 29 September 1892).

Most of what we hear about America are reports from those emigrants who are doing well over there. We seldom if ever hear anything from those who are not doing so well. Hence, this could be interesting.

I know a strong, capable young farmer who went to America with the intention of working there, looking around a bit, learning something, and coming back after two years. He was then twenty-three years old. He came home after the two years were up, but he almost resembled an old man, weathered and worn out. For about six months after he came back he lived with relatives and regained his strength. Had he stayed in Yankeeland with its blazing summers and bitterly cold winters, he hardly would have lived to be an old man. At least he can look forward to that in Denmark. Because of his skill and industriousness he is doing well here.

One of his brothers emigrated later but soon returned. Another brother, who is also a strong young farmer, is currently over there. He left last winter and had in mind to stay two years and get American equality, of which he had great expectations. Let him speak for himself:

> I'll be back before long—by November—unless I get lucky in the meantime. I have tried several places over here, but never have the good fortune of having enough to eat. The place where I am now working is the worst of all. I get all the water I can drink and all the potatoes I can eat. Once or twice a week I get a piece of meat, but it is so small that a bird could fly with it in its beak. That is all that is served me at the tables, but I manage to get a little extra outside of mealtimes.

Whenever I milk the cows, morning or evening, I take the half-full pail and drink as much as I can pour down my throat.

Another thing that can't be helped is the bad weather. One day it is so hot that I don't need clothes, and sometimes the next day is so cold that I shiver, even if I have my jacket buttoned.

It hasn't been easy to find friends over here. In fact, I haven't met anyone I really liked since I was in Chicago. As I mentioned earlier, I'm considering coming home as soon as possible. I've had enough of this "land of robbers," as you call it.[2]

I shall only add that I have written about my own brothers.

R.

A satisfied worker offered glimpses of life on a farm in Missouri. (Source: *Demokraten*, 20 January 1892.)

Stiklerville, where I work, is about three hundred kilometers inside Missouri. The towns here are not like the ones back in Denmark. Most of the people here are farmers, and each one lives out on his own farm. All of the houses are wooden, but our yards are not nearly as big as they are back home and there is no luxury here. The most prosperous farmers go into town in their work clothes, although they are never tattered. The farmers are no better than the servants. Whenever we have to go out, we get a horse to ride.

The fields here are very hilly, and there is a lot of forested land. All in all the soil is the best that can be found. We cleared part of the forest last spring, about twenty *acres*. There were a hundred loads of wood on it. We just piled it up and burned it. Too bad the wood wasn't back in Denmark! We plowed the land immediately and planted corn on it. The first year the grain is the best you can imagine.

The winters are very cold here, and the summers are hot. But the livestock always go outside all year.

We make our own syrup here, and it is clearly better than the stuff you get back home in Denmark.

2. Unfortunately, the writer does not indicate towns in either Denmark or the United States.

As far as the animal kingdom is concerned, I don't think we have any wild animals except wolves. They don't bother people—they're afraid of them, in fact. There are also several kinds of vipers and some rather large snakes.

The workers here are very well fed. We eat three times a day. The meals consist of pork, beef, and eggs, together with several kinds of bread. I also get as much milk as I can drink.

The livestock prices are on the average: a five-year-old horse, one hundred dollars; a good cow with a calf, twenty dollars; a live pig of two hundred pounds, six dollars. The pork is just as good as back home.

We drink water instead of beer, and we can't get enough hard liquor. A small bottle costs half a dollar and can't be bought without a prescription. It is used only as medicine.

The harvest begins early in July. We thresh oats and cut hay. The corn is harvested in October. The yield is thirty to fifty *bushels* of corn per hectar. In the autumn a bushel of corn costs from twenty-five to thirty-five cents.

In the winter the farmer has nothing to do, so he can just sit inside with his wife. But he earns enough during the summer so that he can take it easy five months a year.

An immigrant in Nebraska chronicled the origin of a Danish settlement. (Source: *Langelands Avis*, 13 June 1872.)

Dannebrog Settlement
17 May 1872

Dear Editor,

If I remember correctly, I touched on the Danish settlement in Howard County, Nebraska, in one of my earlier letters. Some readers of your worthy newspaper might be interested in hearing more about "Dannebrog," which is now one year old.

About two years ago several prominent Danes in Wisconsin decided to ask the state government for permission to form the "Board of Directors of the Danish Land and Homestead Company." They intended to raise money by selling shares of stock and gather bold, effective Danes to found a Danish settlement somewhere in the western states. Governor Fairchild of

Wisconsin was happy to grant the request. Even though the board
of directors did not get the support it deserved in the West, it
elected a committee in March 1871 to find a suitable location for
founding a Danish settlement. After some trips the committee
decided that the prairie north of the Loup Fork River in Howard
County, Nebraska, was best and offered the most advantages for
achieving the goals of the company. The region is about twenty
English miles north of the great railroad to the Pacific.

Around 1 May the first Danish settlers, of whom I was one,
arrived at the Loup Fork River. After wading across it we saw one
of the most fertile prairies in the West. It had previously been
seen by few human beings other than Pawnee and Sioux Indians.
They had sold the land to the government but still regarded
themselves as the rulers of Howard County. The government
wisely sent a company of soldiers to protect the colony, so the
Indians have been peaceful up to now. A year ago there was not a
single house in the county; now there are at least a hundred of
them and several hundred settlers.

Of course, there are many difficulties and dangers from wild
animals when an uncultivated area is settled. Most of the settlers
live far from the nearest town, many twenty to fifty English miles
away. They have to buy all of their wares and sell their produce at
that distance until shops are built nearer their homes and the
railroads are extended. Then their property will also double in
value. Any reasonable settler can be sure that after a few years'
hard work and frugality his 160 *acres* of land will be worth several
thousand dollars. He and his descendents will have a secure
future. It must be satisfying to know that he has changed a fertile
but desolate piece of land into a comfortable home.

The Danish settlement now has a considerable number of
Danes, mostly young, healthy, strong people who are willing to put
up with dangers and difficulties in order to build homes for their
future. The settlement has the esteemed old Danish name
"Dannebrog" in honor of the Danish flag. Our postmaster is Mr.
L. Hannibal, the former chairman of the board of directors of the
Danish land company in Wisconsin.

The simplicity of American settlers' houses here is remarkable.
In new settlements most of them are made of vertical posts
covered with brush. They have thatched roofs. The furniture is no

less economical; a table, a few chairs, some trunks, and a tile oven
are usually the extent of it. Most of the settlers have rifles,
revolvers, and shotguns hanging on their walls. Hunting is
important in the sparsely populated areas of America, where elk,
antelope, deer, rabbits, and all kinds of birds can be found in
abundance.

After a year or two settlers usually start to crawl out of their sod
huts and build comfortable wooden houses. Several of the Danes
in Dannebrog reached that stage this spring. They don't need
granaries because the grain is threshed by machine immediately
after it is harvested. They don't need the straw as the horses are
fed hay and grain in the winter. The cattle can stay outside most
of the year because the winter is much shorter here in Nebraska
than in Denmark. The pastures are excellent in the summer, so
cattle raising is the chief source of income for settlers.

P. Andersen

Another Dane in Dannebrog described growth in the area of the settlement.
(Source: *Langelands Avis,* 26 July 1872.)

Dannebrog
Howard County, Nebraska
2 July 1872

Dear Editor,

Last year we founded here a Danish *settlement,* as they call it, or
a Danish colony, consisting of fifty families. At the moment all of
them have exceptionally good land for agriculture and cattle
raising, which are quite profitable here. The worst thing is that
many arrive with not nearly enough money and cannot buy
livestock and machinery, which are quite expensive here. Otherwise, they are all doing well and will hopefully be rich within
a few years, because the soil is especially fertile. I have seen
examples of virgin land being plowed on 1 May and yielding a
good harvest, especially corn and potatoes, that year. The next
year it is splendid for wheat or whatever else is planted on it.

Four towns have been founded this year. Before long all of
them will blossom luxuriantly. Dannebrog, the beginning of our
colony, lies seven English miles from here. The others are St.

Paul, eight miles away; Kotesfield, six miles away; and Petersborg, where I live, which is named after a man who lives right next to me. Both of our names are Petersen. This summer the railroad is being built right past our doorways. It will raise the value of our land significantly and ease the shipping of our produce as well as bring in necessary goods. Schools and churches are going up with remarkable speed, one after another. We Danes intend to build a Danish school and gather a Danish Lutheran church.

Whoever has not seen something like this cannot imagine how fast the country is being settled and built up. As soon as construction is underway the railroad comes through. The merchants arrive and build villages and towns. We have our share of speculators who follow and try to get rich quickly at the expense of the settlers. People learn fast to watch out for them.

I won't write any more this time, because I don't know whether you find this interesting. If anyone wants information about conditions here, I would be happy to reply to the best of my ability.

P. C. Petersen

An anonymous Dane in the Dannebrog settlement commented on the immigrant press and other aspects of frontier life. (Source: Langelands Avis, 15 November 1872.)

Dannebrog Settlement
6 October 1872

Dear Editor,

I am happy to report that during the course of the summer no fewer than four Danish newspapers have begun to appear here in the western states. Two of them, *Norden* and *Amerika*, are published in Chicago. The former is a weekly but *Amerika* is both a daily and a weekly. The other two, *Nebraska Skandinav* and *Den danske Pioneer*, are published in Omaha, the largest city in Nebraska. There are many Danes in this state, eight hundred in Omaha alone. The appearance of these newspapers in Omaha has helped them. They are only weeklies but, if they get strong support from the large Danish community here, we can expect at least one of them to begin to publish a daily edition.

Except for strong political agitation, there is little of interest to
report. The readers of your newspapers are probably not interested in the railroad and steamboat accidents. In the vicinity
of Laramie, Wyoming Territory, the Indians attacked a wagon
train and killed about twenty people. Only a few escaped.

The corn harvest is well underway and has been completed in
some areas. The yields have varied greatly in different parts of the
state. Some areas have suffered greatly from drought during the
last ten months. The last few months the only rain has been in
violent thunderstorms. In those areas where it has not rained the
corn will be bad because the heat and dryness have caused it to
ripen too fast. Here in Dannebrog the harvest will be average. The
past few weeks the temperature has been pleasant, almost like a
Danish summer. The thermometer has been between twenty and
thirty degrees Celsius in the shade.

A young man in Nebraska described winter on the prairie. (Source: *Vejle
Amts Folkeblad,* 20 October 1882.)

. . . When winter comes we have to gather fuel. We get it
easily, even though we have neither forests nor bogs. If necessary,
we could use straw, which we leave for the livestock out where we
do the threshing. The horses and pigs leave the corn cobs, which
together with the stalks make excellent fuel. So do the stalks of the
treelike grass that grows out in the brush areas. We are always
ready for the chills of winter. Until now we were able to get some
trees from unsettled land, but it has been bought now. Those trees
were over a meter in diameter. Coal should become cheaper and
be used more in the future.

Christmas isn't celebrated in any big way here. In America it
isn't a public festival, as is the case back home. We go to church
on Christmas, but there is school on St. Stephen's Day. Scandinavians who felt how "good it is to be children at Christmas
time" back home have preserved some of the season's cheer.
Easter and Pentecost are celebrated for only one day each. We
have plenty of time to celebrate Christmas, though, because
we don't have anything else to do in the winter except gather fuel

and watch the cows. We also have time to dabble in household work, reading, and school work.

A farm laborer in central Minnesota agreed that conditions in the United States were better than those in Denmark and added that life on the farm was preferable in the long run to city life. (Source: *Social-Demokraten*, 5 January 1876.)

After reading the steady stream of reports about the difficult conditions for workers here in America that come to Denmark through the press and private letters, and which are gleefully echoed there, I feel compelled to draw a comparison of workers' conditions in the two countries. I shall focus on farmhands.

The conditions under which Danish farmworkers toil are, of course, miserable. In many respects they are worse than those of American Negro slavery, which was condemned by all civilized countries. In a sense the Negroes did not have to worry about feeding themselves. They received a certain amount of food for each member of their family, and as a rule this was more than enough to live on. In addition they received clothing, accommodations, and firewood, and, because their owners had a vested interest in preserving them, they worked a limited time each day.

The farmhand in Denmark, on the other hand, has to toil from morning until evening at the caprice of his employer in order to eke out a grim life for himself and his family. If the work he must do surpasses his energy, his boss does not care, for there are always others to take his place. He has to send his children away from home as soon as they are able to work. This forces them to neglect their education, so they never develop into citizens capable of looking after their own interests in a free society. In most instances the worker cannot even consider improving his conditions. If he happens to reach old age and is no longer able to work, he is not entitled to a trouble-free retirement, but rather is sent to the poorhouse. From that vantage point he can watch his children follow in the footsteps of his own miserable life.

Compare this with the position of the Danish farmhand after his arrival in America. Let us assume that on his arrival in the West he has used up all of his money. He can find a place to leave his family while he goes out and works. After earning some money he can choose a piece of land. If there is no unclaimed government land in his area he can get a farm under the *Homestead Act*. If he wants to go elsewhere he can find land almost anywhere in the West and buy it on long-term credit. If the land he has selected is forested or lies in an area where there is a lot of timber, he can build a wooden house for next to nothing. Then he can divide his time working for others and improving his own farm. Gradually he can buy a cow or two. Firewood is free. After a while he can cultivate enough land to feed himself, and in the course of a few years he becomes independent. Then he can keep his children home, and they can help him cultivate the land. He can send them to school now and then, because schooling is free between the ages of five and twenty-one.

Of course, here as anywhere else a man can become sick or grow old and not be in a position to provide for his family. In such cases, though, they will be taken care of here better than in Denmark. I have lived in this area, which has nearly three thousand inhabitants, for six years. During this time only one family, as far as I know, has applied for and received aid. The family was Norwegian and the man had been ill for a long time. As evidence that the family did not suffer any deprivation, I might add that the man kept his sixteen-year-old daughter at home, even though she was big and strong and many people wanted to hire her. The girl's father said she should go to school instead.

Conditions are different for the worker who chooses to settle in town. He does not suffer any of the settler's deprivations, because he can immediately rent a house and live comfortably. As a rule he earns a higher wage than do those in rural areas. His children get a better education than they would in sparsely populated regions. He has access to many enjoyments and pastimes that were unknown for him in Denmark.

If one looks only at the positive side, it seems undeniable that urban life is more comfortable. But a closer examination reveals that his long-range prospects are far less favorable than those of the man who has taken a home in the country. All kinds of food are more expensive in the cities, and firewood must be bought at a high price. Rent is also high. In the densely populated industrial cities there is more sickness than in the countryside, and every financial crisis brings a wave of unemployment. One should not believe that there cannot be unemployment in a country with millions of *acres* of fertile, uncultivated land, or that unemployed city workers can make a living from agriculture during such times. That is far from the case. Many wince at the thought of exchanging the comforts of city life to which they have gradually become accustomed for the hardships of farming. Besides, most of them have some money tied up in city property, which is not easy to sell during times of crisis. As a result they stay in the cities, wait for better times, and contribute to unemployment.

> Jens Peter Andersen
> Becker, Sherburne County
> Minnesota

K. C. Bodholdt (1855–1931), a pastor in the Danish Evangelical Lutheran Church, related how he participated in founding a Danish colony in southern Minnesota. (Source: *Kolding Folkeblad,* 29 and 30 December 1885.)

The great influx of Danish settlers in Nebraska and Minnesota has significantly increased the work of the Danish clergymen out here on the prairie as well as up in Minnesota. Every year a large number of Danish farmers sell their property in the eastern states and buy larger tracts of uncultivated land in Nebraska and Minnesota. Since it is important for the Danish church over here to get as many members as possible, we have considered forming a large Danish colony for a long time. Now we have found favorable conditions in Lincoln County, Minnesota, where approximately thirty-five thousand *acres* of land have been bought. It is now open for colonization, so Pastor Anker[3] and I went out there together with fifteen farmers. I assume that many friends in Denmark would like to know what this land looks like, so I shall report on it a bit.

After I had been in Omaha last summer on a business trip, I was informed about this excursion and went to Elk Horn, Iowa,

3. Kristian Anker (1848–1928).

where the Danish folk high school is located. There I met Pastor
Anker and a few farmers. We departed by train from Audubon in
pouring rain, but all of us were in good spirits, and even though it
was evening the farmers sang all night. Perhaps that was because
the day before two criminals had been lynched. It would have
taken too long to hang them legally, but in America that kind of
news has no influence on people's spirits or on the outcome of a
journey.

We traveled all night at a speed of thirty to forty English *miles*
per hour. By morning we were in northwestern Iowa and pressing
farther north into completely unfamiliar territory. Terrible storms
had hit the area only a few days earlier and overturned several
houses. I saw the strange sight of buildings "lying at anchor."
They had been built of wood on sandy ground and anchored with
strong ropes to pilings driven into the ground. In that way they
were bobbing around with their inhabitants and other material
inside. Nevertheless, the region appeared to be fertile and had
many well-cultivated fields and attractive farms.

The trip continued northward, and at 11 P.M. we reached the
Minnesota border in pouring rain and furious thunder, the likes
of which I have never experienced. Our entire party decided to
spend the night in the little station town. In the morning we
continued westward through eastern Minnesota, where the area
offered a rich mixture of crystal-clear rivers with luxuriant forests
lining their banks and beautiful lakes and scattered woodlands,
interspersed with partly flat and fertile prairies. Several million
acres of fertile soil had lain there for centuries waiting for the
current of civilization to reach these fruitful regions.

At noon we reached our destination, Lake Benton, a small town
next to a lake of the same name in Lincoln County. At the station
we hired wagons to convey us out into the country. After we had
bought some food we drove off across the pathless prairie and
then over hills to meadows with streams of various sizes.

A humorous episode occurred when we drove across a large
pasture area that several days of rain had flooded. Without
imagining there might be a brook or stream there we drove right
out into the water. Suddenly the horses pulling the first wagon
disappeared and all six men had to jump off in order to lighten
the load. The horses swam toward land, still pulling the wagon,

while the men had to swim or wade ashore. The rear wagon went in another direction, thereby avoiding the involuntary bath. Our friends used the time to lay their clothes out to dry in the sun. Wearing only their "birthday suits," except for cigars and hats, they inspected a section of land until we met our party in the best of health and good cheer. An older Danish man who had recently come to America and was always "putting down" everything he saw, was so shocked by all of this that he probably wanted to "put down" the clergymen who could participate in such a group. But after all, this was America.

The trip went well the rest of the day. That evening another group arrived, consisting of four pastors and twenty other people, so it was quite a squeeze at the local hotel. In America one soon learns to accept conditions as they are, however, so without arguing about it I slept soundly on the floor with my suitcase as a pillow.

The next day we went up to the northern part of the colony the same way we had done before, but this time we did not have to do any swimming because most of the water had soaked into the ground and we could see where we should drive across the pasture. A great deal of the land was bought at seven or eight dollars an *acre*. Many intended to move here in the spring, and I am certain that many farmers from the eastern states want to sell their property and get some of this fertile but very inexpensive land. Many of my countrymen who come over here with a little money could work hard for a few years and get a comfortable home in this attractive landscape that is best described as "forest, lake, and pasture" with luxuriant grassy meadows.

After we had inspected the land and taken care of the purchases we went back to Lake Benton and made an excursion to a small, wooded island in the middle of the lake. It was Saturday, and the trip out there was very pleasant. The local band played some tunes on board and in the pavilion on the island. We ate dinner in small groups out there, and then did some singing, playing, and fishing. The lake was full of fish, especially northern pike.

The next day we Danes sailed back to the island, where we had a worship service. Our happy stay ended when we climbed aboard the train that evening. All of us were in good cheer and happy to have seen with our own eyes the land that had been offered at so low a price in Minnesota. It was not a bunch of American *humbug*, something that exists in abundance.

We must admit that there are not yet too many people in the western states. On the contrary, there is room for millions of capable, hard-working farmers to create attractive, pleasant homes on the almost endless northern and western prairies. The climate is good and healthy, although it must be called a mid-continental climate, and our usual varieties of grain do well here. For the marketing of produce the Northern Pacific Railroad runs through Minnesota and now connects New York and Chicago with San Francisco and the Pacific Ocean.

A traveler in North Dakota described an immigrant funeral on the prairie. (Source: *Den nye Verden,* 28 November 1890.)

Fargo, North Dakota
4 November 1890

The Dakotas are a strange place, lying between the setting sun and the smiling waters of Minnesota. But stranger still are their marvelous customs. About a year ago I was traveling out on the prairie and spent a quiet Sunday in a rural village. The day was one of those when all of nature seems to be keeping the Sabbath. The sun shone in all its magnificence, the grassy landscape smelled fresh, and birds sang enchanting melodies while fat grazing cows mooed to express their contentedness. Everything was in harmony.

Early in the morning a funeral procession came slowly down the road on the way to the cemetery, where the primitive little church looked more like a Norwegian mountain cabin. A young man had died. His friends had come, some in wagons, others on foot, all filled with a feeling of brotherhood and sorrow.

Many of the wagons were drawn by oxen. In one cart four women, all dressed in black, sat on some prairie hay. One of them was crying, and the words of consolation did not seem to comfort her.

The deceased had come from Denmark. He was born amid the dunes and sandbanks of Jutland. But he had been in America for seven years and was completely Americanized. He had claimed a farm under the *Homestead Act*. After toiling on it for a year, he had written home for his sister, who was to come and be his housekeeper. Big and strong, with red cheeks, she had arrived only a month before his death. Now she sat in the cart and wept over his coffin.

She inherited his newly founded home, 160 *acres* of land with a small wooden house. She had to do two persons' work, but received a lot of help from sympathetic neighbors. In six months she learned the meaning of the word *love*, and is now married to a young school teacher, who will quickly help her expand her knowledge of the language. Sorrow for the deceased created love for the living. Black crepe gave way to flowers, and dark clouds to bright sunshine.

The young farmer had been elected to the state legislature this year, and it is more than likely that he would have had a seat in the Congress of the United States within a few years. Then the redoubtable Danish girl who wept in loneliness over her brother's coffin in a foreign country and who would not let herself be consoled would have become a fixture in the social scene of the nation's capital, Washington.

Yes, great is the inspiration and mighty are the possibilities in *the grand republic*.

Thomas

A young Dane in Dakota Territory lamented the shortage of girls on the prairie. (Source: *Den nye Verden*, April 1888.)

Sanborn, Barnes County
Dakota Territory
January 1888

. . . There is a Scandinavian settlement here, and, although things do not always look so bright, it seems to be making progress. Almost all of the Scandinavians who have settled here arrived penniless and had to begin with their bare hands. But those who began with little and did not incur terribly large debts are doing better every year, despite the low wheat prices. On the other hand, those who began on too big a scale are losing. It would be good if more energetic Scandinavians would begin to farm here. There is a lot of railroad land here that can be had at a good price. The winter is severe up here, but then we have a better summer than most other places. We never get sunstroke.

What we miss most are girls! There are nothing but half-grown children here. There are a lot of old bachelors here just waiting for the girls to get old enough to marry. The innocent lasses don't even celebrate their fifteenth birthday before ten old bachelors in their thirties are on their knees proposing to them. But the girls choose those who have the most gray hair, so there is no point in a young man proposing here. If an immigrant from Fyn writes home to his girlfriend, he can never be certain that a Jew has not gotten to her first and snatched her away right before his nose.

A Happy Boy

An immigrant commented on the hardships of farming in what he anachronistically called "Dakota." (Source: Den nye Verden, March 1890.)

Grove City, Minnesota

Dear Editor,

As an old subscriber to your paper I request that you print this piece.

In recent times I have read and heard a good many contradictory things about Dakota, "the second promised land." I did not really know what to believe and, tired of all the rhetoric, decided to take a trip out there and examine conditions.

So I said farewell to hearth and home, climbed aboard a train, and departed. The trip was especially comfortable. One part of the landscape dissolved into the next in rapid succession. We went through town after town, which testified to the progress and prosperity of the area. Toward evening we reached Northwood, where we were to spend the night. The land in that area is well cultivated and suited for wheat, as the magnificent wheat fields revealed. The farmers seemed to be doing relatively well, despite their rather limited funds. The capitalists seem to be in control

there, just as in many other places. In such a young colony little
or no business is done on credit, unless one is willing to put up
one's land or personal property as collateral. That needs no
further comment. What seemed especially tragic to me is that if
the farmer cannot pay back his debt within a certain time he has
to pay a premium, the size of which the creditor determines, in
order to get an extension of the deadline. In addition, he must
pay 12 percent interest! It cannot be denied that that smacks of
usury.

From Northwood I went on to Towner in McHenry County,
where I found my brother, Thomas Thomsen, in the best of
health.

The landscape in that area is quite attractive. It can probably be
best described as a slightly undulating prairie with scattered
sandhills that are not so little. The soil is not so rich because it is
mixed with sand. In order to get a good harvest a lot of rain is
needed, and there is hardly a surplus of that here. When you also
take into consideration that *Jack Frost* seems to have a special
affinity to the area up here, this region does not seem very
promising for agriculture. Of course, it also has its advantages,
among which I must mention access to good water, which lies only
three to five meters below the ground, almost always on a sandy
bottom.

Firewood is cheap, as is hay. Hay is sold for only two dollars a
stack. But that is not enough to compensate for the negative
aspects of Dakota. Of course, one can live well there, as elsewhere,
if one has enough money. But what happens when the money has
been spent, or if one does not have any in the first place?

That is my impression of Dakota. Perhaps someone else can
come here and get a different, more positive impression of
conditions here. I have not written this in order to run the area
down. As far as I am concerned Dakota can be heralded as a
second paradise. But I must tell my countrymen that if they are
considering moving up here, they would do well to investigate this
paradise first. If they do not, they might be buying a pig in a
poke.

Henry Thomsen

A farmer in Texas found that dairy farming in the United States fell short of the modern techniques that were being developed in Denmark. (Source: Vendsyssel Tidende, 16 November 1885.)

Everything is going as usual here. There has been an intolerable heat wave this year, which has done me some damage. The various kinds of grass I planted for the cows last winter have withered, and the hay I got from the grass does not amount to much, but one must have patience. This has set my dairy farm back, of course, but maybe we will have a mild winter and the cows will have enough to eat in the pasture. There are a lot of problems involved in keeping a dairy farm going in this country, because in the summer the temperature is around sixty degrees Celsius in the shade, and milk becomes thick within a half hour. In order to keep it liquid, one must have a large icebox to set the milk into immediately after it is milked, but here we have only manufactured ice, which melts very fast and is terribly expensive. The price a farmer has to pay for ice can amount to more than he gets for his butter. Then winter comes with its often biting cold (which, however, does not last more than three days at a time), and since the buildings here are made of thin planks, the milk naturally freezes. Then we have to wait until the cold spell is over and the milk has thawed before we can skim it. That is how most of the so-called dairy farms are run around here, but I've remedied that by building a house with double walls and roof, which the heat of summer and cold of winter can't penetrate. In the middle of the house is a large basin where the milk is cooled. It is pumped full of water five or six times a day, and in this way the milk keeps very well. On the other hand, the milking of cows is very bad here. As soon as they come home from the pasture, and the milking begins, the calf is brought to the cow, and then one sees the milkmaid with a little tin pail milking half-heartedly on one side, while the calf sucks energetically on the other. They're competing to see who gets more milk! Needless to say, the calves are fat here, but the price for them is so low that it hardly pays to let them drink water, let alone milk. But the American farmer doesn't think about that. If he can make enough butter from ten cows to use at home, and have a little cream in his coffee each morning, he is satisfied and thinks he is *doing lig* [*sic*] *business.*

A brewery owner from Brabrand near Århus described the settlement of Danish farmers in Washington. (Source: *Demokraten,* 19 October 1892.)

From Portland I took the train down to the steamer that ferries people across the Columbia River, about two kilometers wide at the point. Then I was in Washington. A few years ago this state was the destination of a large number of migrants, from other parts of America as well as from Europe. They believed they would find instant happiness and prosperity. For most of them, however, that was not the case, especially for the farmers.

It was a different story for people who speculated in the founding of business centers, which sprang up like toadstools. This artificial speculation could not sustain itself, though, because the land was still partly wild and uncultivated. It had to be worked, minerals had to be found, mines had to be opened and worked, and all of this takes time. Consequently, the towns sank again. Some became complete failures and remain so to this day.

What Washington demands is a hardy, patient farmer who is willing to clear the forest and till the soil for many years and expect nothing more than his daily bread. Only in the distant future will he or, more correctly, his descendants, be able to reap the fruits of several years' arduous labor. The tide of settlers has largely stopped, and the state is now in what I would call in Danish a "standstill" [*stampe*].

That part of Washington bordering on Puget Sound, which cuts deeply into the state, is clearly one of the best and most valuable. The production of small grains and hops is excellent there, and there are two large, bustling cities, Tacoma and Seattle. A lot of coal from the region's mines is shipped from the latter. Lumber production is also significant in several areas, and an entire fleet is kept busy taking it out. Finally, there are a great deal of trade and steamship connections with British Columbia, Alaska, and so on.

Quite a few Danes live in this state. I believe many of them are prosperous, especially those who came with the first settlers and were able to get land. I hardly need to add that the value of both commercial and agricultural land has risen ten or twentyfold in a very few years. This has been the case in many of the best western states, although it reached its peak ten to fifteen years ago and the game is nearly over, except in a few scattered areas. Now successful speculation requires a detailed knowledge of local conditions, and settlers need considerably more cash than was once the case.

I left Washington after a tour around the state, because I could not find any appropriate business opportunity there, and went back to Portland and from there took a steamer to San Francisco. We sailed 70 kilometers down the Willamette River to the Columbia, and from there nearly 200 kilometers out to the Pacific Ocean. From Portland to San Francisco it is about 870 kilometers by that route.

Valdemar Wahl (1861–87), the son of a prosperous farmer from the Silkeborg region, emigrated to a Danish settlement in New Brunswick in 1883. A few months later he became a father. (Source: Benedicte Mahler, ed., *Catherine og. Valdemar—et udvandrerpars Skæbne skildret gennem breve* [Copenhagen: Fremad, 1975], pp. 49–50.)

Grand Falls, New Brunswick
6 November 1883

Dear Parents,

Today I can report the joyful news that yesterday, 5 November, Cathrine added to the world's population a fat little daughter. It started at 5 P.M., and before evening (it doesn't get dark here before 7 P.M.) both mother and daughter were doing fine. Cathrine is feeling spry and lying in bed talking. I didn't have anything to do with it, thank God. I could hardly have delivered her before Mr. Esquire and his wife came flying in and did it. His wife really knew what she was doing, and she almost had to hold Cathrine for the two hours it lasted. This afternoon Mrs. Petersen is here again with one of the young girls, Laura Hansen. She's delighted with the little girl, especially when she cries—presumably because she doesn't do that very often. She didn't make a sound all night, but she can if she wants to. They say she looks like me, especially her mouth. We have a woman here keeping house during these most demanding days. Later, Mrs. Petersen will be here.

We have arranged things with the Esquires so that they help us whenever we need something, and whenever they need something that we have, we help them. I think I can say that all of us have found the arrangement both useful and enjoyable.

Among the English people here a doctor usually handles childbirths, but in the settlement there are two Danish women who do it. I don't know one of them, but the one we had was very good. She asked only a dollar for her services, but I gave her two. The doctor would have charged ten. The doctor in Grand Falls is bad, and we have to drive fifteen kilometers to fetch him. But everyone says Mrs. Johansen is capable, so the only reasonable thing was to get her, even though she hasn't been officially approved. We saved eight dollars, and that's no small sum.

But enough of that. I have to answer some of Father's questions from his last letter. Danish is the only language spoken in this settlement, and English outside it except, of course, when two Danes meet. Danes go into Grand Falls practically every day. Everyone has his own transportation, either oxen or a team of horses. Last summer a lot of people bought horses. I know at least six who did so. When we came here, the only people who owned horses were the Esquires, and that's a sign of progress. I'm mighty proud of my two gray ones; they're probably the best team here. Now I have to find work for them this winter. It's crazy to feed two horses all winter. It's impossible to use them in the fields after the snow falls. If the map I sent home seems hilly, then it deceives, because only five or six *acres* are hilly, and they can still be cultivated, and I have plowed them. We like to put off long trips until winter, since it is much easier to travel by sleigh than by wagon on these roads, which can be very rough. People say there is never a shortage of bridges, because all of the rivers and creeks are frozen over and the snow is so light that we can drive through all of the drifts *ohne weiter* [German, without difficulty].

Wahl's younger brother Tobias had to notify his parents of Valdemar's accidental death. (Source: Mahler, ed., *Catherine og Valdemar*, pp. 123–24.)

Vanceboro, Maine
17 July 1887

Dear Parents,

I am doing well and still have the same job. Jodden[4] has also
found a good job here, and they're all doing well, both Cathrine
and the children. And I hope, dear old Mother and Father, that
that will lessen your sorrow over the sad news that I must now
give you.

You will soon have your precious little grandchildren and their
poor mother with you in Denmark. Cathrine became a widow on
Wednesday when Valdemar was killed in an accident in the forest
where he worked. This is not the first time I have had to send you
bad news from over here. I hope God will allow it to be the last
time and give you the strength to bear it as well as you have borne
so many other sorrows and disappointments.

I thought it best to tell you the whole truth immediately. I
feared that if I tried to prepare you for it gradually, then Mother
might assume something even worse than the sobering truth.

As you know, Valdemar worked on the railroad and chopped
down trees wherever the line was to be built. He was killed when a
tree that had been cut fell and struck a dead tree, which in turn
fell and hit him in the back of the head as he tried to run away
from it. He died immediately.

We received a telegram about it here Thursday evening. I went
down there on the next train.

Of course, it was a grievous message to bring to Cathrine and
now to you. We were almost afraid that she would not be able to
bear her grief, but to our great joy she has composed herself
somewhat and can do everything that must be done to prepare for
her future. The same day she received a letter from Valdemar
and one from her brother Michael, and, remarkably, Michael's
letter was almost exclusively about his willingness to take care of
both her and the children in case anything should happen to
Valdemar. She thinks she will travel to him as soon as possible.

I went immediately down to Moosehead Lake to a small town
named Greenville, ten kilometers from where the accident
happened and where his body had been brought. I was happy to

---

4. "Jodden" was the nickname of the writer's twin brother Johan, born in 1864.

be able to report to Cathrine, and now also to you, how well they treated the body and how well they greeted me and arranged the funeral, which took place down there. I did not arrive there until noon on Friday, and because of the heat it was impossible to move him. When I went down there, I was met by a local merchant who led me to the church where the minister was, and they led me in. Valdemar's body was well dressed and placed in an elegant coffin in front of the alter. They offered to have the funeral whenever I could be ready. We buried him at 1 P.M. Quite a few people attended. We sang hymns, and the minister delivered a beautiful sermon in which he mentioned you and asked that you be ready to bear the sad news from distant America. May God be with us all for the sake of Jesus. Amen.

Tobias

Ditlev Frederiksen, a native of western Jutland who had been in the United States in the 1890s, emigrated to Canada in 1910. He described the solitude of the prairie. (Source: H. F. Feilberg, *De derovre. En Række Breve fra Canada,* I [Copenhagen: Glydendalske Boghandel, 1917], pp. 32–33.)

Saskatchewan
10 August 1910

Dear Wife,

It's been a whole month since I heard from you, and I'm becoming lonesome. As far as I can see the prospects of making our future home here are good. I've built a small, modest house that will suffice until we have our own cabin. At the moment I'm working for a good man who pays well. On the whole a capable worker can earn a good wage here. The harvest has just begun so the busiest time of year lies ahead.

I've traveled around on the prairie quite a bit and think it is beautiful. Both the vegetation and the wildlife are fantasic. Back home we're not accustomed to predatory birds perched on the side of the road watching people pass by, or prairie dogs standing as motionless as a stick until somebody almost steps on them—then they suddenly disappear into the ground. The badger also pops up and stares at strangers; if you kick at him he hisses and disppears into his burrow. Like most of the other wild animals over here he is somewhat more purely colored than the ones in Denmark.

Ditlev

Frederiksen's teenage son told his grandfather about his trapping and aspiration of becoming a farmer. (Source: Feilberg, ed., *De derovre,* I, pp. 166–67.)

8 January 1914

Dear Grandfather,

The weather has gone up and down. Yesterday and the day before it thawed, and all of the snow melted. But last night it snowed again. I shot a rabbit and today we had it for dinner. I built a rabbit trap today and am going to catch some that way. The rabbit can enter it from one end if it wants to get the potato I use as bait. As soon as it takes the potato a peg snaps up and tightens a wire around the rabbit so it can't get away. I've sent some pelts in and bought traps with the money. It's easy to catch muskrats in the spring after the ice is gone.

Today I wrote to the government in Regina for a map that shows which *homesteads* havn't been claimed yet. There are some not so terribly far from here, and if I like them I'm going to get one. After all, I'm almost nineteen years old. I can work this summer and earn enough money to start farming. I already have a horse and a cow that is going to have a calf this spring. Some day I might be able to buy a few more horses. We'll have to see what happens. I know a great fellow named Frank Morris who had a *homestead* west of here. He says there are more *homesteads* available in that area. I also have an Icelandic friend named Andy.

Henning

Young Frederiksen found his job as a farmhand disillusioning. (Source: Feilberg, ed., *De derovre,* I, pp. 175–76.)

Dear Brother,

I've begun to work for a man named Alexander. A fellow I know, Frank Morris, said Alexander was all right, so I took the job for a month. I'll get twelve dollars, which is regarded as quite a good wage in the winter. I'm starting to regret it, though, because every morning I have to drive into town to get all the water they use, regardless of how bad the weather is. The town is three kilometers from here. In the morning I take the children along, and when I come back I have to water the livestock. In the afternoon I have to drive back to town to fetch the children. The two girls are fourteen and eleven years old, and the boys are nine and six. The older girl is really strange and always seems to be irritated. The younger one is ugly but cheerful. The two boys are spry little rascals.

I asked a man who had been here for a month what kind of person their father is. "He is a devil," was the answer; "I have to work outdoors all day, and besides he yells at me all the time." But I havn't found Alexander to be so bad. The first night I had to sleep here we went into a little room where there was just enough room for us and two wide beds. One of them had some blankets on it, but the other had only a pair of sheets. He said the second one was for me. I blew my top and told him that I would rather walk home in the middle of the night than freeze to death in a bed without blankets. He replied that we could sleep together, but I didn't want to do that, either. So I went to bed with most of my clothes on and managed to stay fairly warm that night. The man's nose and cheeks have been frostbitten, and I hope that doesn't happen to me.

I can play all of the tunes you sent me on the ocarina except "I Went Out." Could you explain a little better how the halftones go and also copy some more for me?

Your brother,
Henning

·III·

Danes in the Wild West

As early as the Gold Rush of the late 1840s Danish immigrants began to migrate west of the Great Divide; the census of 1900 found Danes in every county of California, Idaho, Montana, Utah, and Wyoming. All but one county in both Oregon and Washington reported Danish-Americans at that time. But in only a few regions, including the San Francisco Bay Area, Puget Sound, northwestern Oregon, and Utah were there real concentrations during the nineteenth century. And even in these exceptional regions far fewer Danish immigrants lived in the West than in Iowa, Minnesota, and Wisconsin at the turn of the century.[1]

The writers of the following letters represent a fairly broad spectrum of the male Danes who settled in the American West: a foot-loose argonaut who trekked from Texas to northern California, a young man who found the Lone Star State unbearably primitive, a carpenter and a former emigration agent in the boomtowns and mines of Colorado, and several farmers and city dwellers in Oregon and Washington. Danish women often accompanied their male counterparts westward, although in much smaller numbers. Several of their accounts of the hardships and joys of life on the frontier are given in Chapter VIII.

Letters from the West have several common themes. Among the most obvious is hope of increased prosperity, an extension of the vision that initially drew the immigrants to North America. Another central motif is the rough-and-tumble life in a region not yet stabilized by deeply rooted social conventions; Danes struggled for survival and upward mobility along with other settlers who, like themselves, sought to exploit the opportunities the region offered. Finally, disillusionment from unfulfilled dreams is apparent in many of these and other letters from the West.

1. For the distribution of Danish immigrants, see the decennial reports of the United States Bureau of the Census, which provide a county-by-county breakdown of the data as well as information about intermarriages between ethnic groups.

Jens Storm Schmidt (1819–1908), son of a miller from Horsens in Jut-
land, emigrated in 1846. He left Texas three years later to join the Gold
Rush. (Source: Karl Larsen, ed., *De, der tog hjemmefra*, I [Copenhagen:
Gyldendalske Boghandel, 1912], pp. 74–83.)

American River, California
16 March 1850

Dear Parents and Family,

I have finally come back to civilization. By that I mean I am
once again in an inhabited place where I can send you a letter. I
sold my property in Texas for a tenth of what it was worth,
bought three horses, rode on one and used the others as pack-
horses, because I had decided to travel overland to California.

I left my home on 6 March 1849, well-equipped with pistols,
rifles, food, and clothes, as much as my horses could carry. For
several days I rode alone, but then I joined a group from New
York. We traveled together to San Antonio. When we got there
nearly half of the population had died of cholera, and more were
dying every day. To make matters worse, a Mexican came into
town and reported that Indians had killed six of his countrymen
and that he was the only survivor. It had happened 160 kilometers
ahead on my planned route. My traveling companions decided to
go back, so I was alone. What could I do? Staying in San Antonio
and getting cholera would be worse than going through Indian
country. At first I traveled during daylight. When I had almost
reached the site of the murders I went deep into the forest during
the day, and after sundown I mounted and rode on. One night I
suddenly came to a place that smelled terribly. In the moonlight I
saw small piles of embers. Can you imagine what it was? The place
where the murders had occurred. You can imagine how I felt. But
enough of that. I traveled on.

I met many immigrants on their way to California. We traveled
and traveled, but it was terribly difficult to cross the Rocky
Mountains. We reached Paso del Nort after one hundred days. We
numbered one hundred men and chose Colonel Haecs as our
leader and captain in case the Indians attacked. Haecs had orders
to make peace with the Indians. To achieve that he sent a man
who had been brought up among them up to their camp in the
mountains. He would not say where it was, but he was to befriend

them. He told us where we should meet them. When we got there we couldn't see anything. The next morning we heard shooting and screaming in the mountains. We didn't know what it was, but we thought they had come to attack us. But about ten o'clock a large army arrived. They were Mexicans who had just come from a battle with the Indians. They raised their flag and told their story. They had taken several prisoners, including babies hanging in baskets from their saddle horns, a new way to transport children. They had cut scalps with long black hair off the Indians and stuck them on the points of their lances. They had a long string of ears hanging from their cannon. The Indians had fled, so we continued our journey.

We reached a Mexican post called Tucson, where the bad news began. There we were; most had wagons, some drawn by mules, others by oxen, and several by horses. Everyone began to feel the difficulties of the journey and looked a little emaciated. But now the people there told us that 130 kilometers without grass or water lay ahead. Well, we ventured on, no longer as a company, but each person fending for himself. We reached a river called the Gila. There was water, but little grass. Then we came to another road from Missouri called the South Pass, along which thousands of wagons had come.

We traveled to an Indian village called Da Pimos. A large number of them were almost naked and had pearl rings in their noses and ears. A day later we came to another Indian village called Mariposa, but still no grass. Horses, oxen, and mules lay dead on both sides of the road. There were human graves, burned and abandoned wagons, and clothes. After two more days without any grass I had to throw away all of my clothes. My horses were nearly dead and had almost nothing to eat. I had only two *blankets* to wrap myself in. After three more days we reached the Colorado River, but still no grass! My horses ate leaves. There was something called muscat beans on the trees. I picked them, and my horses and I ate together. I ate Indian-style. Two other men and I killed a panther and ate the meat. I thought I could eat anything I saw. My horses, the only things I could rely on, were nearly dead.

That was the condition I was in when I stood on the east bank of the Colorado where the Gila flows into it. I won't tell you how difficult it was to cross this big river, but on the west bank we saw what is called the really big, desolate desert, the world's largest after the one in Arabia, I believe. Where I had to cross it it was 150 kilometers wide, and I was in a bad humor when I heard that. But I was fortunate enough to be able to buy some horse meat from the Indians, along with an excellent horse. I traveled on, but I cannot describe all of the misery, and I, Jens Storm Schmidt, would not be alive today to write this letter to my parents, brothers and sisters, and friends to let them know what had become of me, had not this kind-hearted, noble-minded, and concerned *government* sent into the middle of the desert a large amount of food and shared it freely with these many starving people. They not only satisfied our hunger but also gave us enough to go on to San Diego, a coastal town on the Pacific Ocean. They probably knew the country better than we did and had foreseen what would happen to us, and taken the necessary measures to relieve our misery.

The Mexicans stole my Indian horse. Except for that and a few other things, I arrived here in Sacramento happy and healthy after a year of difficult travel. A little more than half of that time I had a tent to sleep in, but the rest of the time I slept under stars, sometimes in pouring rain and cold weather, but thank God I am in good health.

Upon arriving in Sacramento, my first question was how far it was to the gold mines, and was told fifty kilometers. I walked around in mud up to my knees to look at this year-old town just after the flood water had receded and the river had returned to its old channel. The town is situated on the river of the same name, about one hundred kilometers from San Francisco, a town of more than four thousand. The river overflowed its banks, flooding almost the whole town. When I refer to the population I mean men, since I don't think there are more than one hundred ladies in the whole town, and it is the same all over the country— no women except for some yellow Mexicans and red Indians.

I bought the food I needed, built myself a gold machine (which is like a cradle), loaded my horses, and departed. When I got there I saw several people wriggling their machines and watched them for a while. The place is ugly. Small and large stones have been cast aside. Under them is some red soil, which one puts into a bucket and carries to the machine, which must be close to the water. I pitched my tent and began my new profession as a prospector. Ha, ha, ha, who would have believed I would become a prospector? The first day I tried it I wasn't able to find anything. The next couple days I found a little, but not much the first week. The next week I worked only four and a half days because it rained, but I made 240 Danish dollars, not bad for a beginner. Now I want to work on the big stones, and I don't doubt that I can make 30 or 40 Danish dollars a day after the water level falls.

People from all over the world are mixed together here, even from China. There are people from all walks of life—generals, colonels, clergymen (many of whom have put their books back on the shelf, probably thinking that people did not have time to listen to them), merchants, captains—in short, all kinds of people. If there is freedom and equality anywhere in the world, it is here.

P.S.: Since the day I wrote the above I had a fight that I want to tell you about for the fun of it. The day after I wrote I began as usual to dig for gold when an American came up to me and asked how much I had found. I told him. He began to dig a hole about four meters from mine according to the rules. Then he worked in the direction away from me, but found nothing. He came up to me, looked at what I had found, went back to his hole, and worked in my direction. I went over to him and told him he could not do that. He replied that he would dig wherever he wanted without asking, since I had no right to dig at all. (There is supposedly a law that only American citizens are entitled to dig.) I decided to show him that I had some rights, and he decided to press the issue. We clashed. In an instant I was on top of him. When he called for help several people came and separated us. The oldest men on the site got together, saw what had caused the trouble, and ruled that he had deserved it. That didn't please him at all. He said I had struck the first blow and crossed the river to where he lived to send for three law officers, who arrested me and took me to a court, which is usually held in the middle of a field or in a tent. The inevitable result is that the accused has to pay the sheriff for his trouble and that is that. The whole procedure isn't worth two cents. At that time I knew practically nobody except my old captain, who swore he would shoot them if officers bothered me, regardless of how many they were. But now I have many more friends. Every single one of them has assured me that they could not get me unless they had a company large enough to defeat them all and take me by force. The officers saw there was nothing to do and left me alone. Today my neighbor has two loaded pistols lying beside him, and I also have a pair, but mine have twelve bullets. Don't think I am a troublemaker, but out here the law isn't strong enough to preserve people's rights. If a man is a coward and can't protect his rights, he doesn't have any.

A Dane who settled in Texas found that state too primitive for his liking. (Source: *Bornholms Tidende,* 17 January 1882.)

. . . I can already give you a bit of information about the state of Texas. It is quite a fruitful country, although only a quarter of it is cultivated. I had imagined the prairies here to be much different from how I found them. Most of the ones I crossed were barren, and the grass consisted of only brittle stems. The prairies were completely different over in Louisiana, where the grass grew so high I could not even see the cows. In the valleys and forests of Texas there is a great deal of fertile soil and plenty of water, but in the higher areas the soil is mainly sand and there isn't enough water. I have yet to see any fruit trees. The horses and cattle roam freely after being branded. When the ranchers need them, they simply ride out and round them up. All of the horses are small and mangy, so mules do most of the heavy work.

The rural roads are so poor that they must be called nearly impassable after a hard rain. Yesterday I took a drive to exercise my two horses, but in some places the mud was so deep they sank in up to their stomachs. Here and there tree trunks were lying right in the middle of the road.

The small farmers here are, on the whole, in poor shape; they usually don't produce enough to pay their hired hands, if they have any. Usually they do most of the work themselves.

The towns here look much different from those back home. Most of the houses are built of wood, and when it rains the streets become a dreadful morass, because not a single one of them is paved. It is just about as warm here as at home during the summer, although a bit colder when the north wind blows.

The railways are so poorly constructed that the cars shake tremendously, and the trains don't go any faster than back home. One English mile costs five cents, which certainly is not cheap. The Americans eat three meals a day, but only two on Sunday, namely at nine in the morning and three in the afternoon.

I am working in town for an English banker. My salary is only ten dollars a month, and as soon as I have saved enough to travel farther, I plan to go north, because I don't like it here at all.

An immigrant lost his health while working as a carpenter in the mines in Colorado. (Source: Danes Worldwide Archives, Julius Petersen MSS.)

Russell Gulch, Colorado
6 March 1898

Dear Parents,

I received your letters of 15 December and 2 January quite some time ago. I see you received the ten dollars I sent you for Christmas. I have also received letters from Jens, Karl, Peter, and Cousin Jørgen, and shall reply to all of them as soon as possible.

Since the beginning of January I have been very unfortunate. I was down in Denver from Christmas Eve until 3 January and had a good time. After coming back here I worked for only six days before developing rheumatism. I'm still not completely over it. I lay in bed for more than a week, and the doctor visited me three times. It was a kind of rheumatism that causes the joints to swell. My hands and feet were swollen to three times their normal size. That lasted three or four days. They had to lift me into and out of my bed, and I couldn't even take my own medicine. I went back to Denver to take Turkish baths. After two weeks down there I was almost healthy. I came up here again on 3 February, and since then I have worked half of the time and been sick the other half. I was sick all last week. My feet hurt so much that I couldn't take two steps without crutches. This week I've worked every day, even though I could feel some pain now and then.

The entire mess has cost me about sixty dollars in addition to lost wages on the days I couldn't work. Had I been well, I could

have worked every day since 1 January. The pain is so unbearable
that a person who has never had rheumatism can't imagine it. The
first time I was sick in America (just after I came over here) was
child's play compared to this. I hope the worst is behind me now.

Petersen who visited you in 1893 is now in Alaska. He left
Russell Gulch a month ago. A few days ago we received a letter
from him. He left Portland on 27 February and had just arrived
in Alaska.

Congratulations to Mother on her sixty-ninth birthday! I didn't
write earlier because I was sick. . . . .

Julius Petersen

*Alfred Bjørnbak, son of the Danish politician Lars Bjørnbak, described the
sprawl of boom towns in a mining area of southern Colorado.* (Source:
Vendsyssel Tidende, 2 June 1892. This letter initially appeared in *Aarhus Amtstidende.*)

Since my last letter not much has happened here at the camp.
One day passes just like the others. But what a change! We
arrived here on 11 December and camped on an open field
midway between the towns of Creede and Jamestown, which are
about three kilometers apart. On 2 January we moved into our
new house. For a long time it was the only one there. But then
one house went up after the other, and today Creede and
Jamestown have grown together to form one town. But that's not
the only thing. Both Jamestown and Creede have undergone such
radical changes and are still changing so rapidly that it is difficult
to recognize either place from one evening until the next morning. Jamestown was founded only two days before we arrived,
so I have known it since its infancy. At that time the town consisted of a few small wooden buildings, only one of which—a
saloon—stood out among the others. But now the *saloon* is the
smallest building in town. All of the old ones have been torn
down, rebuilt, and remodelled to make them newer, larger, and
more elegant. One hotel has been erected after the other, as have
shops and restaurants.

The prices have gone up just like the skyline. A German from
Frankfurt who had just completed his house sold it one evening

for five thousand dollars. The next morning he received a
telegram offering him eleven thousand dollars. One of my
acquaintances sold a building for eight hundred dollars. A few
days later the same building went for three thousand dollars.
That's how it is. People are streaming in with their pockets full of
cash, hoping to make millions.

The town is packed with people, and far out on the road, as far
as from Viby to Aarhus, they are encamped in large numbers.
They live like nomads. The area will be sold on 26 February and
people cannot homestead it even though it is government land. It
has been leased to a man named Mr. Waalsu who has three years
left on his rental contract. Now he is trying to sublet it in small
plots for the remaining period, but the government is having it
surveyed and divided into lots and streets.

But Mr. Waalsu is not the kind of man who will take anything
lying down, not even from the government. He has even rented
out the streets, so it appears that people are building on them as
well as on lots and it's difficult to know which is which. Nevertheless, many people live out there and say, "Let it be." They
don't have much to lose, since their houses are only tents stretched
across a square frame a meter high. But others have been bold
enough to erect two-storeyed buildings.

As I mentioned before, tents are important here, despite the
severe winter. They are used as restaurants, hotels, and dormi-
tories. Such an apartment isn't very big. It has a cot with blankets,
a mirror, a wash basin, soap, and a comb. Pullman is doing
a profitable business with his sleeping cars. By paying $1.25
to the Negro porter a *gentleman* can spend the night in one of
these cars, which stand on the railroad tracks, wherever there is
room. I guess everyone is trying to make a fast buck wherever he
can. The most profitable places are the taverns, which have
sprouted like toadstools. Carpenters are doing well, of course, but
they are at a disadvantage because the railroad can't bring in
lumber fast enough to meet the demand. . . .

Every bit of land is used. A photographer had to set up his
studio on a high cliff, but in order to get a stairway built part of
the cliff had to be blasted away. Dynamite caps are used right in
town, even though the streets are narrow and there is a lot of
traffic. Some men yell "Stop!" and then it explodes. Pieces of stone

and wood fly about, and then it is over. On the whole it's like living under a constant bombardment. . . .

This is a crazy place to live. One day there is prosperity, the next day poverty. Last night there wasn't any petroleum, candles, or coal. But there certainly wasn't any shortage of whiskey and beer.

Disaster struck this hastily constructed mining town, which rose again with equal speeds. (Source: *Aarhus Amtstidende,* 25 June 1892.)

Creede Camp, Colorado
7 June 1892

It has been a long time since there has been a good reason to write to you, but finally one came: Jimtown burned to the ground Sunday morning, 5 June, Pentecost and Danish Constitution Day.

This was the second time I've seen an entire town go up in flames. The first time was in 1865 when Nørre Sundby burned. Then the fire broke out at 4 P.M. and was not under control until 4 A.M. the next day. This time it broke out at 6:30 A.M. and by 8 A.M. the town had burned down. It would be wrong to say that we gained control of the fire. Actually it was just the opposite. It ravaged and raced through the town taking everything in its path, and when it stopped everything was over—completely over. There were not even enough ashes left from the immense quantity of wood to show where the buildings had stood. The only recognizable things were the vault of the First National Bank and the foundations of a bakery. Everything else was flat. Now the river twines through this dead place.

In December, when the mine was discovered, there was a dense forest of willow trees here, but they gradually gave way to the axe. Only a few small, charred willows are still standing to testify to the once luxuriant vegetation.

The fire began in a building that housed a saloon and a barbershop. This was at a point that separated the two streets to the north and where, remarkably, most of the water is located. Both of the streets are flooded as high as the hubs of the wagon wheels. In a moment both sides were in flames. Then the fire went a little ways north, but ran into an area that was not built up. It turned south and went even faster. The only thing we could do was save everything that could be saved. The train resolutely pulled up with two baggage cars, which we filled and drove to Creede Depot after it became too hot for the engineer. Then the stations burned down, as well as the tent warehouse, ticket office, and sleeping cars (not Pullmans, but temporary quarters for the railroad personnel). The fire spread from the station down to the last row of houses at the cliff on the west side of town. The foundation of one house caught fire, and the house tumbled down the cliff and went up in flames in the lumberyard down below. Four drugstores, three banks, and a large number of shops, restaurants, and hotels were also destroyed. All of the horses, mules, and donkeys were rescued, but several wagons burned, along with some stacks of hay. One small child succumbed. Damages are estimated at over one million dollars. Liquor was flowing in large quantities, but a police force was quickly organized and the saloons were closed. Nevertheless, people stole like ravens and fought tooth-and-nail. A large number of businessmen left town on the first train, but others immediately rented the empty buildings in South Creede and the bankers were doing business on Monday. The post office was already functioning at a new location when the Sunday afternoon train arrived. The train that should have left Creede at 7 A.M. had to stop in Jimtown at 10 A.M., but the tracks were already repaired after being destroyed two or three hours earlier. On Monday morning the foundation and floor for a new general store were built, and today people are busy constructing houses, even though the ground is still warm and burning in several places. Now there will be work for several months.

People had been predicting a catastrophe for a long time, but of course nobody knew exactly how it would come. Most predicted it would be the river, which crested on 22 May. I was the only one who had horses north of Jimtown and had to stay up until late in the evening pulling houses, boards, and timber out of the river. In Jimtown the water washed out the bridges and flooded the streets, making travel impossible. Then the water level dropped for a week and we had some cold days. On Monday, 29 May, I was up in the mountains. There was hail, which did some damage.

Farther down the entire forest was covered with snow, and in the
valley it rained so much that the river reached a critical level, but
not nearly as high as on the previous Monday. Then Sunday, 5
June, came and prevented the buildings from being washed away
as had been predicted. . . .

Some Danes visited me that day and we celebrated Constitution
Day as well as we could, but that was not very well, I'm afraid.

Alfred Bjørnbak

*A group of young farmers left Nebraska in 1887 in search of greater pros-
perity in Washington. One of them wrote the following spring.* (Source: *Den
nye Verden,* June 1888.)

Six of us Danes from Nebraska came out to Washington
Territory last spring in search of a better home. I had been told
that when we arrived here we would see green grass and the trees
would be budding. That seemed incredible to me, however,
because it took us only a few days to travel here, and winter was
still raging in Nebraska. But now I'm a believer, because I have
seen it.

After working at various odd jobs during the summer, we went
to Douglas County, 125 English miles west of Ritzville. We arrived
here on 22 November and adapted quickly. Each of us staked two
claims, or 320 *acres,* next to each other. I settled down on my land
on 24 November. The others went back to Nebraska to fetch their
families, leaving me here alone.

Our winters are not as cold as those in the East. The older
settlers claim that last winter was the coldest they have had here,
but I believe it was the mildest I have ever seen. Many of the
horses have not needed hay or grain all winter. I think this place
is good enough for anyone. The grass grows all winter, although
not very much, because we have a frost now and then. But it is
good for the cattle to have something green on the ground.

It is sixteen kilometers to the forest and eight kilometers to
Okanogan Post Office. The first settlement of any significance
began only last summer, but it is growing fast and will soon grow
even faster. Our government is in Waterville, as is the land office.

A lot of building is being done. There is a sawmill, and lumber costs twelve to fifteen dollars per thousand board feet.

The railroad has not reached us, but it is coming. After it comes you will discover that there will not be much unclaimed land left. This will be a good market, because all of the land to the north and west is either forested or rich in minerals. There are coal mines fifty miles south of us, and gold and silver mines to the north. There is plenty of work available now, and there will be more when the railroad comes.

I realize that many will say that it is too far north and therefore must be cold. Nobody has to believe me unless he wants to. It snows frequently, but it melts soon so the cattle can still graze. Crop raising is also better here than in most other areas. There are probably some who shudder at the thought of traveling so far, but a young man can buy a little horse cheaply and travel like many others. Otherwise, you can come together in the summer and either buy wagons here or bring them along. Machinery is much more expensive here than in the East.

I have not had to worry about accommodations every night. In fact, I was not in a house last year from 8 July until 1 December, when I finished my own little house. Until then I slept in a tent or a strawstack, and I am healthier now than when I first came out here from the East, where I had a little fever every summer.

I would be happy to see some of my old friends here next summer. Perhaps we could build up a little Danish settlement, since six of us are already here.

The land south of me is not for sale yet, but soon will be. It can be settled nevertheless, because it has been surveyed. Here and there forty *acres* can be had, but most of it is taken. I believe this area is as good as any other in Washington Territory.

C. M. Petersen
Okanogan Post Office
Douglas County, Washington Territory

A Dane in Tacoma sought to promote emigration to Washington, a territory to which immigrants and native Americans were already flocking. (Source: Den nye Verden, November 1889.)

Half a day's journey west of Omaha on the Union Pacific Railroad the terrain begins to rise considerably. Instead of compact, fertile prairies there are dry, sparsely populated plains. Closer to Denver one sees artificial irrigation from the mountains, although there are only a few settlers. After passing the snow-covered mountains of Colorado one descends into the large, fertile valley of the Mormons, where already in early spring the fruit trees are in full blossom. In Idaho one sees large flocks of sheep and herds of cattle grazing on the slopes of the mountains. The countryside is sparsely populated and the vegetation is thin.

In Oregon there are lush meadows between the forests; they belong to the Indians who live there in large numbers. Portland is a large, attractive city with lots of traffic, but it is crowded with Chinese. There are even individual hotels and shops built in the Chinese style, and inside they are decorated in the Chinese way.

The regions north of Portland are beautiful, and the area along the Columbia River is densely populated. There is not one large, unbroken forest, but several smaller ones interspersed with bountiful fields and well-kept farms. Up toward Tacoma the terrain becomes more hilly, and on the prairies the gravel is so apparent that it looks like a road.

There is very good soil in the valleys, and along the railroad one town has risen after the other. Between the trees and the mountains the whistle of the locomotive competes with the buzzing of the sawmills. In the valleys human hands and fires compete for the merciless clearing of the forests. The same procedure is repeated everywhere, but not always in the same tempo.

The influx of people from other states is great. Most come out here with the thought of building a home on a farm. They are happy to have said farewell to winter forever. But there is always something in the way—out here, the big trees.

In the mountain areas all of the land has been taken, either as "*homesteads*" or "*preemptions*," or is owned by the railroads, which sell it for six to ten dollars per *acre*, in fact twenty dollars in some areas. One hundred miles north of here, near Watdom, the soil is better, but the trees are bigger and everything is expensive.

Most of life's necessities are brought up from California, especially fruits and vegetables. We do not have the joy of seeing corn fields here, and generations will pass before the plow will come into full use. In all other respects Washington is booming. The sawmills are buzzing constantly everywhere, but not fast enough to meet the demand for lumber, either to be shipped out or used here for building. There are not many places where as much building is being done as here.

Railroads are being constructed, a port is being built; sewers, brickyards, and factories are being added. The forests are being cleared and the soil tilled. Nevertheless, now and then there are more people than jobs. Some of them leave. But towns grow fast, and all of modern life's luxuries can be found in them. The railroads and steamships in Puget Sound do a lively business, and the Sound itself is very beautiful.

A mason can earn six dollars a day, while his assistant makes two; carpenters get three to three and a half dollars a day, common laborers about two. The sawmills pay thirty dollars a month plus board. The work is hard, however. Board costs about five dollars a week, and rent is high, so many people build little houses in the forest. Smiths earn two and a half to three dollars per day, while hotel personnel are paid twenty-five to thirty dollars a month plus board. There is a great demand for servant girls, who get twenty to thirty dollars per month.

It is easier for a bachelor than a family man to get a "*homestead*" here, because the short time he must live on it each year is easier for an unmarried man. Most just let the house stand unoccupied and sell the farm after five years. They bring a good price here. In my opinion it takes quite a bit of money to run a farm out here, but wages are somewhat better here than in Omaha. Most workers get along well here, if they want to.

The climate is comfortable, with practically no frost in the winter. It rains a great deal, however. But after it has rained for four or five days (and generally we get only half a day of rain with intermittent sunshine) the sun shines beautifully again for several days. The livestock can stay outside all year. There is very little difference between autumn and winter. Last summer we had only one little thunderstorm and rain a few times. Otherwise it was dry for four months. The nights are cool and comfortable. Now a smokelike fog from the Pacific has enveloped the region. When it is warm here we do notice the heat as we did in Omaha. There are not many storms, but the dust will continue to be bad until the streets are paved.

I wish to extend my greetings to my friends in Omaha and all of *Dannebrog*'s readers. If you have any questions, send me a letter, enclosing stamps, and I will be happy to answer them.

R. Pedersen
1301 "J" Street
Tacoma, Washington Territory

Harald Andersen, a baker's apprentice from Zealand, emigrated in 1893 and settled in Washington. After his wife's death there, he married a girl of partly Indian extraction twelve years his junior. (Source: Karl Larsen, ed., De, der tog hjemmefra, IV [Copenhagen: Gyldendalske Boghandel, 1914], pp. 194–95.)

14 September 1893

Dear Mother,

For the past two weeks I have put off writing to you. You know that I realize you will share my grief. Annie had surgery and died two days later. The doctors in Walla Walla and Spokane (the best doctors) told her and me last June that she did not have long to live.

During the summer we went to several places because of her health, and at harvest time she seemed to be improving a bit, but it did not last long. So we went to Yakima.

Right until the end she was the same dear, understanding Annie. She didn't seem to suffer much, and she always talked of days gone by. Only an hour or two before God closed her eyes, she said she was tired.

Believe me, Mother, it is a joy to know that we never said a harsh word to each other and that there was always love between us, and that until the end I did everything in my power for her. Now she has gone to her eternal rest where there is no sorrow or pain.

Annie was buried in Walla Walla in a cemetery owned by the International Order of Odd Fellows. I couldn't stand to stay on the farm alone, so I rented the whole place to an old Danish friend named Joe Madison.

The town here is new. There is a lot of construction, buying and selling, and teamwork. You can understand that my thoughts are always a bit hectic.

I hope these lines find you, dear faithful Mother, in the best of health.

Harald

A Danish journalist in Astoria, Oregon, described the rugged life of Danish miners in the Pacific Northwest. (Source: Politiken, 7 June 1893.)

Astoria
May [1893]

There are some real giants among the Danish immigrants one meets here in the West—big, robust, suntanned individuals who literally have been able to overcome all obstacles with their bare hands. If there were any weaklings among them, they have simply disappeared.

In almost every city in the West one runs into five or six wealthy farmers who have become assimilated in American society and more or less forgotten how to speak Danish. These chosen few came over here just at the right time. They and their fortunes are topics of discussion back in Denmark. The rest, those anonymous thousands, toil in the mines or have modest jobs in the towns. Usually they are not satisfied with what they have achieved, because they expected greater prosperity when they migrated westward.

In reality the situation is much different from what we in Denmark imagine our emigrated countrymen's lives to be. For example, when we speak of a goldminer, we mean a kind of King Midas who simply has to thrust his spade into the ground to find a nugget.

But that is not how it is. A goldminer is a common mine worker who labors for a company. Sometimes he has the ambition to strike out on his own. Accompanied by a partner, who carries their tools, and a mule, which carries their food, they ascend the most distant peaks of the mountains. Other vacant mining places are not to be found. There he begins to dig and bore, and he perseveres until the tools are worn out and the food is used up. Then he and his partner, both exhausted, descend the mountain, and are fortunate if they can get jobs with one of the large firms that conducts its goldmining not like a scavenger hunt, but like a profitable industry.

But it is extremely difficult to find employment with one of these companies, because they operate only during the summer. Furthermore, conflicts of the most violent sort frequently break out between their managements and the American workers' bellicose unions. The work itself is done as in European coalmines. The only difference is that when the workers come out of the mines in the evening, they do not receive permission to return to the bunkhouses until after the supervisors have searched every stitch of their clothing.

Work in the mines is extremely demanding but also well paid at three or four dollars a day. Needless to say, the unions are responsible for maintaining this high wage. Only a handful of the miners are married; consequently, the mining towns are meccas for flocks of female vagabonds of the most vulgar sort. A wild life is the norm in these mountains. The crack of a pistol can often be heard at the card tables. Such a life gives the men of the West their characteristic robust appearance. We often meet here Danes from Vendsyssel with faces that resemble Viking profiles from the time of Haakon Jarl.[2]

In the winter many of the Danish miners go down into the towns, where they meet large numbers of their countrymen. In every town there is a Danish society where they gather on Saturday evening for a party and dancing. It is moving to see the solidarity that exists among the members of these societies whenever one of the fellows has to be set on an even keel. Apparently it has never happened that a Dane in the West has been deported. It is also touching to see the love with which these good people remember their mother country. Here, about twelve

2. This name is ambiguous and could refer to any of several Viking earls (Old Norse *jarl*) named Haakon.

thousand kilometers from Denmark, one can see an amateur production of "Prayer Day Evening," and when the chapel bells chime over the embankments of Copenhagen, one can feel that the finest strings of the soul are being tugged behind the callous exterior of these miners.

In general it must be said that this part of the West is not now what it was a few years ago. There is no longer a shortage in the labor market, and while the flow of immigrants from Norway and Denmark has decreased, the Swedes continue to come here in growing numbers. It would be irresponsible to advise Danish immigrants who lack personal funds to settle down in the vicinity of Portland, Tacoma, or Spokane Falls.

Of course, the Danes have been lured out here not only by gold, but also by the majestic natural surroundings. When the sun rises like a melting metal shield behind the snow-covered mountains on a spring morning and casts millions of drops of gold across the fruit trees in the garden that is Oregon, and when the flowers open their beakers to release their sweet aroma, and the birds chirp joyfully in the light green forests of the mountains, it is easy to understand why newcomers exclaim: "This is fantastic! Here we will forget our homeland and live for the rest of our lives."

But in the evening, when the Pacific breeze whispers between the leaves of the trees, they feel like foreigners, and a vague longing for Denmark arises from the depths of their souls.

Ignotus [Henrik Cauling]

An immigrant found Washington and Oregon beautiful, but because of unemployment warned his countrymen to stay in Denmark. (Source: Vejle Amts Folkeblad, 4 November 1897.)

Astoria, Oregon
15 October, 1897

Dear Editor,

It might interest some readers of your worthy newspaper to read a few words from the Far West, the land that in the fantasies of many people flows with milk and honey and where gold can be picked up by the bushel. That is a disappointing illusion, however. When they arrive here they soon discover that the struggle for their daily bread is just as hard—I believe even harder—than it was back in Denmark. Last summer conditions were especially bad, although I believe they will improve next summer. A lot of people are thinking about going up north to look for gold, which is undoubtedly to be found in large quantities up there. Many left from Astoria last summer. Steamships leave here regularly for Alaska's coasts. They encounter tremendous difficulties trying to reach the gold mines, but American energy conquers everything. There is already one town in a polar region that numbers eight thousand inhabitants. The migration will probably reach large proportions, but that is all the better for those who stay behind. But it was not my intention to write about Alaska.

The most important occupations here in northern Oregon and southern Washington are fishing, cattle raising, and lumbering. The best salmon in the world are caught right here in the Columbia River. This river is more than thirty kilometers wide in places. The farmers around here produce some butter, for which they presently get about fifty cents a kilogram. Pork goes for about twelve to fifteen dollars per hundred kilograms. The usual wage on a farm is from fifteen to twenty dollars a month, and in the towns one and a half to two dollars per day without board.

The forests are amazingly luxuriant here. Oregon and Washington have more timber than any other state in the Union. The trees reach an incredible height and thickness. The climate is pleasant. Summers are not much warmer than in Denmark, and the winters are exceptionally mild and rainy. In fact, it rains a lot here. One wag claims it rains "only" thirteen months a year! But in reality it is not quite that bad.

There are a lot of Scandinavians here. I have lived in the Midwest and in California, but I have not found a place where Scandinavians are better off than here. Nearly all of the fishermen are sons of the North. Sons of the Celestial Empire are also numerous here. They cause a lot of problems by bringing down the wages paid to white men who cannot work as cheaply as the Chinese, who can live on rice and water. The law forbids Chinese to enter the country, but they come anyway. They are simply smuggled in.

Astoria is only a small town with fifteen thousand inhabitants, but it is beautifully situated at the mouth of the Columbia River.

Many people come here in the summer because of their health.

I suppose I have written enough. I only wish to say this to my countrymen: Do not come to America now. It might be better some day. It is impossible for men who cannot speak English. The good old days when all foreigners were welcome are past. Now they are regarded with aversion. My advice is: Stay home!

S.T.S.

·IV·

Danes in Urban America

As noted in the Introduction, Danish emigration to North America was to a considerable degree an extension of the flight from rural to urban Denmark in the nineteenth century. Consequently, many immigrants had lived on farms as well as in cities in their native land. Others migrated directly from over-crowded rural districts to the United States or Canada. More than half of the Danish immigrants in the United States settled on farms or in small towns, but a large number remained in New York (the usual port of arrival) or took employment in other cities. A higher percentage of Danish newcomers came from cities than did Norwegian or Swedish immigrants, and a larger pro-portion appear to have sought out the urban communities of the New World. By 1900 there were more than 10,000 first-generation Danish-Americans in Chicago and 5,621 in New York City. The Twin Cities of Saint Paul and Minneapolis had a total of nearly 2,700 Danish immigrants, while Racine, Wisconsin, perhaps the most markedly Danish small city in the United States, had 2,815 and Omaha had 2,430.[1]

These communities, while by no means large, became the focal points of the group's cultural life. Danish-language newpapers thrived in all of them, and mutual benefit and social organizations, such as the Dania Society, were founded to serve immigrant interests.

It is difficult to generalize about the joys and miseries of individual new-comers in bustling American cities during the nineteenth century. In his Pu-litzer Prize-winning book, The Uprooted, Oscar Handlin painted a dismal picture of immigrants torn from the soil of supposedly stable European vil-lages and thrust into the turmoil of urban life in the United States, where they were exploited and miserably allienated. Firsthand accounts by Danish-Americans, however, suggest that a more moderate view is closer to the truth. Unemployment during the nadirs of the business cycles ruined the American

---

1. Andersen, *Hvor Danskerne i Amerika findes*, pp. 25–30. These statistics include only the immigrants, not their children born in the United States.

experience of many newcomers in industrial centers, of course, and the wages they received generally fell short of what Yankees were paid. The quality of housing varied greatly, and some Danes complained about violence in American cities. On the other hand, many letters include comparisons demonstrating the superiority of American wages, excited descriptions of the wealth of entertainment opportunities that urban life offered, and awed accounts of the marvels of modern technology. Indeed, some immigrants clearly expressed their preference of city to farm life.

The letters in this chapter reflect Danish immigrant life in most of the cities where these newcomers settled in fairly large numbers. Written by factory workers, businessmen, a pastor, and others, they touch on many aspects of municipal life and mirror the opportunities that booming cities offered as well as disillusionment with the tawdry side of urban living.

❖

Torben Lange, whose letters describing his three transatlantic voyages appear earlier in this book, sold books and moonlighted as a cigar maker. (Source: Lange, Fra Roskildefjord, pp. 209–11.)

St. Louis
26 August 1849

Dear Mother,

We are once again at that time of year when vegetables are sold, and neither Grethe nor I can let fresh peaches and melons go past our noses! Grethe thinks it is wonderful that we can buy a large melon for five cents. We have two peach trees right outside the door, and Grethe is almost too good to them.

It is certainly good to see Grethe so happy all of the time. When I come home in the evening I have a nice face to look at. I usually work from nine or ten o'clock in the morning until after sundown. When I come home she usually has something good for supper, such as stewed apples with sheep milk.

We just received a letter from Jette,[2] and are happy to hear about her son. May Andriis grow and become an able boy.

A long time ago I read in the newspapers that the Danes had won a decisive battle against the Germans and captured all of their

---

2. Jette was the sister of the writer.

cannons. Was that a lie? I also read that a ceasefire had been arranged.

I am now selling books again and will probably continue because it is very profitable and my time is at my own disposal. Nevertheless, I'll keep on making cigars early in the morning and late in the evening. I like to earn my breakfast before I eat it.

There was a ruckus next door Sunday evening. The people took the law into their own hands and burned down a place where fourteen or fifteen ladies of the night worked. At ten o'clock they broke into the house, chased the madame and her hirelings out, threw the furniture out into the yard, and set the torch to it. The establishment had disappeared by midnight, the last of its kind in St. Louis. Recently two dandies were shot dead on the street after they tried to hustle married women.

A year ago today I was sick in Frederikssund, and my leg is still not quite as it should be. I notice changes in the weather more readily. Even though Grethe says it is cold, I am sitting here with the windows and doors open and she is walking outside in the moonlight without anything on her arms.

She is upset this evening because she broke her little silver knife peeling peaches and I spilled ink on a clean shirt. But I think she is feeling better now because she is sitting in her rocking chair reading Oehlenschlæger's tragedies aloud to me while I roll cigars.

A former convict from Zealand found a new life in the New World and encouraged other criminal offenders to emigrate. (Source: *Berlingske Tidende*, 1 June 1866.)

New York
18 February 1866

. . . I am to be despised by others. Although I received a good education, I lost my father when I was little, and my poor mother did everything for me—too much, perhaps—because I was an only child. Even though she was poor she didn't deny me anything, because I was all she had. But my mother died when I was twenty-one. I went into the service, became a sergeant, and tried to keep up with my buddies who had more than I. Dancing, women, and

billiards were my nemeses. I got into trouble, was demoted, left
the service, and took a job as the servant of a married couple. I
didn't have any clothes; those that I wore were borrowed from a
friend. I pawned some of their silverware, believing I could
redeem it gradually, or, to be honest about it, thinking I would be
lucky enough to get away with it completely. But I was arrested
and served four years in prison, being released in March 1860.
While in prison I didn't have much to do with my fellow inmates.

What was my fate upon being released? I had practically no
clothes and money, and where could I find a job? In need, I
wrote to a nobleman for whom I had worked for four years
before I entered the service, partly as a servant, partly as a clerk
in his office. He is a gentleman in the fullest sense of the word.
God bless him! He put me up at his house for two months and,
because he didn't have enough influence to get me a job, he gave
me some clothing and sent me to America. When I left I promised
him that he would never regret helping me, and I kept my word.
Six years have gone by, and by living an orderly and stable life I
have realized how unworthy I previously had been to be in the
company of decent people. I am also several years older now
(thirty-four) and don't think I'll ever break my word. Nevertheless,
I have never forgotten to pray every evening, "Lead us not into
temptation, but deliver us from evil."

When I arrived in New York I was not able to find any work
immediately, but I went south and was fortunate enough to get a
job in a large firm. I stayed there a year and earned good money.
Then the war broke out. The Union fleet sailed to New Orleans
and blockaded the harbor. A German in New Orleans sent me a
telegram informing me that the price of coffee there had risen to
$33^1/_2$, while it was still 20 cents where I was working. My employers loaned me some money, and I bought five hundred dollars'
worth. Within three weeks the price of coffee had shot up to
52 cents. I sold mine and earned seven hundred dollars—quite
a financial coup for a beginner.

In the meantime, the Confederate government was trying to
turn everyone into a soldier, following the time-honored maxim
that "whoever is not with us is against us." My employers advised
me to go to New York and, if nothing turned up there, back
home, assuring me that the war would be over by March 1862 and

that I could get my job back then. I went to Copenhagen and from there to Hamburg, where I worked for a Dane who had a brokerage. In 1862 I went back to America. But the place where I had worked before, Pensacola, Florida, had been burned down; now I live in New York, where everything is going well for me.

I wish the Prison Society back home had the power to help more people then it presently believes it can, because many souls would be saved. I'll tell you why. He who comes over here without any desire to work is forced to work. He has no funds, no family from whom he can freeload, but has to work simply to keep alive. To his surprise, he realizes that only the first step hurts, and that he earns twice as much as in Denmark. Suddenly he sees that "honesty is the best policy," and things begin to fall into place. Finally he is forced to work, to pull with every muscle, if he does not want everyone to despise him. The old saying is true, that "I don't care what you have been, but rather what you are." If I waste my money on rum and whiskey at a tavern, I'll never amount to anything. As an able worker I can probably get work. I can be useful, not if I give up, but if I try to work my way up in society. In that respect it is like a kind of Freemasonry, where everyone can be promoted.

The Yankee notices everything. If I attend to my work and don't waste what I earn, I will be sought after; if not, I will be shunned. For example, if a well-regarded person wants to try some undertaking or another, he can easily get a loan of four or five hundred dollars. Why? Because he is diligent, sober, and industrious. Recommendations are important in America.

This should awaken the interest of one who is not completely lost. If he has the slightest degree of honor he will know he has obligations to the Prison Society or a private individual who sends him over here to work under his auspices. And then what a change spiritually! Pastor, when I arrived here everything looked pretty dark for me. Do you know what strengthened me, so far from my friends and relatives? Yes, of course you know, but in case you meet anyone who intends to come over here, and who has been in my position, tell him not to lose his courage, because prayer to God can make him strong. Faith in God the Father will never abandon him, if he has the desire to better himself—that will make him strong. I am ashamed to admit that when I arrived here I didn't realize what hope and strength one can gain through prayer.

Please forgive me for writing such a long letter and describing things that cannot be of interest to you, such as my time in prison. You are the first person to whom I have ever expressed myself about these things, and now, after so many years, it has done me good to ponder what was such a troubled but yet such a blessed time for me.

What can the former convict do in Denmark? Work? Impossible! No, and again no, and that is the case in other European countries too. Prejudice against him is too strong. His career is stamped "Convicted Man." He is despised among the peasants, from whose social class he came and who should really help him. They refuse to work with him. The professional criminals try to woo him back into a life of crime, since it is an outrage for them to see a cohort who has been "behind bars" become a respectable person. They watch him seek employment and be turned away, then they come to him with a bottle and say, "Don't be a fool! You know it won't work." He listens and falls again.

I have a friend in prison, my only one there, I might add. He was released two weeks after me and found work as a bricklayer's assistant. When I sailed to America, he followed me on board. "On," he said, "if only I could come along!" When I returned eighteen months later I intended to give him one hundred dollars so he could come to America. I went to his mother, who began to cry when she saw me. Two months after I had left Denmark he had been imprisoned for another ten years—good God, ten years! And there he shall stay, a misfortune that we regret, but about which we cannot do anything.

An anonymous writer in Perth Amboy, New Jersey, found the many Danes of that community given to drink. (Source: Den nye Verden, 29 August 1890.)

Perth Amboy, New Jersey
10 August 1890

May I ask you, Mr. Editor, whether you remember Perth
Amboy, or you have completely forgotten us? We remember you
very well from the political campaign. Whenever a few issues of
Den nye Verden are received here in this town, we look at them
carefully to see whether they contain anything about us, the Danes
in Perth Amboy. We have not been able to find anything,
however, so I have decided to tell old Denmark how we live here,
providing you are willing to print my rather unstylish lucubrations.

Perth Amboy is a small town with approximately ten thousand
inhabitants. Of these at least three thousand are Danes who, with
only a few exceptions, are employed at the large terra cotta
factories here. The exceptions are grocers, butchers, craftsmen,
tavern owners, and so on. It seems that Danes are especially suited
to a *beer saloon,* or perhaps a *beer saloon* is well suited to Danes,
judging from the large number of Danish *liquor dealers* around
here.

Previously the Danes lived rather individualistically, but we have
now formed a society. It serves both political and entertainment
purposes. It already has quite a few members and a capable
chairman in the butcher, Christian Krogh. He is well liked and
respected by all as a hard worker for Danish interests. He had
been here for nearly twenty years, and before coming to America
he was a cattle exporter and butcher in Aalborg or that area, I
believe.

We have thought about remodeling our church, but we do not
have enough money yet.

Work has been in short supply the past year, so I must advise
people not to come here, at least for the time being.

Some of the Danes in Perth Amboy are quite prosperous, and a
few well-to-do. The majority, however, are living only hand-to-
mouth. This can be attributed partly to all of the entertainment on
which people spend a ridiculously large part of their weekly
wages. The problem is that there is only one pastime here,
namely, going to the tavern.

With a greeting from America to the readers of *Den nye Verden* and to you, Mr. Editor, from your many friends and acquaintances here, I conclude these lines.

J. B.

A Dane in Philadelphia felt swamped by American advertisements. (Source: *Kolding Folkeblad,* 21 August 1876. This letter originally appeared in *Jyllands-Posten.*)

There is hardly a place imaginable where one cannot see in words or pictures the magnitude of competition here. No individual person or organization can keep its fortune large enough, its reputation solid enough, or its position secure enough, without reminding other people of its business day in and day out. Human weakness must be considerable, because so many ways of doing this have been invented. Not just the endless newspaper columns or walls of buildings and desolate billboards convey the announcements of the competing millions; if you buy a steamship ticket for a Sunday excursion out of the city, you can be sure that one side of the ticket will be covered by the address of a tailor or brewer. If you use a fan to cool yourself in the blazing sunshine, you can be equally sure that at least one side of it will be crowded with advertisements for an *ice cream saloon* or an establishment that sells cooling drinks. Except for those places where the owners or other authorities have expressly forbidden the posting of bills, no place seems to be sacrosanct in this respect. The stately tree trunks along a boulevard or in a park as well as the beautiful landscape along the railroads are tainted by immense placards or inscriptions in yellow on a black background. They proclaim that *Brixby's Blacking* shoe polish is the world's best and *will shine 'em,* or that *Gurgling Oil* is the best medicine against everything *for man and beast.* At the moment it is impossible to avoid these two advertisements for more than five minutes. Nobody is quite sure what *Gurgling Oil* is, but nobody doubts that the manufacturer intends to become a millionaire with the help of his mysterious, meter-high yellow inscriptions, and that he is just as sure to reach his goal as his predecessor Helmbold did by advertising Helmbold's Bucleu constantly along the Pacific railroad.

A Social Democrat in New York compared American millionaires to medieval robber barons, a comparison frequently made in the Gilded Age. (Source: *Demokraten*, 20 February 1892.)

New York
3 February 1892

As my fellow Social Democrats in Denmark perhaps know, there was a dynamite assassination attempt on the millionaire Russell Sage a while ago. He escaped without a scratch. It sent a chill up the spine of all our millionaires over here, and also stimulated the wildest rumors about their fear.

One day while walking down Broadway I met a detective whom I knew. I stopped him and wanted to chat with him, as I had done on many previous occasions. But he kept on walking down the street and whispered to me, "I don't have time. I have to take care of that millionaire over there." That's how it is; the detectives in New York don't have any time because they have become babysitters for the rich men. Hardly any of the big capitalists dare to go for a walk, to the theater, or to the stock exchange without their bodyguards. Whenever they walk along Broadway or Ficotte Avenue they have security people both in front of and behind them. Every officer gets thirty crowns a day for protecting these fellows. The capitalists keep revolvers in their trouser pockets, and their bodyguards are armed to the teeth and keep a sharp eye on every suspicious-looking individual who comes near the millionaire. The capitalist never feels safe. If he meets a partner with a suitcase or a messenger with a package, he immediately high-tails over to the other side of the street. There could be dynamite in the suitcase or package intended to separate him from his millions.

Needless to say, the situation is not any better at the mansions where these financial princes live. Their servants are chosen with the greatest care; the doors and windows are bolted and watched day and night. Under no conditions are unknown persons allowed to enter. The police keep constant watch on these barricaded fortresses.

The New York millionaire especially dreads going for a drive, because his elegant carriage and horses attract so much attention.

Besides, his babysitters, the security people, cannot follow him so
easily. Some of them have completely armored their carriages.
There are thin steel plates between the exterior and the plush
interior walls. The windows are made from a kind of glass so thick
and strong that a bullet from a normal revolver can't penetrate it.
Inside, the owner of millions of dollars sits with a loaded revolver,
trembling for his precious life.

It is even said that some have had bullet-proof vests or coats of
mail made, which they wear under their normal clothing, just like
knights in the Middle Ages. It is difficult to determine whether
that is true, however, because they don't unbutton and reveal what
they have inside their vests. In any case, the comparison with
medieval robber barons is very descriptive. Just as the robber
barons in coats of mail plundered people on the roads or ravaged
through the country, the capitalist millionaire, the person who
maintains contemporary society, plunders the workers. The result
is the same, even though the systems are much different. In the
Middle Ages robber knights built their castles on high ground that
was nearly inaccessible by road. There were walls and defensive
installations around them to protect the robber and his booty.
Today the millionaire turns his house into a fortress in which he
and his lackeys watch over his treasures.

E. F.

*A Danish merchant in New York City was impressed by the volume and
methods of retailing there. (Source: Holbæk-Posten, 30 January 1892. This
letter initially appear in Sorø Amtstidende.)*

The kinds of businesses and the ways they are run over here are
much different from what I have seen in Scandinavia. Shops
usually do not sell only one product (except grain, butter, coffee,
and petroleum). Most businesses carry an assortment of all kinds
of merchandise.

A so-called *grocery* store can provide all kinds of edible things,
from potatoes and cabbage to the most exquisite tropical fruits,
beef and pork, cod and flounder, wild fowl, French bread, and
cakes. Everything is together here—merchant, baker, butcher, and
gardener. These stores are open from five or six in the morning

until ten or eleven at night. They are very poorly decorated; in Copenhagen one of them would be regarded as a warehouse.

Dry goods stores, on the other hand, are extremely elegantly appointed. All of them have electric lights, of course. It is a pleasure to see how exquisitely the fabrics are displayed. I am especially enchanted by the window displays illuminated by electric lights. The dry goods stores are not specialized, either.

There are department stores here similar to Bett and Wessels in Copenhagen. They gross eight to twelve million dollars annually. These stores employ between one and two thousand men and women. Customers can get everything imaginable in them, from furniture to knick-knacks and perfume. A prince's palace could be outfitted from top to bottom from their shelves.

There are four large companies here that import silk. They gross fifteen to eighteen million dollars annually. The amount of business they do is incredible by Danish standards. The buildings in which they trade are magnificently decorated and are worth between one and a half and three million dollars. Dry goods are at least 30 percent more expensive here than in Denmark. Everything that is regarded as luxury goods is fantastically expensive. The most attractive and elegantly decorated places of business are the *drug stores,* or apothecaries. They have all the comforts that money can buy. Most Danish pharmacists would be able to learn a great deal from them. The business is not regulated. All medicines, even such things as opium and strychnine, can be bought without a prescription. The prices are only half what they are in Denmark; this can probably be attributed to the stiff competition.

Mr. Garben, brother of the former teacher in Slagelse, has a rather large drug store in Brooklyn. In every respect he is *all right.*

An anonymous Dane in Chicago described unemployment in the Windy City. (Source: Bornholms Avis, 31 March 1870.)

The desire to emigrate from Denmark to America has unfortunately increased significantly in recent years. No doubt one reason for this can be found in the glowing but completely false reports that are often sent home in irresponsible writings. Even

more guilty of this are *humbug* purveyors who go back to Denmark
in order to lure gullible people to the New World. These characters get paid by emigration companies for every person they
bring over here. This is a racket that would be forbidden back
home.

If the unfortunate victims had any idea of the terrible struggle
they must go through from the time they leave dear Denmark
until they have toiled long enough to gain the bare necessities of
life (and seldom does a Scandinavian get any further here), the
vast majority would certainly stay home. . . . The most pitiful
sight are the many fathers, some fairly old, who come over here
with wives and children, often nearly penniless. As soon as they
arrive in this unknown, partly lawless country whose language
they do not understand, they are surrounded by thousands of
scoundrels who are only conniving to deceive them and cheat
them out of their money and clothing. Even if one is fortunate
enough to reach his destination after a lot of difficulty, he usually
cannot find a job, but is forced to go perhaps several hundred
kilometers farther. The wife has to do whatever work is available.
The children are farmed out to various quarters, thereby breaking
up the family, usually forever. If the husband goes to an employment agency he is immediately promised work at a high wage,
but always at a distant location. If he pays a fee to the agency
he is given an address, which usually proves fictitious. That is
terrible, but it happens to thousands who come here, and many
of them disappear completely.

Artisans and unskilled laborers are the most fortunate. The
situation is bad for farmers, and there is never anything for
merchants, office clerks, or members of the academic class. These
people are completely unhappy. Wages are higher here than in
Denmark, but all necessities are twice as expensive. A good worker
is just as well off back home as here. Besides all this, there is the
very unsettling fact that nobody is sure of his own life. Murder
and theft are routine. In shops and private homes the lights must
be kept on all night, and night watchmen have to protect the
larger warehouses and factories.

Nor is there any help for those in need. If they cannot help
themselves they die, for human life has no value here. More than
fifty thousand are unemployed in Chicago this winter. They do

not have any money, and business is at a standstill. Nobody knows how things will go next spring, but all indications point to hard times.

N.G.A.

In a letter to a friend in Denmark, an immigrant described his job conditions and the excitement of living in Chicago. (Source: Den nye Verden, 3 October 1890.)

Chicago, Illinois
14 September 1890

. . . As you know, I came to America last February and was briefly in Philadelphia before I moved to Chicago. Since the job market was not so favorable and I had traveled with a person who was a real scoundrel, I decided to move on. Now I am quite well situated if you don't look at it through European eyes—a habit quickly broken in this country.

The smattering of English I learned at school was far from sufficient to help me land a suitable job, so I did the reasonable thing and took the first acceptable work I was offered. It was as a machine operator at a farm implement factory that employs three thousand men. That job lasted only three days, though, because it was very tiring and I am not accustomed to physical work. Through a painter named Riis, who had previously lived in Odense, I found employment as a painter. If I may say so myself, I was quite good at painting billboards and decorating buildings. Then a carpenter's strike brought that painting work to a standstill, so I unfortunately had to leave that field and finally landed in my present job at a window, door, and jalousie factory. My official title is now "wood cutter." With the help of a little machine I cut the wood that is used to make doors and windows. It is relatively good and pleasant work. I earn 41 crowns a week, which makes 2,127 crowns a year. That's quite a good beginning wage. Of course, the cost of living is higher here than in Denmark, so I believe my annual wage would correspond to 1800 crowns back home. To be honest about it, my current position surpasses my expectations, and I am amazed at how quickly I have become familiar with working under demanding conditions. But fancy expectations are completely out of order here in America, where work and workers are more highly regarded than back home where so many have petty, warped attitudes. I don't mean to say that I am completely satisfied with my life here. Far from it. Often it seems quite difficult, especially when I think about and long for all of you back home. But I have to accept things as they are, and although I'm hardly an optimist, I hope to do well here. A person can go a long way if he has a good will and is willing to work hard.

What makes life naturally easier over here is that a man can do almost anything he wants without having to take a thousand things into consideration. If I want to get *well dressed* from top to toe in the evening or on Sunday and go to a concert in one of the city's many *fashionable* parks, nobody cares at all or can smell that from 7 A.M. to 5:30 P.M. I am a *sandpaperingsman,* which I'm not ashamed of anyway. You can do that in a city of 1.2 million inhabitants. If a man works hard and uses his head, he can do much better here than in Denmark.

There are a lot of things to see that will amaze a newcomer here. Chicago is truly a magnificent, grandly constructed city, and can be called cosmopolitan in the strictest sense of the word. It has its faults, of course, but considering that it is hardly fifty years old it is surprising how well-developed Chicago is. Some parts of the city certainly match the elegance of the best neighborhoods of Europe's capital cities. I live in the large Scandinavian quarter, right next to well-kept Humboldt Park. It can hardly be called an elegant neighborhood, but it is quite pleasant, bright and friendly. In many respects it reminds me of the residential area of Copenhagen. Here we have none of those huge, ugly tenements like back home. Every family has its own little house with a garden. That is why the city sprawls out so far. Chicago has streets thirty English miles long. Getting from one side of town to the other is a journey in itself. But at least there are trams in nearly every part of the city, and they go as fast as the sleepy railroad trains in Denmark. They make transportation easier and we hardly notice the distances.

Chicago is without a doubt the world's largest railroad junction. I don't know all of the lines that spread out from here. Traveling by train is sheer pleasure in America. Large, well-ventilated parlor cars equipped with every imaginable luxury make even long-distance travel as comfortable as staying home in one's own living room. The train I took here from Philadelphia (twelve hundred miles) had an elegant dining car and a no less elegant Pullman sleeping car with cozy little berths. There are both first- and second-class cars. As far as equipment is concerned, second-class here is at least as elegant as the venerable first-class cars in Denmark. I had an exceptionally pleasant journey through the hills of Pennsylvania. It took only twenty-four hours, averaging fifty English miles per hour. Rather fast! The express train from Copenhagen to Korsør rolls along at the blinding speed of fourteen miles per hour. A Danish-American lady who was born here but was on a visit to Denmark, told me that while traveling through Zealand she was absolutely certain that the train was having mechanical trouble and consequently had to go at half or quarter speed.

What I miss most is a good friend. The only one I associate with is a young Norwegian who is also a sander at the factory. He is incredibly naive, but so lively and open that I can't help liking him. He is the son of a school principal in northern Norway, and is amazed by everything he sees in Chicago, because he has never been away from home before. To him Chicago is a marvelous place. He is also a fantastic admirer of female beauty, and often expresses his appreciation in a rather direct and obvious way. When we meet a pretty young lady he is usually silent for a moment, then grabs me and says loud enough for her to hear: "Wow! Just look how beautiful she is!" Naturally, that is often extremely embarrassing. One evening he made quite a scene at Barnum's Circus when three hundred very scantily clothed dancers appeared in the final number. That was a beautiful sight to behold in the electric illumination, but only a person from Bodø would express his enthusiasm in such a way as to make a laughingstock of himself.

There is a lot of good, inexpensive entertainment here in Chicago. On Sundays I usually go to Lincoln Park, which is attractively situated on Lake Michigan. It is the most beautiful and most frequently visited of Chicago's seven major parks. It's fun just to sit on a bench for an hour and watch all those who drive, ride, or walk past. There is a large zoo in the park with free admission, and a magnificent electric fountain that one of the city's millionaires erected for a mere 120,000 crowns.

When evening comes my Norwegian friend and I go to an elegant restaurant where we have a really fine steak or other meat dish for fifteen cents, then we pay ten cents to get into another place where we have a glass of beer and listen to a fine ten-piece orchestra with various first-rate male and female artists. The place is similar to the *Concert du Boulevard* in Copenhagen. Here in America no lady would dare to sing unless she had a good voice. There are surprisingly good, well-trained voices here, and a fine repertoire for both orchestras and vocalists.

I have often thought that America really is the place for you, my friend. I know from experience, as you do, how hard it often is to get by back home. But here everyone who wants to work does far better. You are a carpenter by trade, and here in Chicago there are eight thousand carpenters working under very favorable conditions. They get paid thirty-five cents an hour, which makes $2.80 for an eight-hour day.

Room and board cost only about two hundred dollars a year, so there is a lot left over. There are many Scandinavian employers here, so the language need not be a hindrance for you. The trip from Copenhagen to Chicago can be done cheaply. Think about it. Needless to say, I would be very happy to see you here, and the venture is not so ominous that you cannot go home again. I dare say there is no better time for you than the present. . . .

S. A.

In a letter to a younger brother, Julius Petersen described the hubbub of Chicago and festivities on the Fourth of July. (Source: Danes Worldwide Archives, Julius Petersen MSS.)

Chicago
5 July 1887

Dear Brother,

I received your letter on 30 July and thank you for all the news it contained. I see that you had a lot of snow after the warm weather at Easter.

Hans Kristian told me he wanted to come to America. On Palm Sunday Rasmus received two letters from him. You write that he is in Colorado, but that's wrong. He is in Woodbury County, Iowa. That's up in the corner where Iowa, Nebraska, and Dakota meet, right on the Missouri River. He is working for an Irish farmer and seems to be doing quite well.

Thank you for the news about Constitution Day, the national festivals, political meetings, the market, livestock exhibitions, and so on. The first news I received from Denmark was that the conscription law was abolished the day after I left the old country. No doubt it was lifted because of me! Congratulate Kristian Larsen and give him my regards. Maybe I'll write to him in a while.

Here in the capital city of the cities there is a lot to see. The *courthouse* is a real palace of marble and sandstone. Christiansborg Palace in Copenhagen is only a shadow of it in size and magnificence. Then there are the post office and the water works with the water tower. The water works are right next to Lake Michigan in a little park, and have the largest steam engine ever built. It has two enormous flywheels. I've been up in the water tower, which is accessible as an observation point. It is 244 steps high, each step being about twenty centimeters. (I measured them.)

All of Chicago is covered with parks. Lincoln Park, the biggest, is right next to Lake Michigan north of the downtown area. Washington Park, the second largest, is on the lake just south of the center. There is one park after the other all over the city, and a wide boulevard runs through all of them. It is fifty kilometers long. Throngs of people are in the parks every Sunday. They can rent boats on the lakes in them, and there are flowers, greenhouses, and statues. Lincoln Park has a zoo that dwarfs the one in Copenhagen. Everything is free.

There are countless viaducts over the railroads and bridges over the river. There are also two tunnels, one from the South Side to the West Side, the other from the South Side to the North Side.

The police and fire departments are excellent. Chicago has eighteen hundred policmen stationed in thirty precincts throughout the city. Whenever a policeman on duty arrests somebody, he reports it immediately by telephone to his precinct and the paddy wagon is sent out in less than a minute to get the person.

The fire department is even faster. Whenever a fire is reported (something that happens twelve to fourteen times daily, as a rule) the department knows immediately where the alarm was sounded. They can tell from the signal whether it is sawdust and firewood, petroleum, or ignited by electrical wires. The horses stand already harnessed behind doors that are automatically opened. The horses are trained to run to their places in front of the fire engines, so the men need only fasten some straps. Then they are ready with various hose-and-ladder wagons. If it happens at night while the firemen are asleep (except those who are on duty), electric wires remove their blankets so they awaken. They sleep with their clothes on. To avoid wasting time they slide down poles through holes in the ceiling instead of running down the stairway. Half a minute after the alarm is sounded the horses are galloping down the street with the fire engine. Anyone who fails to get out of the way is driven over, and it is his own fault. The trams stop, and cabs, coaches, and workcarts pull off to the side like chickens. While I have been here there have been two large fires, one at a large lumberyard and the other at a slaughterhouse. Each caused a million dollars of damage. Both were on the far South Side, about 20 kilometers from us. There are about fifty fire stations.

Yesterday Rasmus and Marine were finally married. Their wedding was a crowning touch to the Fourth of July. Already by the middle of last week boys began to shoot fireworks on the streets. All of the shops were full of flags ranging in size from five by eight centimeters to four by six meters. It became worse and worse every day, and on Sunday there was a lot of noise. But Monday, 4 July was a bright day, a grand day for many, especially Rasmus. I almost thought the world was coming to an end (joke), because beginning at 4 A.M. I could hardly hear myself speak because of the noise. The houses were almost completely hidden by the flags, and were literally shaking from the cannon volleys. Many windows were broken. There were flags of every imaginable kind. Of course, 90 percent of them were the Stars and Stripes, but there were several Danish flags and many Norwegian and Swedish ones. In the morning seventeen Scandinavian societies marched in a parade here on the West Side. The first one was the "Danish Veterans of Chicago," about one-hundred fifty strong, all wearing memorial medals. Street urchins had literally filled the streetcar tracks with firecrackers, so there was a constant cracking under the wheels.

The Danish church where Rasmus and Marine were married is in a very quiet street, so fortunately there was some peace and quiet outside her aunt's house, where we were served wine and cake. We male guests drank a lot of it in honor of them. The bride and groom changed clothes and we followed them on the streetcar down to the Racine steamer, which they boarded at 8 P.M. to begin their honeymoon trip. Here in America it is customary for a bride and groom to begin their wedding trip the same evening they are married. All steamships and trains have so-called "bridal chambers."

When we came back home from Lake Michigan the fireworks had begun in earnest. Firecrackers were thrown into the streetcar where we sat, and salvos were fired right in front of the horse's noses. They didn't know what was happening, of course. The poor motorman had to stand with his hand on the brake all the time in order to stop whenever the horses were frightened. Several times they nearly turned over the streetcar. Finally we arrived home.

Right next to where we live there are fire and police stations, and fireworks worth eight hundred dollars were to be set off. We arrived just in time to see it. Two balloons went up, and an enormous number of rockets, golden dragons, and flaming wheels exploded. The remarkable thing is that people stood right next to where the fireworks were ignited, so some recieved small burns and many had holes burned in their clothing. We stood way over on the other side of the street, but nevertheless Juul's daughter, who had come to the wedding with us, had her new dress destroyed. A rocket came right at us and hit her. Those of us who stood next to her helped brush the sparks off, but they burned several larges holes in the dress, so it was completely ruined. She had paid fourteen dollars for it eight days ago. But enough of the Fourth of July.

Rasmus and Marine will be up north for ten days. Maybe I'll go up there for a couple days and accompany them home. Perhaps they will have themselves photographed later in their wedding clothes so you will be able to see that Marine was a pretty little bride.

I have learned enough English to make myself understood at
the factory where I work.

Greet everyone who knows me. . . .

Mr. Julius Petersen
in care of *Folkevennen*
W. Indiana Street
Chicago, Illinois

*Pastor Thorvald Lyngby described the Danish working class in Racine,
Wisconsin. (Source: Kolding Folkeblad, 22 December 1882.)*

Racine is a city of twenty-two thousand inhabitants one hundred
kilometers north of Chicago on Lake Michigan. According to
general estimates, between four and five thousand of its inhabitants are Danes. There are also many Norwegians and some
Swedes. Racine has a lot of factories, and a large number of the
Danes work in them. For example, eight hundred of the approximately one thousand employees of the Mitchell & Lewis
wagon factory are Danes. Some of them are smiths, others are
wheelwrights or carpenters or do body work. In addition to the
wagon factory, there are two others that employ many Danes.
There is a plow factory and a kettle factory where the workers do
so much hammering that one can become partially deaf just by
walking past on the street. Certainly not all of the Danes work at
these factories, even though they are quite large. Racine also has
many other factories as well as transportation work, farming, well-
digging, and so on. I don't have a guidebook at hand so am
mentioning only the most obvious things. Besides, I have been
here for only two months and during that time have been too
busy to see the entire town.

Most of our countrymen are doing quite well here, but wages
have gradually gone down somewhat, because there is a steady
influx of workers from "the old country," as we call Denmark and
the rest of Europe. I have to repeat what I said earlier, however,
that in material respects America is far more favorable to the poor
man than Denmark. It is a fact that a man can work his way up

over here. It is not at all rare that a man comes from the old country, oppressed by poverty and sometimes also by the power of the nobility, and over here gets a chance to develop his resources and lift himself up to the point where he can live his life according to the ideals that he shares with the more fortunate.

Poor people ask for counseling just like other people, and we deal with them just like the others. The opinions of the poor are respected just as much as those of the rich. We notice that favorable conditions make for progress, because a wretch— especially a spiritual wretch—has a difficult lot here. On the other hand, I have to admit that many of our countrymen sink into crudeness, animal lust, and willfulness. So certainly not in all cases do we see happy results from the change. On the contrary: there is probably nowhere in the world with more evil and greater immorality than here, where all extremes converge. Hence, I can't advise anyone unconditionally to emigrate, because the difficulties and temptations overwhelm so many people. . . .

An immigrant commented on Danish life in the rapidly growing lumber town of Manistee, Michigan. (Source: Aarhus Amtstidende, 15 August 1872.)

Since there are many Danes from the Aarhus area in this town, it will no doubt interest readers of *Aahus Amtstidende* to hear a little about the place.

Michigan is the state with the highest wages in America and the only place where work can be found all year. It is only the sawmills, though, that employ hundreds of thousands of people. Wages for newcomers are only twenty-six to thirty dollars a month plus board, but married men who know the language and have a skill earn forty to fifty dollars a month and get accommodations for their families. Energetic laborers can earn four or five dollars a day piling logs. Cabinetmakers, carpenters, painters, and masons get from three to five dollars a day, plus board.

Until November the work is at the mills, but after that time it is in the forest, and we are paid thirty-five dollars a month plus board. The work consists of felling trees, sometimes with axes, sometimes with saws. The tools are so well designed and light that a boy of sixteen or eighteen can do the work as well and earn as much as a man of twenty or thirty. The only regrettable thing here is the law or rule that says no wages can be paid between 1 November and 1 June. But we can get everything on credit from the mill owners, who all sell all kinds of wares. According to reliable reports the Scandinavians are considering a *strike* against the law. They are also demanding that the work day be reduced from eleven to ten hours. We now work from 6 A.M. until 6 P.M. with an hour off for lunch. The food that we get at the restaurants and from the mill owners is extremely good. Those who cook for themselves are paid a food allowance of fourteen dollars a month. An entire family can live respectably on that sum, even if it consists of six or eight persons. Firewood is free. Pork costs about ten cents per kilogram, beef about twice that much. Butter is thirty to fifty cents per kilogram, while eggs cost thirty-six cents a dozen. Cotton clothes are much cheaper than in Denmark.

The streets of Manistee are covered with sawdust, two or three meters deep in places. All of the bulwarks are made of byproducts from the mills. The town burned down last year, but almost all of it has been rebuilt. Manistee has five thousand inhabitants, including fifteen hundred Scandinavians, fifteen hundred Germans and two thousand Frenchmen, Poles, Bohemians, and Americans. There are no fewer than five churches, including a Scandinavian Lutheran congregation whose minister is Mr. Nørgaard, who once was a teacher in Uldum. He also runs a restaurant that serves beverages and tobacco, and a reading society, which costs eight dollars a year to join. Sometimes a preacher comes here from Wisconsin. He can make fifty dollars in just a few days by conducting weddings and baptisms and absolving people of their sins.

There is also a Scandinavian workers' society with a health insurance program whose chairman is Jørgen Linderup Sørensen, owner of the Copenhagen Hotel. That hotel is truly a home for us Danes. We live, eat, and drink in the Danish way there, but without liquor. Michigan has a so-called "temperance law," and there is not a single place in all of Manistee where anything resembling spirits or liquor can be bought, only selzer water or soda pop. Not even Bavarian or lager beer is sold. Of course, there are all kinds of ways to get around this, and ingenious people among the thirsty souls can always find one of them.

The hotel owner Sørensen is currently on a trip to Denmark to recruit workers for the sawmills and the forest.

Among the things we need most in Manistee is a Scandinavian reading society. If some immigrant or other can afford to bring one or two hundred good Danish books, he will certainly be compensated by the workers' society for his expenses and make a little extra, besides. To illustrate how great the need in that area is, just think that it costs seventy-five cents per month to read one or two books.

The heat has been very severe this summer. Nobody has died of sunstroke here, though, unlike New York, where no fewer than 280 people have succumbed to it. From everywhere there are reports of people "kicking the bucket," especially in the eastern states. There are also many fires, especially in the southern states, where some people lack all feeling for human life and the other damage that is caused.

On 4 August the Scandinavian sewing society had a forest party, called a *picnic* here. It lasted until 2 A.M. The young people, who otherwise have no entertainment, enjoyed themselves immensely. The chairman's wife had sewn a stars and stripes banner. Next to it waved our Danish Dannebrog as well as Swedish and Norwegian flags. The ballroom was decorated as splendidly as possible with green foliage and banners. A former teacher named Myrup had organized an orchestra, and Danish national songs rang through the forest. The speakers included J. L. Sørensen, Valdemar Camillo, M. A. Sommer, and the major, Mr. Fowler, who spoke in English, which Sommer interpreted.

According to an immigrant in Minneapolis, the Danes of that city were not highly regarded. (Source: Holbæk Amts Avis, 8 May 1885.)

Minneapolis
14 April 1885

Dear Editor,

If the readers of *Holbæk Amts Avis* are not completely occupied with the political controversy in Denmark, they might find it interesting to read these lines from the promised land, which is called America.

My first word of advice to Danish workers is this: If they can tolerate their miserable existence back home, then they should not come over here. They cannot expect anything good over here. This is especially true for men with families and people who are getting up in years. It is more difficult for older people to learn English, and in general they find it more difficult to adapt to all the new conditions that they find here. How about young people? All right, but they should be especially educated for America. A young man who has been trained in agriculture can, as a rule, find some kind of gainful employment in the summer, but he is lucky if he can earn a living in the winter. Usually the winter months use up whatever is saved in the summer. An artisan can, of course, be lucky enough to find work in his field immediately, but that is such a rarity that I have never met anyone who has not had to do some other kind of work first. It is therefore important to be able to do other things, or at least not to be completely ignorant of other trades. Unfortunately, as a rule that is the case with artisans from Denmark. In many cases they have never used a shovel or a spade; they cannot even bridle a horse. Just yesterday I saw a Swedish merchant trying to get a job as a teamster. He was simply unable to put the harness on the horses, so he did not get even that modest job.

No, he who wants to emigrate to America should be specifically trained for it. For example, he can work for a wheelwright for a year and a half, and during that time use all of his free time to learn English and German. Then he can work for a farmer for a year. Following that he can go to Sweden or Norway and learn how to construct wooden buildings. After doing that for a summer, he can go out into the forest and cut down trees for a winter, and the following summer work on a railroad gang. Finally, he should get some practice working in the mines. If during all this he has not neglected his language studies, he is ready to go to America around the age of twenty. He will not have learned how to do anything very well, but that is not necessary over here. He who can do a little of everything gets along best. He must not shirk hard work, and he must not shirk being treated like a dog. He must be willing to be anyone's servant, just like any other newcomer here. . . .

There are very few who prosper here, although one must try.
Here in Minneapolis there are a thousand Danes, many of whom
have been in this country for several years. But of all of them only
four or five have attained a better standard of living than that
which they could have reached back home if they had undergone
all of the difficulties and privations that they have experienced
here.

In this regard I have to add that the Danes have special
difficulties to overcome here in America. It hurts me to have to
say this, but as a matter of fact our people are not well regarded
by the Americans. They maintain, and I can hardly deny it, that
after the Irish the Danes are the most given to drink and similar
evils. Of course, that does not hold true for all Danes, but all of us
have to pay the price, nonetheless. Some, indeed the majority, are
orderly, but nobody pays attention to them. But everyone notices
when the police arrest Danes for drunkenness, fighting, indecency,
and the like. This is what the bad individuals among us are guilty
of, but that is not the only thing. For example, if a Dane wants to
open a business, he cannot count on any support from his
countrymen as customers, because they are so few. It is a completely different story with the Germans, who are like a city within
the city, because there are so many of them.

Another thing that hurts our reputation among the Americans is
the Danish-American press. It uses the most disgusting language.
There are exceptions, of course, such as the little newspaper I
read, *Folkets Avis,* published in Racine, Illinois [*sic*]. It is a respectable paper, in contrast to *Den danske Pioneer* in Omaha,
Nebraska, which is the worst conceivable rubbish.

On Friday evening the Dania Society here in the city held a
mass meeting to discuss the current issue of constructing a
building that would serve the Danes of Minneapolis, something
similar to the soldiers' homes that have been built recently in
Denmark. The idea, as it was developed at the meeting, is
exceptionally attractive, and it would certainly be a considerable
benefit if it materializes.

The Danes in Minneapolis have a Lutheran church but no
sanctuary, so we have to rent a building. Our pastor, Adam Dan,

is a remarkably good preacher and an outstandingly respectable
and kind man.

Yours respectfully,
Peter Sørensen

*A group of immigrants from various Danish communities reported on
unemployment in Omaha.* (Source: *Bornholms Avis,* 5 April 1870.)

We have heard that the Montreal Ocean Steamship Company
has sent some Danes back to Denmark to encourage people to
emigrate to America. We believe it is our duty to the working class
of our native country to express the following: Immigration to
Nebraska has been great in recent years. At present there are
many people who cannot find jobs. It can be said that half of
them are unemployed, and prospects for the future are very dark.
It is true that land can be had at a very low price for free, but if a
man doesn't have money, he cannot do anything with it, because
he cannot till the soil with his bare hands. That's how conditions
are here, and we hear the same from people who come from
other parts of America. Because of this, we want to advise our
countrymen to stay put for the time being.

J. Jørgensen, Sipperup	Christensen, Giislev
R. Rasmussen, Baalse paa Falster	F. Carl Andersen, Copenhagen
Niels Larsen, Karbæk Parish	Hartvig Jonsen, Risbykke
Lars Petersen, Rynkebye	Olsen Jane, Liunge
Niels Larsen, Copenhagen	P. C. Larsen, Velle paa Fyn

*A Dane who had previously been a farmhand in Iowa had to accept a job
at a slaughterhouse in Omaha.* (Source: Danes Worldwide Archives, Ole
Andersen MSS.)

Omaha
1 December 1890

Dear Brother-in-law,
    Today I want to write a few words to you and tell you how
things are going. I like to get a little mail from the old country

once in a while and I realize I can't expect any if I don't do some writing myself.

I'm still well and have a job, but I'm no longer in Iowa. I'm in the state of Nebraska. Larsen, the tailor from Skibby, and his son live here. In fact, I met them the day I arrived in Omaha. I was mighty surprised to see the old tailor here. I had heard that his son lived here, but I hadn't seen him before I came to Omaha. They want me to pass along their regards, and the older Larsen says he owes you twenty-five *øre*, which he will pay you when he gets back to Denmark. I live at a boarding house not far from where the Larsens live, so I get to talk with them almost every day. He is working as a tailor but doesn't have much business. He claims he will get more orders after he becomes better acquainted with conditions here. Larsen also says he was happier in Denmark than he is here.

I'm working at a slaughterhouse where pigs and cattle are butchered. Three hundred men work here. I get paid $1.50 a day, and room and board cost $3.75 a week. There isn't much work to be had right now because the ground is frozen. We haven't had any snow yet, but it is quite cold now and we have to expect snow soon. . . .

Ole Andersen

PS: Write soon and tell me how things are going back home.

A few months later Andersen offered a few more insights into working-class life in Omaha. (Source: Danes Worldwide Archives, Ole Andersen MSS.)

Omaha
24 April 1891

Dear Brother-in law and Sister,

Today I want to take a pen in hand and write a few words to tell you a little about how things are going here. I don't have much news. I'm well as always. Thanks for the photographs, which are really pretty and look a lot like you. I'm going to have my picture taken soon and I'll send you a couple of copies.

Well, it's just about summer back home. Here it's already quite warm, but we had a bad autumn last year and only recently have people been able to begin work in the fields. I'm still working here in Omaha, but I'll probably move back to a farm because it's impossible to save any money in town. You see, Nebraska isn't a "dry" state like Iowa was. Here we can get as much liquor as we want.

We Danes have an insurance association here. It's a good thing, because a person needs some support if he gets sick. I paid two dollars to join, and the periodic fee is half a dollar. If a member becomes ill he receives a weekly benefit of five dollars, and if he dies his survivors get fifty dollars to pay for the funeral.

I want to pass along greetings from Anders Peter. I talked with him recently, but he isn't well. He said he wanted to go home to his parents as soon as possible. I'm also supposed to greet you from Larsen the tailor and his son. They are well, but the tailor doesn't have much work. His son can feed him, though, since he makes two and half dollars a day as a plumber. . . .

O. L. Andersen

Andersen took a cynical view of a Danish actor who visited Omaha. (Source: Danes Worldwide Archives, Ole Andersen MSS.)

South Omaha
9 December 1901

Dear Sister and Brother-in-law,

Today I'll take up my pen and write a few words to you. I should have written to you long ago, but because I'm such a lazy correspondent, a long time passes before I take up that dangerous weapon, the pen.

First of all, I wish to thank you for the photograph of Laurits and my brother-in-law. It's really nice. And Laurits has grown so big! I'm looking forward to seeing the big boy and Agnes again. They were such nice little children when I left home. I certainly hope that I'll be able to make a trip home sometime and see all of you. My wife isn't interested in going back to Denmark, because all of her family is over here. I'm sending you a photograph of the children. It's not as good of Myrtle as it ought to be, but it resembles Anders well, even though it wasn't easy to get them to stand still, since they are so small.

There isn't much news from here. Actually, something is always happening, but I believe you read about most of it in the newspapers at home. A royal Danish actor stopped here last summer on his tour of the United States. My wife and I went to hear him when he was in Omaha. He was an impressive person who tried to express how happy he was to meet so many of his countrymen, but I suspect he was equally glad to fill his pockets with American dollars. After all, that was the main reason he came here.

We want to wish all of you Merry Christmas and a Happy New Year, and many fond greetings to you from my wife and children as well as myself.

Ole Andersen

A socialist in Washington described aspects of the workers' movement in the Pacific Northwest. (Source: *Demokraten,* 4 February 1892.)

Out here on the Pacific Coast the fight for the just demands of socialism is going on. I enclose a copy of *Tacoma Tidende,* in which you will find a speech by Christian Michelsen regarding this.

Just like back home many people over here have strange ideas about the legitimacy of socialism and its advance. Fortunately, however, there is always someone who is willing to reply to the accusations when such opinions are expressed. The peculiar fantasies are thereby properly illuminated.

I was amazed when I first came here last autumn to see capitalists marching together with the working class through the streets of Tacoma in the Labor Day parade. That happens in most of the towns out here. Obviously they are trying to pull the wool over the workers' eyes by flattering them. It is not difficult to see that they are not doing it out of love. Those sneaky foxes deliver speeches flattering the workers because they cannot get along without them out here in this new country. They tell about everything capital and labor have accomplished together, but they forget to mention that after these new towns and mines have been opened and people to work in them recruited, they try in every

way possible to steal the worker's hard-earned money through
flattery, threats, and so on. If the workers do not obey their
capricious decrees they telegraph Chicago and get Pinkerton's
secret police (or the "bloodhounds," as we call them) and have
them shoot down without mercy their "friends," the workers.

Such an episode occurred five months ago between Tacoma and
Leathe. The owner of the mines had hired several Negroes, who
did not understand what was going on. They were supposed to be
scabs and replace the white workers. But the citizens of Tacoma,
chiefly the middle class, rose up resolutely, saddled their horses,
and galloped out to the mines to protect the workers. They were
not afraid of Pinkerton's bandits, the guardian angels of capital-
ism. Armed with rifles and revolvers, they ordered Pinkerton's
men to leave the place immediately in accordance with the laws of
the *United States*. Pinkerton's henchmen were forced to obey. It is
great that the will of the people is far more powerful and
confident over here; otherwise there would be no end to the
terror in this land with all its capitalists.

Greet all the comrades back in the third district of Aarhus. I still
believe we should agitate more for truth and justice, the principles
of socialism. The more we do so, the deeper the impression we
will make on the people. Then all of those who respect truth will
feel it is their duty not to yield to minor problems but rather to
march forward to victory.

L. Hansen

*A sailor from Bagenkop on the island of Langeland related the difficulties
into which his crew fell after a smuggling incident in Cuba.* (Source: *Langelands Avis,* 11 June 1872.)

. . . I'll tell you about my most recent voyage. As you have
probably heard, I sailed to the West Indies last autumn. In
Philadelphia I signed on with a bark on which I had worked
before. We sailed down the coast, took on a load of lumber, and
proceeded to Cuba. We arrived in Cienfuegos on 19 October. On
the evening of 22 October, while the customs official was dining
with the ship's officers on board, the cook put some gunpowder
into a boat to smuggle it ashore. A little while later a mate rowed

the boat in because he wanted to bring some chickens to two young men who were waiting on land. Two customs officials who had come down to inspect the boat found the gunpowder and confiscated everything, including the young men. They demanded that the boat be rowed to the customs office, several kilometers away. They came on board the ship to get more men to help row. Three men, including me, were ordered down into the boat. We did not have the faintest idea what was happening. About nine o'clock that evening we reached the customs office. All of us, together with the gunpowder and the chickens, were taken inside. Twelve soldiers tied us up like sheep and dragged us away under arrest. That same evening the ship was inspected. They found several items that belonged to the captain. The entire ship was placed under arrest and the crew was forbidden to go ashore.

We were under arrest fourteen days before our comrades on the ship got permission to visit us and bring our blankets and clothes so that we could change. During all that time we had to lie on the bare floor. For food we were given two small loaves of bread every day and water. In the meantime the bark had been unloaded but not released. Only the navigator and three sailors were on board, because the captain, the cook, the foreman of the place, and the customs official had been arrested the day after us.

At the hearing nobody claimed ownership of the gunpowder, since that meant death by firing squad. We were under arrest for three months and twenty-three days until finally the mate who was in the boat when the gunpowder was discovered was found guilty. They were not certain, however, so he was not executed, but together with the captain, the foreman, and the two young men he was sentenced to eight years of "chain labor." That means that they were placed into leg irons and forced to work in the streets and forts.

Each of us had a lawyer who was an officer in the Spanish army. We were finally set free. The day our sentences were to be pronounced, 25 January, we were marched down to the governor's house, and on 13 February the papers releasing us arrived from Havana. We were sent back to the bark and finally, on 2 April, left for New York. The cook and a sailor deserted, however, because they feared they would be thrown overboard on the way

Until the twentieth century Danish peasants typically lived in simple wattle and daub houses like this one on the island of Læsø. (Courtesy Gunnar Knudsen)

Pastoral xylographies, such as this one depicting the town of Ry in 1893, revealed little of the population explosion and social problems that bedeviled rural Denmark during the nineteenth century. (Courtesy Gunnar Knudsen)

Though public social services did not keep pace with the need for them, free meal tickets were often available for the droves of unemployed persons who queued up to receive them in Copenhagen. (Courtesy Gunnar Knudsen)

Thousands of Danes embarked for North America at Larsen Square in Copenhagen, here depicted in Edvard Petersen's painting of 1890. (Courtesy Danes Worldwide Archives)

The flagship Thingvalla of the Thingvalla Line steams out of Copenhagen harbor in the 1890s in this painting by Vilhelm Arnesen. (Courtesy Danes Worldwide Archives)

Dans ombord.

The Danish Thingvalla Line attracted emigrants with advertisements depicting the joys of life on board its ships. (Courtesy Norwegian Emigrant Museum)

For the majority of emigrants who booked accommodations in steerage, the Atlantic crossing failed to live up to their expectations which advertisements by shipping companies had raised. (Courtesy Gunnar Knudsen)

The Thingvalla *limped into Halifax, Nova Scotia, after colliding with the* Geyser *in 1888. (Courtesy Gunnar Knudsen)*

*Weary immigrants while away the time aboard a train as it departed St. Paul, Minnesota, in 1886. (*Harper's Weekly, *13 September 1886)*

Life in Custer County, Nebraska, was no doubt lonely for this immigrant family that posed in front of its sod house in 1887. (Courtesy Solomon D. Butcher Collection, Nebraska State Historical Society)

Half a dozen cats and an oleander tree provided some measure of solace for John and Hannah Christensen in Kansas. (Courtesy Nebraska State Historical Society)

In both the Upper Midwest and the Pacific Northwest forestry provided seasonal employment for many Danes. (Courtesy Minnesota Historical Society)

Partridge, Minnesota, sprang from cutover timber land and was later re-named Askov after a well-known town in Dennmark. (Courtesy Minnesota Historical Society)

Ethnic churches provided spiritual homes for a small number of Danish immigrants. St. John's Lutheran Church near Cozad, Nebraska, featured a familiar pulpit, communion rail, altar, and altar painting, but its wooden walls would have seemed strange to those accustomed to the white masonry interiors of sanctuaries in Denmark. (Courtesy Nebraska State Historical Society)

Parishioners at a Danish church in Nebraska celebrated Lent by staging a play in 1912. (Courtesy Nebraska State Historical Society)

Letters from friends and relatives in North America quickly became centers of attention in many Danish towns and were frequently printed in local news-papers. (Courtesy Gunnar Knudsen)

back. We were happy to arrive in New York on 2 May. I am
thinking about sailing on the coast again this summer.

*Frederik Andersen (b. 1864), the son of a teacher in southern Jutland,
gave up his incipient career as a baker to become a sailor. Shortly after
emigrating, he asked his family to take care of his modest earnings.* (Source:
Karl Larsen, ed., *De, der tog hjemmefra,* IV [Copenhagen: Gyldendalske
Boghandel, 1914], pp. 149–150.)

Boston
3 June 1884

Dear Parents, Brothers and Sisters,

After an enjoyable journey to Philadelphia on board a three-
masted schooner named the *William G. Lewis,* I am back in Boston.
The captain wants me to make a second voyage on the same
schooner. I am well and satisfied with my situation here.

I received the enclosed letter along with twenty dollars from
Stuvert Freeman last Sunday. I am sending them and a little of
the money I saved from the last voyage to you. It amounts to
thirty-seven dollars. Please deposit this money in your savings
account for me until I can send more. Today I tried to withdraw
the thirty dollars I have in my account at Boston Bank, but they
insist on an eight-day advance notice. I don't know anyone who
can withdraw my money for me while I am at sea, so I'll have to
leave it in until a convenient time.

Things are going badly for Robert Jonsen. I don't want to room
with him any more. When you write to me, address the letters *care
of* Mr. Albert Bray. I like him, and he is my only real friend here.

Please give five crowns of the enclosed money to Dagmar for
her nice letters to me. In the hope that all of you are in good
health and fine spirits, I remain

Yours faithfully,
Frederik

·V·

The Danish-American as *Homo Politicus*

Danish immigrants comments on American politics must be read in light of both nineteenth-century Danish politics and the social status of most immigrants in the United States. The Danish "age of absolutism, " which began in 1660, came to an end on 5 June 1849 when the nation received a moderately liberal constitution. Universal male suffrage and other civil and political rights in harmony with contemporary liberalism were granted and a parliament was created, but the monarchy was retained (albeit in a greatly weakened form). During the second half of the century, however, election to one house of the bicameral parliament required property ownership, and conservative governments frustrated most attempts at further reforms—parliamentary democracy was not introduced until 1901.

During the third quarter of the century the Industrial Revolution began to be felt in Denmark, and a Social Democratic party was organized during the early 1870s to represent the interests of the growing urban working class. The radical organization was persecuted, however, and in 1877 the Copenhagen police apparently bribed two of its key leaders, Louis Pio and Poul Geleff, to emigrate to America. Several other socialists followed when their fledgling party foundered.

When Danes migrated from the Old World to the New they took considerable interest in American politics, as their newspapers indicate. At least two factors, however, limited their political power during the nineteenth century. First, Danes in general arrived a bit later than Norwegian and Swedish immigrants; as a result many lacked the standing usually needed to run for office, and even to gain American citizenship, before the era of William Jennings Bryan. Secondly, the diffuse settlement pattern of Danish-Americans prevented them from wielding much clout as a voting bloc in most areas. These two factors help to explain why few Danish immigrants gained prominence in the political arena.

While it is now impossible to measure accurately the party preferences of Danish newcomers, their correspondence and newspapers suggest that they tended to be more Democratic and Populist than their Norwegian and Swedish counterparts. These two other Scandinavian groups were decidedly Republican from the days of Abraham Lincoln until the 1890s, when economic exigencies shattered their loyalty to that party. Among the Danes, though, allegiance to the Republicans was apparently never pronounced during the Gilded Age, and certainly not in the 1890s, when farmers as well as laborers and artisans pitched their tents in the Populist and Democratic camps.

Generally speaking, Danish immigrants preferred the American form of government to that of their native land, in which the peasantry and urban proletariat exercised even less control over their destiny. Some, however, especially socialists, objected to American campaign techniques and viewed the United States as essentially a plutocracy.

In a letter to his sister, Torben Lange commented on American issues of the 1840s. (Source: Lange, *Fra Roskildefjord til Mississippi*, pp. 150–55.)

St. Louis, Missouri
28 February 1844

Dear Henriette,

. . . I remember that you are interested in politics, so I will tell you a little about our domestic politics. There are several different parties here that are quite hostile toward each other because the presidential election of next October is approaching, especially the Whigs and their opponents, the Democrats. The Whigs are for maintaining the existing banking system, which is advantageous to rich people. It serves only to make the rich richer and the poor poorer. The Democrats, however, oppose the banking system. They want to close all the private banks and organize a national bank. The Whigs are pushing Henry Clay as their presidential candidate, the Democrats Van Buren. Personally, I am a Democrat in regard to the banking question, but in other respects a Whig.

Another party that is currently active and gaining strength every day is the so-called *anti license men,* of which I am a member. According to the existing legislation, what is called *tax* or *license* is paid in this way: A man who, for example, opens a grocery store or something similar has to pay a fee to the government of fifty dollars annually, regardless of whether he begins with fifty dollars or five thousand dollars of capital. A man who drives a *dray* or other vehicle in the towns must pay ten dollars annually to the government, regardless of whether he owns one horse or one hundred. The principle of the *anti license* men is: *any man, rich or poor, shall be taxed according to the value of his property.* Be assured that this party is strong. The last time license fees were collected, there were hundreds here in St. Louis, who simply refused to pay. Instead, they paid 0.5 percent of the value of their property. Nobody dared to do anything about it. The first man who refused to pay (that was about three years ago) swore that he had never paid and never would pay for a license. The name of this man, the first *anti license* man who amazed everyone with his boldness, is S. C. Hoyt. At that time he sold oranges that he carried in a basket through the streets. Now he owns a fruit shop. If thousands of prophecies are fulfilled the world might someday hear of S. C. Hoyt, *President of the United States of America.*

A fourth party, the most dangerous of all, are the so-called *abolitionists* or *anti slavery men* who are opposed to Negro slavery. Negro slavery is a great evil and a blemish on the nation, but emancipation of the Negroes at once would be an even greater evil. They are an abominable race of people. It would be right to set them free, but not irrationally all at once. That would be the ruin of this proud republic.

There are a large number of religious parties (although I don't belong to any), such as *Methodists, Presbyterians, Episcopalians* (like the Danish state church), *Unitarians, Catholics, Baptists, Rationalists, Mormons,* and many others. The Mormons are generally the lowest scoundrels, thieves, and robbers. One of their doctrines is that a man can have as many wives as he desires. They also teach that the produce of the earth is for all people equally, so it is not a sin to steal. This religious sect numbers several thousand members. Its center is at Nauvoo, right across from the mouth of the Des Moines River. Its high priest and America's number one scoundrel is Joseph Smith, a Yankee by birth who founded the religion. They are now building a large temple in Nauvoo, the reconstruction of Solomon's Temple. "St." Joseph Smith, and his holy priests pull the dirtiest tricks in Nauvoo, all behind the mask of holiness and, as they say, to promote *"the only true faith."* These Mormons will not be around for long, though. They are too evil and their neighbors in Illinois, Iowa, and Missouri will not tolerate them for long. They have already fought battles in which several lost their lives. . . .

Today, 3 March, there was a large demonstration that resulted in the crowd tearing down the medical college and anatomy laboratory. The cause was that the doctors had had corpses stolen from the cemetery regularly and also that people [had] disappeared without a trace. This morning a dog was seen running with a piece of an arm. The observer reported this to the *mayor,* but in the meantime the mob had torn down a wooden wall (I always join the crowd on such occasions) and found a pit full of dead bodies. This aroused indignation. Stones began to be thrown at the building. Six people were put into jail and fifty soldiers cordoned off the building. Naturally that provoked the hot-headed Americans. A skirmish followed but the soldiers, who themselves were citizens, did not offer much resistance. As soon as the crowd yelled "Down with the bayonets" they retreated. As soon as the soldiers were out of sight chaos erupted. All of the windows were smashed, the doors were broken down, and everything that could be destroyed was broken to bits and thrown out the windows. Cadavers, skeletons, and so on were carried away to be given a decent burial. Then there wasn't any anatomy laboratory any longer. The mob dispersed singing and shouting "Hurrah." Four or six of the doctors left town early today as soon as the mob began to assemble. A lot of people have gone down to liberate the six who are in jail.

After ten years in the United States, L. Strandskov from Møen, an island in southeastern Denmark, praised American democracy in terms worthy of a Fourth of July oration. (Source: Bornholms Tidende, 2 February 1882.)

. . . I am probably not much better informed about general conditions in America than most of the other people here. During the past few winters I have traveled a few thousand kilometers in various directions, but that is not a great deal in a country as large as the United States. Nevertheless, I dare say that Minnesota,

Iowa, Wisconsin, and Nebraska are the states where Danish farmers will most readily find what they are looking for, namely, good soil, a healthy climate, and, above everything else, a legal system as sound as anywhere else in the world.

I also appreciate greatly the constitution under which we live. We elect our own local officials and city council, every state chooses its own governor and, finally, the president himself is responsible to the people. Whenever we are dissatisfied with the way they govern, we elect new people. There are not any artificial interpretations of the law or any provisional finance laws, and I am certain that if anyone violated the constitution he would be in trouble.

In such a republic everyone is for democracy, of course, and one need not be here long before one begins to view the constitutional monarchies of Europe with anything but respect. Whenever we begin to discuss politics at our hotels, where we Scandinavians meet Americans and people of all other nationalities, we quickly agree that the form of government that makes the least sense is the constitutional monarchy, in which the ministers are theoretically responsible, but in practice not responsible to any legislative body as long as they have the king to protect them. It is difficult for advocates of democracy to believe that any genuine form of popular sovereignty will evolve under such a system.

I shall reserve further comment on Danish politics, though, because it is difficult to keep well informed about the subject, even though it is difficult to avoid, since everyone talks about politics here.

One immigrant criticized various aspects of American society, but nevertheless preferred the United States to Denmark. (Source: *Langelands Tidende,* 7 November 1882.)

Sabula, Jackson County
Iowa, North America
7 October 1882

Are Conditions Better for American or Danish Citizens? No doubt this question confronts many of my countrymen back home and their kin every day, but even though the answer is always in favor of the Americans they do not dare believe it. They imagine all kinds of dangers and difficulties, and are not sure whether they should emigrate. In order to help answer this question with the bit of experience I have, I shall give a little report about immigrants' arrival and early days in America.

Illness and unemployment are the first things that confront immigrants over here. If, while sick or unemployed, they discover that almost every farmer they meet here is more interested in doing us harm than helping us, it will be clear that it is absolutely necessary to have some money upon arriving here. Remember this maxim here: Help yourself and depend on yourself.

Most prospective emigrants are trained in some trade or other and hope to get an appropriate job after arriving in America. They discover, however, that only two kinds of work are available here, railroad construction and farm work. Both are demanding. It is true that the workday on the railroads is only ten hours, but the foreman is always watching and there is hardly time to spit on one's hands. On farms the workday lasts from sunrise to sunset with three breaks for meals. At times the temperature is 40° Celsius in the shade. It is not necessary to bathe over here, because one is bathed daily in one's own sweat. So don't imagine that one can make a living over here by sitting in a rocking chair and getting some fresh air. Hard work is routine.

All of these things that I have described are only physical trivialities. Far worse is the intellectually stifled state of our countrymen over here. Most Danes emigrate at a very young age and with very little knowledge. Many have practically no experience when they enter busy American society, where in many jobs the only serious talk concerns how to make money and humor always degenerates into vulgarity. Regrettably, it is not easy to notice anything Danish about these immigrant brethren. One can commit to the mass grave of false hopes the expectations one might have had of finding a Danish mentality among them. . . .

Conditions are better for Americans than for Danes, but no less is demanded to be a good and useful citizen in the United States than in Denmark. In every society people are appreciated more than machines. I have heard several Americans boast about American freedom and, no less, the equality that supposedly is more widespread here than in any other country. I have not yet been fortunate enough to see some other regions of America, but it seems clear that a man with talent and knowledge can work his way up over here. It seems to me, though, that this is due less to the country's constitution than to the low price of the fertile land that is bought and cultivated every day.

I believe that many who return to Denmark and praise American liberty really mean its good daily wages. Nowhere in the world have I seen more strict police or a harsher judicial system than right here. That is quite natural, because the people are not mature enough for freedom. As far as equality is concerned, the United States is like any other country; intelligence, knowledge, and education enjoy the privileges they deserve. Hence, the Americans have the same goals as the Danes, and dullness, ignorance, and vulgarity are always made to appear like the opposite of what they really are.

It should be clear by now that I am not infatuated with the glories of America and do not overlook this country's shortcomings. You might wonder why, after complaining so much, I still prefer America. The reason is simply this: hunger is unknown in America, and no kind of work is looked down upon here, if it is done by an honest man. These are the two principal reasons why I admire and prefer America. In Denmark nearly every other man has to worry about food and, although there has been a lot of progress during the past twenty years, prejudices have far from disappeared. Not the least of these is contempt for work or, more correctly, for the workingman. Of course, this stems from the days when serfs did the work while the nobility went hunting and raiding. It is strange that such old prejudices continue to haunt the people like a nightmare, but naturally they will be gone some day.

From what I have written it will be clear which attributes I regard as necessary for Danes who intend to emigrate to America. Nevertheless, I shall repeat my opinion. The better the Dane, the better the American citizen he will become. Therefore, I advise young people, both boys and girls, to attend one of our folk high schools for a semester or two. Develop your personalities and

characters and become independent, reflective people, not pawns
of egotistic advisers, of whom there are too many.

A. C. Jørgensen

*An immigrant socialist took a cynical view of the American electoral pro-
cess.* (Source: *Social-Demokraten,* 31 May 1885.)

New Haven, Connecticut
3 May 1885

We have just survived a severe winter, but the breezes of May
are anything but pleasant. It was a sorrowful winter.

In the country this comedy is called the "presidential election."
To describe it is simply impossible, and that is not the purpose of
this letter. One just has to see in person how "the world's freest
people" wade through the mud of the streets almost every evening
on command from their leaders and raise an Indian war whoop in
honor of their future suppresser, whose image is usually suspended from a rope or affixed to a pole and carried down the
street. Every little troop includes a division of drummers. Everyone marches in rows and wears a uniform consisting of a cotton
jacket and knee-length shorts. These are the gaudiest multicolored
things imaginable. The colors correspond to those of the politician
for whom the people are marching. In harmony with all this
each marcher wears a dog license on his chest with a large
number on it, so that the masses can be properly controlled by
their "commanders." It breaks the heart of any freedom-loving
person to see such mummery and eunuchlike servitude.

Such a spectacle tempts one to doubt the viability of the entire
workers' movement here, because professional politicians have
everything in their hands. But for the individual the situation is
quite different. The two large political parties, which hold each
other in check, are currently nothing more than two bands of
robbers who do their robbing "legally" and do their best to gain
possession of such booty as cushy jobs, offices, and the like. Once

such a system is entrenched it either develops further or else destroys itself. Our political parties have already reached that point, so they are forced to reveal themselves for what they are— exploiters.

The vast majority of the people do not realize that yet, but they shall learn to realize it. The powerful weight of the facts is bringing the people to their senses, even though it was not possible to enlighten them with even the best arguments.

There is widespread superstition here that something bad always happens to businesses in presidential election years. Many resigned themselves with that poor excuse all last year, but now they are complaining that times were never worse. The most depressing thing is that there is no prospect of improved conditions in the near future.

At the moment the Germans are playing the leading role in the socialist movement in this country. Agitation is very difficult because there are so many different nationalities and languages, but the movement is making progress nevertheless, slowly but surely. The workers of America understand their place in the class system better than ever before. In the past workers' organizations have either failed to survive crises or else become incapable of fighting. Nevertheless, they have grown, and now there are also organizations that did not previously exist. It is not surprising that socialists play leading roles in most trades, because they are usually the most enlightened workers. But the situation would be significantly better if all social democrats could speak English as well as their own languages. Fortunately, the socialist literature in English has become constantly better and the selection is larger. The best work on modern socialism that has been published here is *The Cooperative Commonwealth* by Lawrence Grønland. It costs one dollar, but a revised, cheaper edition will cost only twenty-five cents. This book will help our cause significantly by clarifying our position.

That is how we are quietly proceeding toward that goal that no power on earth can bring about—the union of all nationalities [two unintelligible words] as socialism strides toward victory.

With socialist greetings,
Fr. F.

Christian Lautherborn (1860–1906), a native of Ålborg, was in Oyster Creek, Texas, when Grover Cleveland defeated James G. Blaine in the close election of 1884. (Source: Karl Larsen, ed., De, der tog hjemmefra, IV, pp. 21–23.)

. . . There was a great deal of excitement in America this autumn because of the presidential election. The Republicans had been in power for twenty-six years, but this year the Democrats were victorious. I am immensely proud to be a Democrat in body and soul and have been one since I became interested in politics. This year I received my citizenship papers and had the right to vote.

What a difference there is between elections in Denmark and the United States! Back home people are more peaceful and sober, but here they don't have enough patience to wait until the votes are counted. They want to know the result an hour after they mark their ballots. Election day was 4 November, and that evening there was a lot of commotion in the streets. Everyone was eager to hear the result. Both of the parties had headquarters where all of the election news was announced, and the telegrams came in very fast. It would have been too difficult to read them, of course, so each party set up a projector on top of a building and hung a large white cloth from the top of a building across the street. That way everyone could read all of the telegrams that came in. I was at Democratic headquarters, and every telegram was in Cleveland's favor. It seemed strange that they knew everything so fast, so I went down to the Republicans' head-quarters to see what the results looked like there. Everything favored Blaine. I concluded that all of this projector nonsense had been arranged merely to satisfy the hot-blooded Americans until the excitement had died down.

It was three weeks before we knew who had been elected president. One day it seemed to be one candidate, the next day the other. Everyone bet on the election, and I saw people bet as much as eight hundred dollars that Cleveland would be the next president. Finally it was clear that Cleveland would be the president. The entire city was illuminated and there was a torchlight parade. That was the greatest sight I've ever seen.

Everyone was present—old men who could hardly walk, boys eight or ten years old, people on horseback, in carriages, and in decorated wagons. They all had torches. Six brass bands were in the parade, as were the old cannons from the Civil War. Veterans of all the old soldiers' organizations were there with their flags and uniforms. It took about an hour for everyone to pass, even though they marched fifteen abreast. . . .

Julius Petersen analyzed how the American presidential election process snatched defeat from the jaws of victory for the incumbent, Grover Cleveland, in 1888. (Source: Danes Worldwide Archives, Julius Petersen MSS.)

Chicago, Illinois
19 February 1889

Dear Brother,

I received your letter on 30 January, more than four months after I had sent one to you, so you can't congratulate yourself for promptness! If you had written earlier, so that I had received your letter immediately after the presidential election, you would have learned a lot about it from me. As you heard long ago, it unfortunately resulted in a loss for the Democrats. It was only a partial loss, however, because the Republicans received a majority only in the electoral college while Grover Cleveland garnered about one hundred thousand more votes than Benjamin Harrison. It is a terrible shame that a man can get a majority among the voters and still not be elected. Since the election many people have called for a change to direct popular election of the president so that this won't happen again.

Harrison can thank Governor Hill of New York for his victory. Although Hill is a Democrat and succeeded Cleveland as governor on Cleveland's recommendation, he opposed the election of Cleveland because they disagreed on some things. Hill had a friend whom he wanted to make postmaster of New York. Cleveland didn't want to appoint him because the man who already held the position was doing his job very well. Hill became angry about this and began to oppose him secretly. He did not mention Cleveland's name in a single one of his election speeches.

But the powerful Democratic organization in New York, "Tammany Hall," founded by Thomas Jefferson in 1789, of which Hill was a member, had large quantities of ballots printed and spread them around the state. They deleted the names of Democratic electoral college voters and substituted Republican ones. These ballots still carried the names of the nominated Democratic candidates for state, *county,* and local offices. The result was that the Republican Harrison received a majority of fourteen thousand votes for the presidency and Hill received a majority of nineteen thousand votes for the governorship. As usual, New York determined the outcome of the election.

This is the third time a candidate has received a majority of the popular votes without being elected. Andrew Jackson received a majority of 50,000 votes in 1824 but John Quincy Adams was elected. In 1876 the Democrat Samuel Tilden received 251,000 more votes than the Republican Rutherford Hayes but wasn't elected. Now it's happened a third time, so it's about time to change the constitution. The candidate who gets the most votes should be assured of being elected, and not have the election decided by pure chance.

I was downtown on election day until after midnight. All of the large English-language newspapers had suspended screens from the second stories of their buildings. When telegrams with election results came in, they projected them from an apparatus across the street so that they appeared in immense letters on the screens. There were twelve screens in all, and the huge crowds standing on the streets shouted "Hurray" or whistled, depending on whether the results were in favor of or against the candidates they supported. It was easy to tell that they were most excited about New York. There were loud shouts of joy at first, because the earliest results were from large towns that are all Democratic. New York City surpassed them all. Cleveland received fifty-six thousand votes more than Harrison there and twelve thousand more in Brooklyn. But in the rural areas of New York the Democrats won in only a few places.

In other respects it's also strange. Cleveland is recommending low tariffs, but the Republicans want to keep high tariffs because they believe low tariffs would hurt the workers. But most workers vote for low tariffs. The farmers, who would be helped by low tariffs, vote for high tariffs. Just wait, though; by 1892 the farmers will be better informed, and then Grover will be back in office! He'll get my vote, if I'm still alive, because just then I'll get the right to vote.

Here in Chicago the Democrats won hands down. In Illinois Harrison won a slender majority of twenty-two thousand votes and Fifer was elected governor by defeating the popular Palmer by nine thousand votes. Right after New Year the various governors were inaugurated. Harrison will be inaugurated on 4 March. Cleveland will then go back to New York and be a lawyer, as he was before being elected mayor of Buffalo in 1881.

Here in Chicago we will elect a new mayor and twenty-four new *aldermen* (city council members) on the first Tuesday in April. If the Democrats turn out as numerously as they did in November they can be sure of victory. But in municipal elections they usually let the Republicans get the upper hand. Chicago's budget is larger than that of Denmark. I recently saw the mayor's official report for 1888, which showed revenues of about 18 million dollars and disbursements of about 15.5 million dollars. In other words, there was a profit of about 2.5 million dollars.

I can't even give you an idea of a hundredth of the huge parades and all of the noise that accompanied the election, so I won't even try. On 30 April there will be celebrations all across the country, but especially in New York. That day it will be one hundred years since George Washington swore an oath to the constitution as the first president of America.

I've read about the celebration *humbug* you're having back in Europe. The French are crazy to stick with Boulanger as though he were their savior. And the Austrian crown prince shot himself. The newspapers over here claim he was the most licentious person of all the European courts, and that's saying something.

We had a very mild winter until February, but now it is worse, but not terribly bad. As you probably know, Hans Christian has gone out to Colorado and is working in a little town named Stout, which is about 120 kilometers north of the attractive city of Denver. He got sick immediately, but now seems to be doing well out there. How has winter been back home? I suppose you have a cold, damp room. . . .

> Julius Peterson
> in care of Mr. R. Peterson
> 332 W. Indiana St.
> Chicago, Illinois

By 1894 Peterson had shifted his loyalty to the Populist Party and its champion, Democrat William Jennings Bryan. (Source: Danes Worldwide Archives, Julius Petersen MSS.)

> Chicago
> 4 October 1894

Dear Brother,

I received your letter a week ago and was happy to read that you are well. I see that you had an early autumn this year. We had an early one last year, when I worked on Niels Carlsen's farm. We began to harvest on 15 August.

Wheat is very cheap, fifty-three cents a *bushel* on the Chicago grain exchange. The times have not improved much. The causes of these hard times are McKinley and the Sherman Act. In my opinion the abolition of the latter was harmful, especially for the West. Chicago got a taste of its abolition, and of the antisilver legislation in general, which the two rotten old parties find too good to continue with. It will take years to rectify. I'll never again vote for either of the old parties because of that, and in fact I only did so once or twice.

The Populist Party is the party of the future. This year it will play a significant role for the first time in Chicago and Illinois. I don't expect us to win, but we should get enough votes to make many Democrats' and Republicans' hair stand on end. Kansas and Colorado are already solidly Populist, and without a doubt the Populists will win in Nebraska this year. They also have a firm foothold in every state west of the Missouri. The Republicans will probably still win in all of the states between here and the Atlantic this year, but for the first time the two old parties have a serious rival. I couldn't care less which one of the two old parties is in power. They're tweedle-dum and tweedle-dee. The two parties haven't done anything for seventy-five years except enact tariff laws. They've written nine tariff laws already and the end is not in sight. All other reforms have been pushed aside in one Congress after the other so that they can waste their time chatting about tariffs. . . .

Please send me my money as soon as possible when you get it on 1 November. I should have it by 1 December at the latest. Remember, money orders take longer than letters.

Carl Christensen, who visited me this evening, asked me to send you his regards. He will probably move back to this neighborhood. He has worked steadily since last spring at a bicycle factory in the northernmost part of the city. But yesterday he began to work at a place where he worked last autumn. It's not far from here. He will almost certainly move down here because he has to travel about fifteen kilometers to work. He has had a good job this past summer, which is more than I had. I worked very irregularly all summer and am still doing so.

I hope this letter finds you well and in good humor. . . .

Julius Petersen

Petersen was bitter after Bryan's defeat in the crucial election of 1896.
(Source: Danes Worldwide Archives, Julius Petersen MSS.)

Hampton, Iowa
5 December 1896

Dear Brother,

. . . As you can see from my address, I am no longer in Chicago but in Hampton, Iowa, five hundred kilometers west-northwest of Chicago. I came up here on Monday and live with Margrete's brother-in-law and sister. Mr. Hansen is a traveling salesman for a company in Chicago. I quit my job in Chicago and have taken it easy since the beginning of October. Hansen was in Chicago two or three weeks ago and told me he thought it best to go home with him. There is nothing to do here, but it is cheaper to live here, and Hansen has three horses that I take care of. He has to cover an area at least fifty kilometers in each direction, including ten or twelve villages. He often drives his own horse and carriage if he doesn't have to go too far.

Hampton has between three and four thousand inhabitants, but it takes up far more territory than a Danish village of comparable size. All American towns are very spread out, even their downtown areas. At this time of year it isn't very attractive, but in the summer it is beautiful because of all the trees planted along the streets and around the houses. I was here in the summer of 1895.

In Chicago the times are worse than I have ever seen. Unemployment defies description. Before the election the Republicans claimed that "if McKinley is elected things will get better." He was elected, but things got even worse. McKinley received 7,053,102 votes and Bryan 6,344,463. McKinley won by 708,639 votes. He received 269 votes in the electoral college and Bryan 178. Colorado gave Bryan a greater majority than any other state, 151,970 to 22,785. McKinley got 604,467 votes in Illinois, Bryan 465,299. In Chicago McKinley got about 201,000 votes and Bryan 154,000.

Had Bryan been elected, my lots in Denver would be worth at least twice as much. The capitalists bought all of the major newspapers and even the clergy to oppose Bryan. Eight of Chicago's eleven daily newspapers supported McKinley while two were for Bryan and one remained independent. That's how it was everywhere in the East. Furthermore, there was a lot of pressure at the factories and so on to get the workers to vote for McKinley. I was surprised that Bryan managed to get as many votes as he did.

Grover Cleveland fired every postmaster and other federal official who said anything favorable about Bryan. But today Bryan is regarded as a hero across the whole country, and his supporters have already organized societies to work for his election in 1900. It was not a partisan struggle even though the old party names were retained. All of the parties were divided on the silver question. The first party to take up the issue was the Populist Party. In that respect Bryan was closer to them than to his fellow Democrats. As one speaker put it during the campaign, "The rich Democrats

have abandoned us, but the poor Republicans are with us." Grover
Cleveland will go down in history as a traitor to his party. I'm
certain that he doesn't dare come out west because there is a
danger that he would be lynched. . . .

Julius Petersen

*Pastor Frederik L. Grundtvig described the divided political loyalties of
Danes in the Midwest.* (Source: *Kors og Stjærne,* January 1892.)

Clinton, Iowa
3 November 1891

Today is election day! Do I have time to write letters? Yes,
because I don't have the right to vote. I'm not an American
citizen. Anyone who intends to live here should get citizenship,
otherwise he cannot have any influence on society. It is not
strange to swear an oath of allegiance, but at the same time one
has to renounce his motherland. That is what makes many people
hesitant. Here in Clinton most of the Danes have the right to vote,
and today is important for both the city and the state. The
majority of Clinton's voters (including almost all of the Danes) are
Democrats. There is a split within the Democratic Party between
the Catholics (especially the Irish) and all of the others. The
schism becomes greater every year and threatens to be fateful for
the future of America. No doubt the Catholics have a good many
misdeeds on their consciences. They are as thick as thieves and are
trying to seize power everywhere. And yet the fight against them
is on such a tawdry level that one is tempted to sympathize with
them. A secret society has been organized (and unfortunately
many Danes have joined it) whose purpose is to persecute and
oppress the Catholics, confiscate their church property, and close
their schools.[1] If this society is allowed to spread, it will probably
lead to a civil war. And we immigrants can be sure that if the
Catholics are put in their place, we Protestants will have to do
everything we can to protect our religious and ethnic heritage!

1. Grundtvig is probably referring to the nativistic American Protective Association,
founded in Clinton in 1887.

Here in the town of Clinton and in Clinton County the Democrats have taken up the cudgel against each other (although not literally). The Irish are on one side and the Danes and Germans are on the other. The Yankees are standing back fanning the flames. Most of them are Republicans, and the Swedes in Clinton support them. This evening the Germans and the Danes held a joint meeting. Speakers alternated in German and Danish.

It will probably not be long before this strife brings about a full schism in the Democratic Party. But in Iowa it has not prevented the two factions from uniting in the state elections. All of the Democrats (and quite a few Republicans) have joined hands. The big issue is whether Iowa should continue to forbid the manufacture and sale of intoxicating beverages, everything from brandy to apple cider. The law has been tried for several years, and whatever one may think of it, it has not had the desired result. Here in Clinton all of the saloons were closed right after the law went into effect. But liquor was still sold; it was smuggled in hay and so on. Later, people bought it at drug stores. Doctors wrote one prescription after another for brandy, whisky, and so on. Little by little people dared to reopen the saloons. The judges are elected by the people, and the people here don't want to obey the law. Hence, the judges don't do their duty. New we have twice as many saloons as we had before prohibition. People no longer try to conceal their violations. The city recognizes this and exacts a small fee, officially a fine. That is harmful. Is it any surprise that under these conditions the young generation is becoming lawless? The law should either be changed so that each municipality can decide whether it wants prohibition, or additional rules should be adopted so that prohibition is effective. But that would mean that the state, with a state police force, would be given the right to interfere in local affairs. The Democrats support the first solution, the Republicans the second. Iowa has traditionally been a Republican stronghold, but this issue will probably cause them to be defeated.

I mentioned earlier that nearly all of the Danes here in the Clinton area are Democrats, but that is not the case with Danish-Americans in general. I believe most Danes in cities are Democrats, but most of them in the country are probably Republicans.

At least that was the case until the Republicans opted for
protective tariffs. Emotions can get high on election day, but
most of the time politics doesn't cause any disruption. There are
many things that divide us Danes, but politics is not one of them.
In those places where there are only a few Danes, they are likely
to stick together through thick and thin.

Frederik L. Grundtvig

*A Dane from Odsherred in northwestern Zealand questioned the political
sophistication of the American population and ridiculed the press after Bryan's
defeat.* (Source: *Holbæk Posten,* 7 January 1897.)

DeKalb, Illinois
9 December 1896

To write a public letter from America without mentioning
politics would be unthinkable after the heated election campaign
that ended on 3 November. The chief issue separating the two
major parties was not the tariff, as is usually the case, but rather
the question of the gold standard or bimetallism. Never before
have I seen an election with such excitement, changes of party
loyalty, or uncertainty regarding the outcome.

On one side were the millionaires, bankers, factory owners,
bureaucrats, and political machines—in short, everyone who was
for tight money and protectionism. They supported McKinley. On
the other side stood the advocates of low tariffs, cheap—and
justifiable—money, income tax, and so on, with Bryan as their
candidate. McKinley sat home in Canton, Ohio, receiving
innumerable "guests" who streamed in on special trains that the
capitalists financed. Bryan, meanwhile, traveled from town to town
and state to state, occasionally speaking twenty-five to thirty times
a day to large throngs of people. It is said that he spoke five
hundred times to more than five million people.

Bryan is said to be the best speaker in America. He represents
the interests of the oppressed against the brutal attacks of financial
tyrants. No previous politician has dared to do that. It is easy to

understand how he won respect, even among many of his political opponents.

As is usually the case in this country, the struggle was between capital and justice. It is more intense here than in any other country. Capital won, as usual, and it did so on election day, 3 November. But the victory was expensive; it cost more than two million dollars and, hopefully, a Republican defeat in the next presidential election. The margin of victory was narrow: Bryan won a majority in twenty-two of the forty-five states in the Union.

The future does not look bright. McKinley, our president-elect, is in the hands of the capitalists. They bought his election, and those gentlemen don't do business without exacting a high price. They want to increase their millions, double them, in fact. Who will have to foot the bill in the final analysis? The middle class, the farmers, and the working class will be further impoverished. We have to expect tight money and higher tariffs, things that always help to make the rich richer and the poor poorer.

And the press? Didn't the great American press enlighten the people? Yes, in a way. But it, too, is in the hands of capitalists. All of the large dailies in New York and Chicago—including the Social Democratic ones—campaigned vigorously for McKinley. The spirit, or rather the antispirit, that prevails in the newspapers here is sensationalistic and produces detailed accounts of all the murders, suicides, assaults, robberies, thefts, divorces, immorality, and other scandals and filth that are part of daily life in America.

Then there is the local press. Almost every village has a newspaper, usually a weekly. Its inside is printed in town and the rest consists of gossip from every hamlet within fifteen kilometers. I can't refrain from giving you a sample of this "local news" that seems to be the newspapers' chief drawing card: "Mrs. A. has had a new door put on her house, which greatly increases its value." "Mr. B. has had his barn painted." "Mr. C. went shopping in town yesterday." "Miss D. was visited yesterday evening by half a dozen friends. They played, drank tea, and ate cake until late at night." "Mr. and Mrs. E. are the proud parents of a new boy." This "news" isn't very highbrow, but it suits the readers' taste, and that is good enough for the editors.

Newspapers usually reflect the level of development of their readers. They reveal that in America morality is not the number one question, but rather, "How much money do you have?" If the Americans were as intelligent as the Danes, McKinley would not be our next president, there would be fewer millionaires, and more people would be equally prosperous.

N. P. Clausen

·VI·

Danes and Ethnic Pluralism

For most Danish immigrants, moving from Denmark to North America was leaping from a relatively homogeneous society to a most heterogeneous one. In their diminutive native land, all had spoken the same language, all were subjects of the same monarch, all shared a common national history, and nearly all were nominal Lutherans. The social and cultural simplicity of Danish immigrants' background contrasted with that of many of their counterparts from the British Isles, the Danube Basin, or the Balkans, for example, where peoples had intermingled various languages, religions, and other folkways for centuries. Indeed, some aspects of the Danes' upbringing resisted harmonious relations with other groups in the New World. Prejudices against Slavs, for instance, ran deep, as did suspicions of Roman Catholics.

Many Danes resented the German expansionism that in the nineteenth century claimed large segments of what Danes regarded as Danish soil. Even relations with other Scandinavians were not always smooth. Sweden and Denmark had not fully left behind their rivalry dating from the pre-Napoleonic era when both countries were powers in northern Europe, and nationalistic Norwegians were seeking to shake off Danish cultural hegemony.

For these and other reasons, immigrant Danes tended to look with disdain on southern and eastern Europeans, resent Germans, occasionally admire Yankees with whom they felt some affinity, and tolerate, if sometimes grudgingly, other Scandinavians. Their comments on Afro-Americans and Indians also provide insights into their own values, prejudices, and aspirations in the New World.

Torben Lange generalized about other immigrants shortly after he arrived in the United States the first time. (Source: Lange, *Fra Roskildefjord til Mississippi*, pp. 96–98.)

131

St. Louis, Missouri
25 March 1842

Dear Family,

. . . The Norwegians and Swedes who come over here usually
settle in Wisconsin or Michigan. I saw only one Norwegian last
year on Lake Erie. The last Dane I saw and heard was a navigator, H. Treschow, whom I met in New York last autumn.

You might be interested in hearing a little about the many
immigrants here and how they usually behave. Most of them are
either German, French, or Irish. The Germans usually land in
New York or Baltimore, although in recent years many have also
come via New Orleans. Even though they land in the East, we get
many of them here in the West. Most of them are either farmers
or professional people. Most bring some money with them and
want to go westward immediately, at least the farmers. But when
they reach America they think, "Now we are in America so things
will be all right." The largest number go immediately to Pennsylvania, where they are cheated out of their money. Finally they
open their eyes and go west. Immigrants who come to America
believe there are only wild people in the West and don't dare
make the long journey out here, so they buy poor land in the East
that nobody else wants. Finally hunger drives them out here.

The French usually go west right away, settle down, and fight
the Indians. That drives them farther west. They attract Yankees
from the eastern states, who migrate and buy land from the
French settlers. The French then go even farther west. Not many
farmers come from France, but those who do follow that pattern.
All of the names here in the West are French, such as Independence, St. Louis, St. Charles, Quincy, Prairie du Chien, La Platte,
and so on.

The Irish settle in various places, but most of them work on the
canals in the East or on the railroads. Many are also doing time in
prison. A newspaper titled *Shall Ireland Never More Be Free?* has
gained a lot of attention here. Queen Victoria certainly doesn't like
it, because it contains powerful material.

By the way, I wouldn't advise anyone to sail to New Orleans, at
least not in the summer. Yellow fever is raging down there,

especially among foreigners who are not accustomed to the climate. Last year many newly arrived Europeans died of it.

Today I saw ten Indians trudging through the streets, apparently trying to trade furs for rings, guns, gunpowder, and so on. These Indians are handsome fellows—tall and erect with glistening eyes and hair as black as coal hanging down to their shoulders. They're good looking. Judging from their clothes, they were Osage Indians. I have seen them before in western Missouri. . . .

Like many other Danes on both sides of the Atlantic, Lange held his German neighbors in low esteem. (Source: Lange, *Fra Roskildefjord*, pp. 234–35.)

St. Louis
16 April 1851

Dear Sister,

. . . I don't have much news for you today, except that sometimes I get extremely irritated at my fellow Europeans. These Germans are real trash. On the whole the Germans are the lowest, most despicable scum ever inflicted on American soil. Until a month ago the American newspapers hardly took notice of the German papers; now they are full of German news. Using the excuse that America allows complete freedom of speech and the press, some of the German newspapers have begun to run down the Jesuit order and make fun of Sabbath-keeping. They preach rationalism.

In the mayoral election in St. Louis last Monday the Germans did everything they could to elect their candidate. Fortunately, he was defeated. Many of the hotheads who have been driven out of Germany in recent years are now trying to improve America's constitution, which is already excellent. That is pure ingratitude. America offers refuge to all the refugees of Europe, but when they arrive here they do their best to stir up dissension among the people. One newspaper recently told the Germans that it regarded it as beneath the dignity of a native American to argue with a

German, and that most of them were too ignorant to have much influence.

One of the few Danes who settled in Georgia observed the wretched lives of rural Negroes there during Reconstruction. (Source: *Langelands Avis,* 12 May 1870. This letter initially appeared in *Næstved Avis.*)

I was not able to find an appropriate job in New York, so in the middle of January I came down here with the hope of finding work on a plantation. I arrived a few months too late, though. All of the plantation owners had already hired workers, so I had to content myself working for a gardener who pays me low wages. The reason for that is that he can hire plenty of Negroes, and they don't demand much. Four Negroes and two Negresses work here. Each of them is paid eight or nine dollars a month and gets one and a half kilograms of pork and four kilograms of flour a week.

It was quite a change for me to come from the cold North to the warm South, where nature blossoms in all its beauty in January and February. There are very few horses down here. Most of the work is done by mules, which have more endurance and can tolerate the heat better than horses. A large, powerful mule costs about two hundred fifty dollars, while a horse costs only one hundred dollars.

The city of Savannah, the capital of Georgia, which I have visited several times, is about thirteen kilometers from the ocean on the Savannah River. It has about sixty thousand inhabitants, including thirty-five thousand Negroes. The streets are unpaved. People walk, ride, or drive in sand. Beautiful, shady trees have been planted everywhere.

An incredible number of policemen patrol the streets, both on foot and on horseback. Their main task is to keep an eye on the Negroes, who are very thievish. People are punished in a strange way here. A few days ago I read in one of the newspapers that a Negro who had stolen a rifle was fined ten dollars for the crime. Not being able to pay the fine, however, he had to work on the streets for a month.

In the forests around here there are an incredible number of snakes, including rattlesnakes. I haven't seen any yet, because they hibernate in January and February. I expect to see them next month, though.

It isn't difficult to buy land here. Good land not far from town can be had for ten dollars an *acre,* and if it is farther away it costs only five or six dollars. It would be easy to acquire a good small farm here, but not many do so because the unhealthy climate leads to dangerous illnesses.

When I am working out in the forest I occasionally go into the Negroes' shacks to get a drink of water. That gives me a chance to see how they live. As a rule two families live together. Their houses are built on top of four pilings about seventy centimeters high to reduce the dampness. They don't have any windows, only three or four shutters on the sides. Beds, chairs, and tables are rare items. There is always some straw in a corner where some half-naked children crawl around, looking more like apes than human beings. Regardless of their poverty, almost all Negroes have a gun and a dog, because hunting is their only pleasure. Usually they hunt rabbits.

Now and then I've found it interesting to talk with the Negroes about their former situation when they were slaves. They tell how they were sold from one man to the next, first for seven hundred dollars but later for five hundred dollars, depending on whether they were young or old, fat or thin. They also tell how slave traders felt and examined them as though they were livestock. Frequently men were separated from their wives and mothers from their children. It must have been an unhappy time for the poor blacks.

Now they have gained their freedom, but they don't know how to use it. As long as they have pork and bread in their houses it is impossible to get them to work. They refuse to work unless forced to by hunger. Even today there are many Negroes who long for the time when they were slaves, but they are the lazy ones. They say that then they always had as much as they could eat, and when they were sick somebody took care of them. Now nobody looks after them. It's not surprising. The man who owned the slaves kept a close eye on them because for him a Negro meant just as much as a horse does to a farmer in Denmark.

An anonymous native of Fyn who drove a wagon through Indian Territory (now Oklahoma) commented favorably on Indians and their relations with other Americans. (Source: *Langelands Avis,* 24 June 1870. This letter initially appeared in *Nyborgs Avis.*)

2 May 1870

My last letter was written in Dwight, Illinois, about 90 kilometers from Chicago, but now I am far from there. The town where I live now is small, but like all American towns it is growing. It is located in southern Texas, about 185 kilometers from the Gulf of Mexico. The railroad runs through here down to the Gulf. I left Dwight last August and took the train through Illinois to St. Louis, Missouri, looked around that town a bit, and continued west into Kansas. About 150 kilometers from the border I stopped and worked for five months, taking any kind of job I could get.

I didn't have any desire to stay there longer than five months, and I received an unexpected offer to take an interesting trip through the country that I had often yearned to see. A merchant who traveled about with thirty wagons needed drivers, who would be paid in addition to getting free travel. The trip was to Texas, so I immediately applied for the job. The trip went southwest through Missouri into Kansas. Then we went through the southwestern corner of that state and headed toward Indian Territory. After three weeks, driving from morning until evening including Sundays, we reached Texas. We ended the trip in northern Texas, and the drivers could go wherever they wanted. I went 100 kilometers farther south, and since my money had gone the way of all flesh, I had to work for a farmer for a month. I liked the job, but he refused to pay me more than fifteen dollars in gold a month plus room and board, and I demanded twenty dollars. Many things are cheaper here than in Denmark, but many things are more expensive. In any case, money goes fast here.

Knowing that I could earn fifteen dollars anywhere, I left the farmer and went south to a town called Hampstead, where I am now. I'm broke again, but two weeks' work will put some cash into my pocket. I intend to go out to the railroad bridge tomorrow. They pay a dollar and a half a day after room and board have been deducted. . . .

Let me tell you a little about Indian Territory, which was very interesting and differs from the rest of the country. This territory is owned exclusively by the Indians. The United States gave it to six or eight different tribes. Before then they were wild and always at war with the whites. The government in Washington made a deal with them: in exchange for the territory they promised to be peaceful and not disturb the whites who travel through or set up businesses there. If the Indians break their promise they will be hanged mercilessly and driven out.

The Indians are decent people. Everything possible is being done to civilize them, and they are making good progress. The government doesn't allow whites to buy land from the Indians, because that could lead to disturbances. But whites can marry Indians and in that way gain possession of large tracts of land and thousands of cattle. A large number of people have done that; it happens every day. These cosmopolitan marriages produce half-breed children who are often quite attractive. The Americans, or the so-called "whites," send their children to schools in the East to be educated. Some of the half-breed women are the most beautiful I have ever seen. They are all industrious and do some kind of work. Desire to work hardly characterizes full-blood Indians. I've seen many of them riding around wildly, hunting with bows and arrows. They're also well acquainted with firearms. . . .

An anonymous Dane commented on ethnic groups in Chicago and praised the stereotypic Yankee. (Source: *Politiken,* 1 June 1885.)

Chicago
6 May 1885

Today the Thingvalla Line's summer excursion to Scandinavia set off with a big procession. It went through the main streets to the railroad station with flags waving and a brass band. The parade was ceremoniously led by a uniformed rider. In front was a large open carriage with a uniformed brass band. Then came some other wagons with the Thingvalla agent *Mr.* Mortensen and the most prominent travelers. They were followed by a caravan of about twenty-five more wagons carrying happy neighbors, another

band, and the baggage, high-quality suitcases by the load. The
lively music and satisfied travelers in the beautiful parade gave the
impression that this *advertising* had been exceptionally successful. It
was well publicized in the entire Northwest that the excursion
would have a large number of participants this year. Our new
ambassador from Denmark, Professor Rasmus Andersen, promised to join it in New York and honor it by taking part.

Under such circumstances participation is barred to the Irish,
Russians, Poles, and similar ethnic groups. I extend my best wishes
to friends and relatives in the old country.

Spring has been very cold and was late in coming this year. The
grass is just turning green, but the buds on the trees are still quite
a way from leafing out. The weather has had an effect on
business. Land sales began late this year. Real estate is one area of
business in which several Danish firms are active here. Because of
their knowledge of the German and Scandinavian languages and
acquaintance with European conditions, they can compete
effectively against American competition. Most of the sales are
made to old farmers who buy land for their grown sons. They also
sell land to workers who have earned money in the cities and
factory areas. As a rule immigrants are too poor to buy land
immediately, but oppressive political and economic conditions in
Europe will cause capital and the intelligentsia to come here from
the Old World. In the older settlements people are moving away
from boring, exhausting manual labor toward more modern
systems of dairying and cattle raising based on European models.
Meat production has been very profitable in recent years for
people who began with sizeable investments.

One should not come to Chicago to find typical American
conditions. There probably isn't any other city in the world with a
more mixed population of all nationalities. The Irish and the
Germans are especially heavily represented and well organized.
Whenever the former serve on a jury, they are said to adhere
consistently to the principle that the Irish are always innocent. The
Germans are an intelligent and pleasant race, although at the
moment their ambition to preserve the German language and
culture here is rather annoying. The native Americans, the old
Yankees, aristocratically keep their distance from the immigrants.
It is almost an honor for newcomers to have any contact with the

venerable stock from New England. A fleeting acquaintance gives
an impression of this sober, *gentlemanlike* race, whose merit is their
harmoniously developed personalities, which have developed as a
result of living in a free society for several generations.

We Danes occupy a modest position in Scandinavian society
here. The most important Danish-Norwegian newspapers are in
Norwegian hands. One exception is the monthly, *Scandinavia.*
Published by a group of Danes, it gets attention and respect from
the Americans. More active connections with Denmark than has
hitherto been the case would be highly desirable for promoting
mutual development as well as for spreading Scandinavian culture
beyond the narrow confines of our language. A monthly magazine
would be an appropriate focal point for discussing aesthetic and
social questions.

*Many Danish commentators, including this one in Portland, found the
Chinese immigrants on the West Coast unpleasant.* (Source: *Den nye Verden,*
December 1888.)

Portland
October 1888

One remarkable thing in Portland is its Chinese quarter. No
other American city other than San Francisco has anything to
match it. The Chinese quarter is right in the middle of the
business district. There are Chinese in all parts of the city, but
they have their shops downtown. Despite the emphasis that the
Chinese put on having clean clothes, the exteriors and entrances
of their buildings are anything but clean. A foul smell strikes
anyone who passes through the quarter. Even the rich and
refined—and Portland has some wealthy Chinese—do not seem to
be much better in this regard. Their buildings are decorated with
a large jumble of Chinese characters and ornamented with some
gadgets that by American standards seem bizarre. The Chinese
feel right at home in this part of the city, and laughter and jokes
can be heard on the crowded sidewalks all day long. Groups of
sons of the "Celestial Empire" sit or walk around as though they
were simply looking for the best and most comfortable way to pass

their time. In no other city have I ever seen people so happy and contented as the Chinese in Portland.

A Dane in New Orleans contrasted the violent behavior of Italian and Irish immigrants with the "peaceful, mild" conduct of Scandinavian-Americans. (Source: *Den nye Verden,* 21 November 1890.)

New Orleans, Louisiana
3 November 1890

Our fine city is in an uproar these days. The peace-loving citizens are alarmed by the bloody reports about the war that is raging here between the Italians and the Irish. According to the most recent reports, the numerous Italians of New Orleans are practicing the same barbarian customs that we have read about in medieval novels. The *vendetta,* or blood feud between families, to which Romeo fell victim in Shakespeare's marvelous drama, seems to be flourishing as a routine thing here in the South, even though Juliet is missing from the picture.

But in America the Italians are more practical. They no longer fight over women, but rather over the fruit business. If an enterprising Italian has been fortunate enough to secure a contract to rent a well-situated street corner for selling fruit, his countrymen do not attempt to compete with him in the usual way. No, they simply wait for him in some dark corner, and when he comes past they thrust a stiletto between his shoulder blades or shoot him with ten revolver bullets in all parts of his body. That is the easiest way to prevent the lucky fruit dealer from reaping any benefits from his new contract and new *stand.* People in the South call that *business.*

The Italians have also been accused of maintaining their language and not wanting to become American citizens. We peaceful, mild Scandinavians are shocked, of course, when we read about such things. Fortunately, there is nothing like that among us.

The fact that the entire city government and the mayor have taken up the cudgel against the Italians suggests that not only the

Irish are opposed to them. In a way the Irish are just as bloodthirsty as the Italians. The latter assassinated the police chief, who
was an Irishman by birth. That was the spark that touched off the
war. No fewer than a score of Italians have been arrested, but
there is not the slightest doubt that all of them will be released for
lack of evidence. All of the witnesses have fled back to Europe.
That trick is well known in America, but it is so widespread here
that all respectable citizens have to protest its further use. Every
day there is another murder and an arrest is made, but every day
a witness disappears. That is how our judicial system operates.

The federal government is considering sending a division of
soldiers down here to restore order. It is our wish that they arrive
soon. For the time being New Orleans is in a state of terrorism.

J. S.

*An anonymous Dane vented anti-Catholic feelings and supported the se-
lective restriction of immigration.* (Source: *Demokraten,* 23 April 1892.)

. . . We still have one great evil, and that is Roman Catholicism.
It is spreading rapidly, and if the Catholics gain power we will be
oppressed for a long time. They have a rare way of working their
way up in America; partly by cheating and partly by cunning they
acquire finances, or rather capital, and use that opportunity to
become employers. Their workers, you can be assured, are an
unfortunate lot. The Catholics also have a strange way of gaining
possession of the best government offices, and through them they
exercise power and influence. Hence we Danes, like others, have
to remember these words: "If you want to get ahead in America,
fight everything that is Catholic, for Catholicism is one of our
worst enemies."

At the same time, there is one other thing we have to fight, and
in all likelihood the government is going to help us in this
struggle. We have to counter the throngs of Italians and Chinese
who come here for the sole purpose of earning a lot of money
and then returning to their native countries. But their attempts to
earn money often result in their applying for unemployment

benefits, so the country has the expense of supporting them and gets nothing in return. That's not the worst of it, however. They come as miserable strikebreakers and lower the wages of other workers. If a worker thinks his wages are too low and asks for a raise, he usually gets this answer: "If you don't want to work for what you're getting, then leave. We can get an Italian or a Chinese for whatever we're willing to pay."

·VII·

Danish Identity in America

Danish nationalism faced several challenges in the nineteenth century. During the Napoleonic Wars Denmark allied with France, a strategy that backfired and led to the British bombardment of Copenhagen in 1807. Six years later Sweden forced the cession of Norway, which for more than four centuries had been the junior partner in a union with the Danish crown. Forces of the German Confederation occupied part of Denmark in 1848, and in 1864 a joint Prussian-Austrian force wrested away the ethnically mixed provinces of Holstein, Lauenburg, and Schleswig.

While Denmark was receiving a drubbing in the international arena, the meaning of danskhed, *or Danishness, underwent a profound transition within the kingdom. During the second half of the century, the Industrial Revolution changed what had been a solidly agrarian society into a rapidly urbanizing one. Secularization eroded the remnant of popular piety that had survived the Enlightenment. Nearly universal literacy introduced the Danes to a spate of new intellectual currents, many of them from abroad.*

Some Danish immigrants clung to the folkways of their childhood, while others drifted with the current of rapid assimilation into the mainstream of American life. Those with ties to the German-dominated territories attempted with little success to foster Danish nationalism in America. Others transplanted Grundtvig's "folk high schools," where youth were taught Danish culture with a high-church Lutheran veneer. Fraternal organizations parallel to those of other immigrant groups sprouted in several Danish-American communities, although their membership was seldom large. Perhaps because Danes in America were so geographically scattered, most rather quickly discarded many of the trappings of their national heritage.

Questions of cultural retention are inherent in many immigrants' letters, but few Danes addressed the matter directly or devoted more than a few lines to it. Several of the letters included in other chapters touch on such issues as the place of the Danish language in America generally and in ethnic churches

143

specifically. Those in this chapter deal with the "folk high schools" and the threat to Danish nationalism in German-dominated South Jutland.

❖

Danish immigrants from South Jutland, lost to Prussia in 1864, met in San Francisco to remember their homeland. (Source: *Kors og Stjærne,* March 1893. This letter initially appeared in *Flensborg Avis.*)

San Francisco, California
21 January 1893

During the past year we North Schleswigians had many enjoyable and successful festivals together with our brothers from the Kingdom of Denmark. On 5 June we celebrated Constitution Day; it was the biggest Danish festival ever here on the Pacific Coast. We rented a big park in the middle of San Francisco (Woodwards Gardens) for the day's events. Two large Danish flags graced the entrance. It was a pleasure to see the happy faces of the old North Schleswigians when they saw the old Danish flag. Here in America there is no law against loving the language and memories of our land; in fact, it would be unthinkable not to cherish the intellectual and moral heritage we inherited from our forefathers. Over three thousand of us were gathered that day. Speeches alternated with Danish songs. A certain Mr. Hansen spoke especially beautifully on behalf of South Jutland. . . .

Twice a month we have Danish-Schleswigian gatherings here in San Francisco to preserve Danish language and literature. Magazines and books are placed at the disposal of the members. We never forget him who so indefatigably fights for our mother tongue and our rights. I mean our beloved spokesman, Gustav Johannsen. The beautiful speech that Member of Parliament Johannsen delivered at the celebration at Skamlingsbanken in June 1892 was printed in all of the Danish and Norwegian newspapers over here. That is proof that the national struggle in South Jutland concerns all Scandinavians. Editor Jessen's book, *Between the Baltic and the North Sea,* is read with extraordinary interest here, and it would be desirable if it found its way into every home in

North Schleswig. With great sorrow we have learned that Jessen
has once again been placed into a Prussian prison because of
alleged misuse of the press. But God will not disappoint those who
remain true to a just cause.

The thing that has hurt us the most is that the children who
have come during recent years cannot even write home to their
parents in Danish, and their parents complain that they cannot
understand their children's German. We cannot understand
whether that is the goal of the German government. Let me quote
what a German speaker said at one of their gatherings: "Let us
maintain our language and fight for it; this is a matter of immense
significance. It is proof of a nation's power when its language is
respected outside its natural borders."

I cannot understand why Schleswigians do not have the right to
fight for their own language and maintain its validity within its
own territory instead of throwing it away as though it were a
foreign coin. I wish the Germans would remember the venerated
words that the unforgettable Member of Parliament J. P. Jung-
green often quoted to them: "Do unto others as you would have
them do unto you."

*The Danish community in Jamestown, New York displayed its binational
loyalty at a Christmas celebration.* (Source: *Bornholms Tidende*, 25 January
1891.)

31 December 1891

. . . The hall that had been prepared for the affair was about
twenty meters long and twelve meters wide. In the middle were
two attractive gaslit chandeliers and a beautiful Christmas tree,
about five meters high with a gold star on top. It was decorated
with thirty-six Danish flags and mousetraps made of red and white
tissue paper. In addition, the boughs were laden with about three
hundred baskets and cones filled with candy, nuts, apples,
oranges, Christmas candles, and so on, completely in the Danish
style.

At one end of the hall, right in front of the tree, there was a stage for use by the orchestra. On it we had built a house with a door and two windows. The house was covered with greenery and attractively decorated with paper flowers and flags. Over the door and windows we had affixed a five-meter-long banner with red letters on a blue background, bearing the inscription *"Glædelig Jul"* [Merry Christmas]. Higher up on the house, in the attic, we had a star on a blue banner. All of this was illuminated by six lamps. The program, consisting of speakers, songs, readings, shadow pictures, and the like, was conducted in front of this house. On the opposite end of the hall we had erected a seven-meter-long cloth sign painted in four colors and bearing the inscription *"Velkommen"* [Welcome]. Garlands of tightly packed flowers and bows hung from it in neat order. On either side of the sign was a Danish crest with three gold lions and nine red hearts on a blue background and six Danish flags. Finally, there was a gilt crown atop it.

In the middle of the third wall we had a Danish-American flag decoration with one of the Danish shields I described on either side, as well as garlands. The fourth wall also had a Danish-American flag decoration with a Danish shield on either side, although those two differed from each other. The two large doors that led out to the adjacent rooms were attractively decorated with greenery and Danish flags. Finally, the American colors, red, blue, and white, were draped from the ceiling around the hall.

The highlights of the evening were *Mr.* Victor Holmes' patriotic speech, *Mr.* Hansen's solos, and the shadow pictures by *Mr.* Westh and *Mr.* Wilhelm Petersen.

The mood was good and everyone was well entertained, especially the children, who said it differed from an American Christmas tree. Most of the Danes in Jamestown were present, although a few were prevented from attending by illness and other causes. The number was estimated at three hundred.

The followers of the Danish theologian and educator N.F.S. Grundtvig emulated him in founding "folk high schools," one purpose of which was to preserve Danish culture in a Christian context. (Source: *Aarhus Amtstidende,* 9 August 1882.)

Elk Horn Folk High School
Elk Horn, Iowa

When I read about all the efforts to reduce emigration from various countries, I do not get the impression that these attempts are based on love of the poor people who are considering leaving for the New World. Rather, it seems that there is fear of a labor shortage that would result if too many emigrated. Hence, arguments to convince the poor to stay home are not based on love, but rather on selfishness. A labor shortage does not harm the worker, but rather the employer. . . .

Surely many immigrant parents, in their concern for their children's material well-being, have neglected spiritual and cultural matters and settled in places without churches or schools. Some people have tried to lessen their spiritual poverty after becoming aware of it. But the problem could be partly prevented if the pastors and teachers in Denmark would give the people information about where the Danish congregations are in America. If they are informed about these things only after arriving in New York it is too late, because they have usually already made travel plans.

The temptation to sink down into a materialistic life is great over here. There are also plenty of other temptations. But otherwise the moral standard of the congregations with which I am acquainted is much higher than that of most of the parishes in Denmark. One does not see nearly as much drunkenness and disorder here as back home. I believe this is evidence that people are greatly elevated by the real hope that they can improve their lot by working their way up to better conditions. Many workers arrive here from oppressed conditions in Europe lethargic and tired. But they are uplifted by being able to reap the fruits of their labor and feel free and independent. They know that the future is brighter for their children. They gradually become optimistic, free, and happy, and appear more at ease. They develop respect for the worth of others and for themselves, and I dare say they become more receptive to spiritual and cultural influences than was previously the case. In view of this, I would never advise anyone against emigrating if he believes that he

cannot get along well in Denmark. It is not my intention to
promote emigration or to advise everyone to leave home. I only
wish to express the right of the individual to do so without being
regarded as one who is obsessed with making money.

The inhumane practice of sending unskilled poor people over
here is completely reprehensible, of course. The government here
has taken measures to send such people back to where they came
from. Those who are given to drink seek out the cities, where they
degenerate very rapidly. No more than unskilled workers should
such people come over here. On the other hand, it is a fact that
some who have served sentences in their native countries come to
America and, aided by better social conditions here, have become
respectable men.

It has been said that people who come here are disappointed
both with regard to making money and in a cultural and religious
sense. Naturally, that depends on what kind of expectations one
has beforehand. I do not believe, however, that as a rule emigrants are disappointed. Anyone who thinks he can get rich
without working will be disappointed, of course. People have to
work here, and in general they have to do manual labor at first.
The poor worker does not demand more, and it is difficult to
have much sympathy for other people. In cultural and eccle-
siastical respects Danish immigrants will need support from
their native country for a long time. Anyone who realizes this will
not be disappointed to see that cultural development here lags
behind that in Denmark. We are making considerable progress in
that field. We are striving as hard as we can to acquire the cultural
heritage of our mother country. It is not *humbug* when we sing
Danish national songs. We can love Denmark even though we live
here. Admittedly, many immigrants do not do so. . . .

Every good, capable student at our folk high school is a
colleague in our cultural and Christian educational work, even if
he or she is a quiet person who only through his or her behavior
shows that there is a better way to live than that shown by the
majority. I do not believe that Denmark will become impoverished
because she gives up some people. The Lord's household is so
richly appointed that the more it gives up, the more there is left.
Such an expense can be put on His account.

One of the men in Denmark who has done the most for

missionary and educational work among his countrymen here
wrote to me a few years ago and expressed his hope that someday
the Danes in America would repay the debt they owe their mother
country. I share this hope completely. But not only the constant
interaction between Denmark and America will have great
significance. It is my hope that if Denmark ever fights to get
South Jutland back, it will prove not to have been *humbug* that we
often refreshed the memory of our native land by singing "I Love
the Beech Forests of Denmark."

*A teacher at the new folk high school in Tyler, Minnesota, described the
role of the immigrant community in its construction and dedication.* (Source:
Den nye Verden, September 1888.)

I wonder whether I am wrong in believing that here and there
there are people who would like to hear a little—preferably
something good—about the Danish settlement in Minnesota.

By the time these lines are read, "Danebod" will be completely
built, or at least ready to be roofed. The work has progressed well
from the moment we began. The cellar took a lot of time. We
wanted a stone-walled cellar under the entire building. That took
150 loads of large stone, a task that gave the farmers around
Tyler a lot of work. I am happy to report that not only did the
farmers do this task without compensation, they also did it with
joy.

I have been met with the same courtesy here as in other places
earlier, and neither my family nor I am tired of Minnesota.

Naturally, I did not have any cash to pay for the lumber for the
school, but five or six able men provided it and gave me four
months' credit. Now there is practically no major reason why the
school should not be ready on time.

The influx of settlers has not been large this year. But a few
have bought land in this area after we began work on the school.

Church people and supporters of the folk high school who have
considered making their future homes here should not wait too
long before buying. There is a lot of land left, but the most fertile
and most favorably situated is not only sold first, but is also often
bought up by speculators who let it lie fallow until they can make

a large profit selling it. There is some good land here in the
settlement, but also some poor land. It is better for people to
inspect the land before they buy it than to take the risk of getting
a piece of worthless property and curse the agent who sold it to
them. We have several agents, so if one of them does not have
what you have in mind, just see another one. Now is a fine time to
visit the settlement, just before harvest. On the Fourth of July,
which is America's Independence Day, we had a little celebration
on Danebod's farmland. There was plenty of shade when we put
our umbrellas up. I gave a speech about our relationship as Danes
to America and American Independence Day. Kristian Hansen,
who is a teacher from Denmark and a fairy tale narrator, told one
of his good old tales, which captured the attention of young and
old alike. Hansen bought land right next to the school the same
day, and I am happy that we have secured an original fairy tale
narrator for our future school. That is how we have begun out
here, and I believe this large settlement will have a bright and
happy future, both in spiritual and secular respects.

If any of our countrymen visit the settlement, they should not
forget to visit the pastor, who lives in a little house just south of
Tyler.

H. J. Pedersen

·VIII·

Danish Women in America

*Women in Denmark were subject to the same economic and demographic forces
that impelled many of their male compatriots to emigrate. Before about 1885
family emigration prevailed, and Danish women most frequently accompanied
their husbands and children to the New World. After that time, however,
emigration of younger, unmarried men and women became more common,
and Danish girls in their teens and early twenties found their way to America
in relatively large numbers.*

*Søren Kjær, a Danish politician, cited one economic incentive for going
to the United States shortly after he visited the country in 1887:*

> The demand for Scandinavian girls, especially Danish ones, is
> enormous. Mr. Lambke in New York told me that I was welcome to
> send 3,000 girls any day I pleased. He promised to get them all work
> within a few days at a beginning wage of seven to twelve dollars [per
> month]. Girls who are skillful at household and dairy work might earn
> 25 dollars. Working in the fields is unknown for women in the United
> States.[1]

*Domestic work was unquestionably the chief form of employment for single
Danish Immigrant women, but apparently not many remained single long.
Since fewer than 40 percent of the adult newcomers from Denmark were
female, they were in great demand as spouses and as servants.*

*Perhaps in part because women were forced to play subordinate roles in
Danish and American society during the nineteenth century, it is relatively
difficult to locate letters written by them, especially by women who occupied
the lower rungs of the immigrant social ladder. The seven included in this
chapter are not a representative cross-section. Six are by women who emigrated to Canada, and the one who wrote from the United States enjoyed
unusual economic prosperity for an immigrant. Nevertheless, these letters reveal several of the experiences that countless Danish and other immigrant*

---

1. Hvidt, *Flight to America*, p. 85.

*girls and women shared, such as spending a holiday with boyfriends, finding
a spouse, toiling to feed the men at harvest time, and caring for sick children.*

*Several collections of immigrants' letters, in which women are well repre-
sented, have been published in Danish. In addition to those edited by H. F.
Feilberg and Benedicte Mahler, special attention is called to the letters by
Laura Borup in Volume II of Karl Larsen's* De, der tog hjemmefra.

❖

*Cathrine Wahl (1860–1943), the daughter of a military physician in Ål-
borg, emigrated with her husband, Valdemar, to a Danish settlement in New
Brunswick in 1883. She described domestic life in rural Canada in a letter
to her older sister.* (Source: Benedicte Mahler, ed., *Cathrine og Valdemar—et udvandrerpars skæbne belyst gennem breve* [Copenhagen: Fremad, 1975], pp. 78–79.)

Castbjerg, New Brunswick
21 March 1885

Dear Alice,

If you are surprised and irritated at us for not writing to you all
year, you have good reason to be. But I hope that if you are
irritated, you will allow me to explain.

I won't go into detail as to why we've neglected to write. These
excuses are always so boring—lack of time and so on.

First, thanks for the Christmas greeting and the present. I think
A Question is a good book, but I don't think it is as interesting as
the other ones by Ebers.[2] Thanks also to you and Mathilde for
what you sent with Tobias.[3] The trousers are just fine. The
smallest stockings fit Josepha already, but we'll put the others away
for a while. The black crocheted scarf that Tobias brought is really
nice. He can't remember who it was from. I assume it is from you,
though, since I remember you used ones like it. The dolls are
much too nice for her now; we won't give them to her until she is

2. George Moritz Ebers (1837–1898) was a well-known German Egyptologist who
also wrote novels. The work referred to, *Eine Frage* (translated into Danish as *Et
Spørgsmaal*), was set in ancient Greece.

3. Tobias Wahl was the younger brother of the writer's husband, 23 years old when
this letter was written.

older. We were especially happy to get the Christmas flowers. I also got some from Nelly, but not the same year as yours.

Believe me, Josepha is funny now. She can walk by herself. Right now she, Valdemar, and Tobias are wrestling on the sofa. I would like to be Josepha because of how they play with her. She causes a lot of accidents, though, and recently she knocked a lamp off the table, smashing it to bits. It wasn't lit, though, so she didn't get hurt. . . .

I think of you very often and wonder whether you will ever come over here. Recently it has seemed so clear that you will come and we will have a good time together. Since Tobias came I have wanted more than ever to have a helper here, both because I need somebody to help with the work and for keeping my spirits up. We could have a great time talking with each other! But I make a lot of plans and in the end I just become melancholy, while my little bundle of joy roots around in everything that she shouldn't touch.

We are waiting for spring here, but it still hasn't arrived. It is disgustingly cold. I can stand it in the winter, but at this time of year it is just crazy.

We have just received sixteen meters of *homespun* that I have to sew into men's clothes before the busy summer months arrive. I've sewn some that could have fit better, but the men console me by saying they're not so bad. Tobias is especially happy with his trousers. Believe me, I am terrified about beginning such a big job, although it is a bit easier because I have a large sewing machine.

I have to greet you from Tobias. You have to excuse him for not answering your letter. He has written so many recently.

My handwriting is worse than usual this time. My hands are completely destroyed and full of cuts and, even worse, deep cracks in my fingertips that hurt. Back home I always had such nice hands.

Valdemar has cut Josepha's hair for the first time, and I am enclosing a lock of it.

Valdemar sends you his best regards. Don't follow my example—write soon!

Catherine Wahl

Marie Eskesen was born in southwestern Jutland in 1876. Her family emigrated in 1891 when her father, Bernt Eskesen, was offered an administrative position in a terra cotta firm in Perth Amboy, New Jersey. (Source: Danes Worldwide Archives, Letters and Manuscripts, Box XXXIII.)

> Perth Amboy, New Jersey
> 15 June 1891 [*sic*; probably
> July, not June]

Dear Julie,

I would have written to you last week, but I put it off because I thought I would get a letter from you. I suppose I can't expect one so soon, even though it seems like a long time. Last time I wrote to you and Minne together, but this time I'll write only to you, and my next letter will be to her. You and Minne can tell each other what I wrote to each of you.

First let me tell you where I've been recently. On Friday, 3 July, I visited Mother's sister, Aunt Marie. The next day the boys, me, Matilde, William, and a couple of others planned to go sailing. We couldn't rent a big enough boat, though, so we had to postpone that until the next day. 4 July is a big holiday over here, American Independence Day. There were fantastic fireworks everywhere. We wish we could have been out sailing that day. Matilde said big balloons were sent up from New York. But on Saturday evening Matilde and I were invited to a tea party where there were fireworks and a dance. First we had some fireworks in the yard at home, then we went down there. We had as much *ice cream* and soda as we wanted. The boys knew so many young men that we didn't know whom we should dance the next dance with. We went home at 2 A.M.

The next morning at 10 o'clock we all went down to the boat we had rented and climbed aboard in good spirits with baskets full of food. Knud, who was our mate, promised that we would reach our destination, South Beach (a large amusement park), by 2 P.M. We were late, though. There wasn't any town at South Beach, but everywhere we looked there were carousels, roller coasters, and other breakneck rides and cafes. We went on the roller coaster once. You have to try it. In went up slopes and thundered down again until the ride was over. Of course, we liked the carousels

best, although I liked the roller coaster, too. Matilde screamed, but
Miss Carlsen (a lady who came along) and I liked it. We wished we
could have stayed more than two and a half hours, but we had to
get home and go to bed. Knud promised we would be home by 11
P.M. , but there has a headwind so we didn't get home until 4 A.M.

We were supposed to get up early on Monday to wash, but I
slept until noon. Matilde washes every Monday and I do the
ironing on Tuesday. I've already begun, and Matilde says I'm
good at it. I've bought material for two new summer dresses. One
of them was ready for the trip to South Beach. The other, which
is very light blue, will be finished one of these days. I have to get
it ready for an excursion, probably in two weeks. Ekardt has
invited me to where he worked in New York. Next Wednesday or
Thursday I'm going with the Sunday school group to a place
called Beuten Beach, which also has a carousel and so on. Adults
can bring whatever they want there.

You can see that I don't have any time to be homesick, but I
always think it would be nice to have you and Minne over here.
Besides Mother and Father and the maids, I have five brothers
and one sister here, and they should help me from becoming
homesick.

On Sunday I was up at Tottenville again. I got some apples that
were not supposed to be eaten raw, so I roasted them. In the
evening I sailed home with Kristian, who was also there, since he
works there. I have a new pair of boots because I've already worn
out the shoes I got when we left (I forgot my old ones), but you
mustn't tell anyone. I also have a new hat. It's terribly big. I use it
for sailing because the sun always burns me so badly. I had the
old one remade because the boys made fun of it and asked
whether I really wanted to go out with it on. . . .

Marie Eskesen

Johanne Frederiksen described the difficulty of taking several small chil-
dren across the continent to join her husband, a farmer in Saskatchewan.
(Source: H. F. Feilberg, ed., *De derovre. En Række Breve fra Canada*
[Copenhagen: Gyldendalske Boghandel, 1917], pp. 48–51.)

28 May 1911

Dear Grandfather,

Please forgive me for waiting eight days before writing. All of us were so busy with the voyage that I wasn't able to accomplish anything besides beginning to adjust to customs here and feeding the family three times a day under very difficult conditions. Now we are getting things into order.

Henning wants to tell about the train trip, which defies description. We were able to stretch out on wooden benches only two of the five nights on the train. The other three there were constant changes. As soon as we were asleep we had to get up again, wait at a cold station, and board another train. The last night I lay the three smallest children on the floor between the seats. They simply couldn't sit up any longer. But the jolting and shaking gave them headaches. Ellen was temporarily deaf, Hans had a pain in the back of his head, and little Niels vomited so violently I thought his intestines were going to come up. He couldn't eat anything, but he is better now. Ellen and Hans are also feeling better. Marie had a sore throat and fever during the whole trip and still looks terrible, but she is starting to improve. Henning is more disheartened, but he was a great support during the long and demanding trip, always warm and willing to help. Now the excitement is over and he too is feeling a bit depressed and is tired and sick, but that has to be expected. Ellen was always the healthiest. None of the children complained or has been naughty. We all cried when we got off at the last cold station in drifting snow at 1 A.M., but my husband was there to meet us.

The wild prairie seems so barren and strange. It's like a sea. We are just a speck in the middle of a circle that grows or shrinks as the weather changes. On a clear day we can see an almost endless distance. Houses are visible in the distance, and here and there are grain elevators. When it rains or snows it seems that our little cabin is the only house in the world. Just imagine how bleak it looks—but it's worse than you can imagine. We've shoveled most of the mud away. It doesn't feel like a home yet, but I believe that will come. Inside these four low walls we and the children should be cozy and we'll survive.

My husband has been working very hard, and his clothes fall off him in dirty clumps. He could hardly get by without us, though, so we had to come over here. It isn't easy for a man to come home from work day after day tired, wet, and dirty to an ice-cold room without any food or a change of clothes.

It is still very cold here, colder than it was all winter in Denmark. Yesterday we had a snowstorm that lasted all day and most of the night. Other people get by, though, and so can we with God's help.

My husband has built himself a little shop behind the house along the north wall. He has an American forge, a drill attached to the wall, an excellent grindstone, and a good toolbox. In the autumn he expects to get work with a threshing crew. That pays really well. Everyone likes him and is willing to lend him a helping hand. My task is to think of myself as little as possible and be everything to him and the children. With God's help I'll succeed, however difficult the beginning may be. My husband is indescribably happy to have all of us over here.

Now the important thing is to get some draft animals. At the moment a horse costs five hundred dollars, a real fortune. We need at least four to plow the prairie soil, which has lain fallow for thousands of years. We have borrowed a wagon and tomorrow we're going into town to buy the most essential kitchen utensils and some food. Over here we cannot simply run to the shop. My husband has bought flour, oatmeal, lard, and a pail of jam. A nice young wife who lives near us gave me a loaf of bread and some butter. Our cow, which cost fifty dollars, doesn't give much milk, but it is rich in cream. We also have seven hens that lay well and two small pigs that Hans likes. All of the animals go out in the snow. Our parlor is five meters long and four meters wide; for the time being it will have to do. A table and bench have been built. We have two large beds, one atop the other. I've hung a curtain around them, so together they look like a four-poster. Since we are settlers we have to live that way. Henning sleeps on top of a chest. This summer he is going to work for our neighbor. They are young, attractive people, educated in a way, and they have the strength and youth that we lack. School will be difficult for Henning. We believe he should have two weeks free to relax and adjust to this new life.

All of the others are sleeping, and I'm tired. Good night!

Johanne

She later described the burden of helping a neighbor at harvest time. (Source: Feilberg, ed., *De derovre,* pp. 36–37.)

22 October 1912

Please excuse the confusion in this letter. I am writing it "between the battles." You can probably remember that there is a little wife in the area, Mrs. Richter, who has lost two babies during the past two years. Now she is very close to having the third and cannot do anything. At the moment she is supposed to be feeding sixteen or seventeen threshers three meals a day, and it is impossible to hire a woman to help her. When she asked me to cook for them I could hardly say no. But it is very demanding. Baby[4] stays home with the boys while I help.

Do you want to hear what the threshers eat? It's different from what we used at home so should be interesting.

Breakfast: oatmeal, eggs, cold ham, potatoes, coffee, bread, stewed apples.

Dinner: roast chicken stuffed with bread crumbs, onions, and sage; cabbage, potatoes, beets, tea, bread and butter, cheese, and apple *pie.*

Supper: stew, browned potatoes, stewed carrots, tarts, boiled fruit, tea, bread and butter, and *pickles.*

We bake seven large loaves of bread every day, five or six *pies,* buns, tarts, cakes, and so on. There are also chickens to be killed and plucked, and butter to be churned, so you can easily understand that when it is time to wash up there is a lot to do. Breakfast is on the table at 6 A.M. and the evening meal is rather late, so you can see that the day is long, especially since I'm already tired from the harvesting. Fortunately, I did a lot of baking and washing before I left home. My husband is home. There is so much for him to do on the farm because he was gone so much this past summer. One advantage of my taking a job here is that it gives Baby some free time. She cannot stand it or manage it. She has worked for Mrs. Richter for quite some time.

---

4. "Baby" was the nickname of the writer's older daughter, Marie, then 14 years old.

The children are well and have plenty to do. They seldom cry, but somebody has to keep an eye on them when I am away from home. Baby is good at that, and everyone is more independent here than back in Denmark. When they sit at the table in the evening, washed and with red cheeks, happy and occupied with the day's events, then they are all sweet. . . .

Johanne

The war in Europe and a drought in western Canada were serious concerns to her. (Source: H. F. Feilberg, ed., *Hjemliv på Prærien. De derovre. En Række Breve fra Canada,* II [Copenhagen: Gyldendalske Boghandel, 1918], pp. 219–20.)

26 August 1914

A letter dated 26 July, which reached us on 8 August, didn't say a word about war, but on 1 August all of Europe was said to be on fire, so our mother country is probably in danger. I think it is terrible that almost an entire generation of strong, young men should be sacrificed. Whoever wins the war and gains power, they will be gone—fathers and sons. One army falls on the battlefield, a larger army overcome by grief, privation, and poverty. Just imagine everything that will be lost along with them!

Even though we have the best garden in the area, and the women come and get what they need from me, there still isn't a tenth of what we had last year. On 8 August it was terribly hot, but that night there was a killing frost that destroyed a lot of what we had. The year 1914 has become a war year for you and a year of crop failures for us. In many parts of Saskatchewan and Alberta there is absolutely nothing to harvest.

Our wheat crop was among the best in this area. The oats were also good, but we didn't get enough. My husband swathed and I shocked the grain. The whole thing didn't amount to more than fifty *acres,* but that was plenty for me. We have a lake on our property, so the grain has to be harvested as soon as possible to save it from the ducks. One evening, when I hadn't finished all of this task, they threshed it for us. Yes, I cried. It has been shown that wheat becomes richest and best on well-tilled soil; it is *Nr. 1 hard*. On the other hand, the harvest is bad if the soil has not been tilled right.

The weather has been very dry this summer. It didn't rain for eight weeks. Hot winds sent the temperatures up into the thirties, and one day it was almost forty degrees. There isn't a shadow on the prairie. The sun blazes down on the house all day, making it like an oven inside. Sickness has resulted, and we have had our share.

Johanne

The Frederiksens' teen-age daughter related the joy of attending a neighborhood party. (Source: Feilberg, ed., *Hjemliv på Prærien*, II, pp. 284–85.)

Dear Sister,

I have to tell you about a little *surprise party* I attended recently. It was the Behrends' tenth wedding anniversary, and since they didn't want to have a party themselves, the neighbors decided to have one for them. About twenty-five of us met at the Stiebel place, walked over there quietly, and knocked on the door. They were surprised, of course. Then the fun began. Mrs. Behrend was given a bridal veil and an old white dress. Mr. Behrend was given a false mustache, glasses, a high collar, and a long, red necktie. Then we played a march, and each of the men was given a piece of cloth to sew into a dish cloth for Mrs. Behrend. It was fun to see them try to use a needle and thread. The one who did the best job received a prize. In the meantime each of the women was given a length of rope to make into a halter without cutting it. I won the prize because I happened to know how to splice a rope and tie knots. Then we played children's games. It's been a long time since I laughed as much as when we were supposed to play a game we all knew, but when we tried nobody could remember more than *"a little red cart painted blue,"* so that was the end of that! We were served sandwiches, cake, coffee, and vanilla ice cream. I brought the ice cream.

You have to excuse me for stopping now. I didn't get home
until 4 A.M. and now I'm drowsy.

Your sister,
Marie

*Even in western Canada farm women began to feel the impact of World
War I.* (Source: Feilberg, ed., *Hjemliv på Prærien,* II, pp. 232–35.)

3 January 1915

I suppose the war must be on your minds all the time. Nobody
has ever experienced anything as horrible as it, and we all wonder
when and how it will end. There is a lot of talk that war will break
out between the United States and England, and that the Nordic
countries and The Netherlands would not be able to remain
neutral.

Even though the war is far away, it confronts us because this
country is basically in it. Canada has sent one million soldiers,
flour, oats, horses, grain, and money to England. We have
something called *The Patriotic Fund* whose purpose is to take care
of soldiers' families. Millions of dollars have been collected for it.
Then there is *The Shilling Fund,* which collects money from
Canadian children to send to children in Belgium. A lot of money
has been collected for it, too, and we have given our mite.

Let me thank you for the long stockings, which are just perfect.
Hans[5] uses them, and they're almost like underwear. He is
overjoyed by them, and every night he hangs them over a rope in
the kitchen so they will be warm and dry in the morning. It's just
wonderful how tidy the boy is. His hook is always clean and there
is never a spot on his clothes. "Niels is free to borrow my coat," he
says, "but he has to ask first." He insists that every tear or hole be
mended immediately. Nobody is allowed to hang clothes on his
hook. Recently he scolded Henning and then said to him in a
friendly way, "This is my coathook. Will you please stop hanging

---

5. Hans was one of the writer's sons, then 10 years old.

your sheepskin jacket on it?" He confided to me: "You can't imagine how badly it smells."

He is a very strong child and is always hungry—not at all fussy about food. He goes outside and plays in the snow, goes into the barn and talks to the animals he loves, and shows how he can hang like a sloth (I don't know what kind of animal that is) from the beams of the ceiling. Once in a while he says to me, "I think tonight is just right for some Indian wrestling," and like a fool I immediately get involved in a test of strength. At first I'm stronger, but after a little while he can *knock me all over the room,* and I can't help laughing at the boy.

For six weeks before Christmas we didn't have any milk, but do you think our neighbors with six to ten cows would sell us a drop? You should have seen the joy in the boy's face at Christmas when we finally had both milk and calves. "It's just great to get full eating oatmeal." He really needs food, exercise, and some learning.

It has been a joy to see Henning become such a big and strong young man. Work is mere play to him, and he really is a good boy. He has very good clothes, and at an auction in the neighborhood he made a very good deal on a nice little spring cart with two sleds and another sled. He brought them home and we're using them. When they butchered on the farm where he works, he brought twelve kilograms of beef home. He is always willing to extend a helping hand and can draw well. Now and then he comes home and plays some *whist* with us adults, and we all have a good time. He is doing well now. Niels is always "Danish-minded" and thinks nothing is any good unless it comes from back home. "But which home?" Hans asks. "Isn't this home?" They each received a book, but Niels didn't read his because it wasn't from Denmark. He was happy to discover that "even though Christmas is past, it is still before Christmas."[6] He thinks, speaks, dreams, makes, and draws only machines.

These days we are reading *Village Children* by Ingemann aloud. One evening I stopped in the middle of a specially exciting passage and, looking at Niels, asked him what kind of impression

6. This apparently reflects the boy's preference for the Danish custom of celebrating the Christmas season until Epiphany, or Holy Three Kings' Day, Jan. 6.

it made on him. He blurted out with delight: "Look, mama, it can go around!" He had been playing with a machine for walking on the ice, so *Village Children* had blown right over his head.

Marie has been sick. I'm a bit worried about her because she is so thin. I think Hommels worked her too hard last summer. Her days were long, often from 4 A.M. until 10 P.M. It can be dangerous for her to be big for her age, have red cheeks, and not be willing to give up anything. We wanted to have her home all of July, but she didn't think she could leave that woman. But both then and now I think it was unjust of us not to have taken better care of her. She is very energetic, and when she discovers anything wrong with herself she corrects it. When she has a job to do, she is almost too conscientious and does everything she can, and then some. Finally we had to drag her home, sick and sorrowful. I cannot deny, though, that she gained something from the experience. She got clothes and made friends, but such labor should not be demanded of young people. If Ellen[7] worked without being paid anything, she would be exploited.

Johanne

7. Ellen was the writer's younger daughter, then 11 years old.

· IX ·

Danes
and Religious Pluralism

Lutheranism replaced Roman Catholicism as the state religion of Denmark in the 1530s and, apart from being influenced by rationalistic and pietistic currents during the eighteenth century, changed relatively little for three hundred years. In the middle of the nineteenth century, however, three phenomena fractured the seemingly monolithic religious landscape of the Baltic kingdom. First, the constitution of 1849, while maintaining the established church, allowed the formation of other denominations. Within a few years several sects, mostly of British origin, appeared and became permanent segments of Denmark's religious mosaic. Second, the state church suffered a de facto schism that has never been completely repaired. One faction declared its allegiance to the ideals of the romantic, high-church pastor, N.F.S. Grundtvig (1783–1872). The other, associated with the Inner Mission Society, stressed Biblical authority, the necessity of conversion, strict personal morals, and the avoidance of what they perceived as worldliness. Both parties professed loyalty to orthodox Lutheranism, but their fidelity to the doctrines of Martin Luther did not prevent them from engaging in mutual recrimination. Third, in the 1850s Søren Kierkegaard launched his most virulent attacks on the state church and its notion that virtually the entire population of Denmark was Christian. His widely read series of pamphlets, Øjeblikket [The Instant], carried vehemently satirical tirades against the clergy, the sacraments, and other trappings of "official" Christianity. For several decades after his death in 1855 Kierkegaard's works continued to supply rhetorical ammunition to the detractors of the Danish Church and its counterparts in Norway and Sweden. Few Danes formally renounced their faith, but attendance at worship services and participation in communion plummeted.

All of these currents were magnified among Danish immigrants in the United States. In the absence of a state church, spiritually active Danes joined a myriad of denominations. Both factions of the established church were trans-

164

planted to American soil; the Grundtvigian wing, influencing the Danish Evangelical Lutheran Church in America, was founded in 1872. The pietistic branch allied temporarily with like-minded Norwegian immigrants, but in 1884 seceded to organize a denomination which, after merging with another breakaway group, was known as the United Evangelical Lutheran Church. Reflecting the spiritual lethargy and anticlerical trends in the mother country, both communions remained small. In 1902 the quasi-Grundtvigian "Danish Church" had a total of 14,792 members, while the "United Church" numbered 16,481 souls.[1]

There is no dearth of either manuscript or printed letters describing the religious life of Danish Lutherans in the United States. But two factors distort the picture that these available accounts paint. First, the vast majority of the most accessible letters were written by clergymen. While their descriptions are invaluable, it would naturally be desirable to have more lay viewpoints. Second, the Grundtvigians, being more interested in preserving Danish cultural identity in America, left more evidence of their religious life than did the pietists. The letters included in this chapter reflect these biases but also mirror several shared themes of Danish-American Lutheranism in the nineteenth century, such as the severe clerical shortage, competition from non-Lutheran denominations, the intersynodical rivalry between the two Danish camps, and the widespread irreligiosity among Danish immigrants.

Owing largely to British influence, but also somewhat to the evangelistic efforts of returned Scandinavian emigrants, there were Baptist congregations in Denmark by 1840, and Methodist ones began to dot the Danish landscape in the 1850s. Under the leadership of the subsequent emigration agent Mogens Abraham Sommer, a number of revivalistic "Christian Apostolic" congregations also appeared in the 1850s. During the following decade the so-called "Catholic Apostolic Church," a British form of the faith drawing elements from diverse Protestant, Roman Catholic, and Orthodox traditions, came to Copenhagen. In the 1870s a returned Danish-American, John Matteson, proclaimed the Seventh-day Adventist faith in his native country. The Salvation Army marched into Denmark in the 1880s, the decade when the Danish Mission Covenant was founded as a cousin of the Scandinavian-American bodies that later became the Evangelical Free Church of America.

Given this multiplicity of denominations in their homeland and widespread

---

1. Andersen, *Hvor Danskerne i Amerika findes,* p. 30. Like most other Lutheran statistics, these figures include all baptized members, regardless of age or whether confirmed.

dissatisfaction with its state church, it is not surprising that spiritually awakened Danish immigrants joined a large variety of communions in the New World, where the denominational constellation was far more complex. Because no specifically Danish Lutheran congregations existed in the United States until around 1870, one of the viable alternatives was to seek membership in Norwegian Lutheran flocks, and many did so. It is impossible to trace with precision those Danes who were received into English-language churches. But specifically Danish congregations were formed representing the Baptist, Methodist, Adventist, Congregationalist, and other traditions.

These immigrant groups shared several characteristics. First, all were naturally based on the principle of "voluntaryism," a fundamental tenet of American religious life that was opposite to the birthright Lutheranism to which most Danes had been accustomed in their native country. Second, a severe ministerial shortage plagued most of these infant congregations, requiring laypeople to play an active role in their leadership. Third, most allied with corresponding English-speaking denominations, often as ethnic conferences within the parent body. The Norwegian-Danish Conference of the Methodist Church, for example, was founded in 1880 but not totally integrated into the larger body until 1943. Fourth, within the framework of these alliances, the immigrant churches usually received some measure of financial support from their Yankee counterparts. Their ministers were often bilingually trained in special departments of the Yankee denominations' theological seminaries. Finally, because they actively recruited members among nominally Lutheran Danish-Americans, these immigrant communions all incurred the wrath of Lutheran clergymen on both sides of the Atlantic, who accused them of "sheepstealing."

Thousands of Danes abandoned traditional Christianity to join the Church of Jesus Christ of Latter-day Saints, making it the chief benefactor, in numbers of converts, of religious freedom in Denmark during the second half of the nineteenth century. The Mormon patriarch Brigham Young dispatched missionaries to Scandinavia shortly after the 1847 trek to Utah; especially in Denmark they were quite successful in proselytizing Lutherans as well as members of the various free churches. Many of the converts subsequently migrated to the supposed American Zion in Utah. Indeed, between 1850 and 1905 more than twelve thousand Danish Mormons departed for the New World.[2] These pioneers came from all social classes and represented a wide spectrum

2. Mulder, *Homeward to Zion,* p. 107.

of occupations, although farmers, artisans, and laborers predominated. In contrast to general trends in Danish immigration, a slight majority were women.

Their journey from Denmark to Utah testified to the organizational skills and camaraderie of the Latter-day Saints. Working closely with colleagues in Great Britain and the United States, Mormon missionaries to Scandinavia (themselves almost invariably Nordic immigrants) accompanied proselytes to England, where they were given free or subsidized passage to America on chartered ships. Regrouping in the Midwest, often in Missouri or Nebraska, they set out across the prairie in well-organized wagon trains, each member assigned specific duties and responsibilities. Upon reaching Utah, these hardy immigrants, now accustomed to working effectively in a highly disciplined company, were quickly integrated into a cooperative social system that demanded hard work but also offered security to all who pulled their own weight and did not challenge the existing order. They were encouraged to assimilate rapidly; apart from a Danish-language newspaper, Bikuben *[The Beehive], most vestiges of Danish culture soon vanished.*

Not all of the presumed converts remained true to the faith or accepted the regimented life of Mormon society. Some found the tactics of Brigham Young and other leaders heavy-handed. Others appear never to have converted at all, but merely claimed to have done so to facilitate emigrating to the New World. These apostates and malcontents wrote a large number of exposés, which Danish Christian clergymen and journalists on both sides of the Atlantic marshalled in their barrage of anti-Mormon propaganda.

Skandinaviens Stjerne *[Star of Scandinavia], a Mormon periodical that began to appear in Copenhagen in the 1850s, is a rich source of immigrant letters. Like nearly all Mormon and anti-Mormon literature of that time they are tendentious, and the degree to which they were edited for publication is impossible to ascertain. Nevertheless, they provide many insights into the journey to Utah and immigrant life there. Letters hostile to the Mormon Church are scattered in other sources as well; they tell of disillusionment with the Mormon hierarchy and polygamy, and the failure of life in Utah to match the glowing descriptions that missionaries in Denmark offered.*

Rasmus Andersen (1847–1930) ministered to Danish Lutheran congregations in Neenah and Waupaca, Wisconsin. (Source: *Meddelelser fra den dansk-amerikanske Mission,* III [1872], pp. 40–46.)

Waupaca, Wisconsin
16 October 1872

In my last letter I told you that Pastor Anderson, who was born
in Denmark but is serving a Swedish-English congregation in
Illinois, had just visited me. He preached here one Sunday
evening in Swedish. Most of the people in church were Swedes,
and they were really pleased with his sermon. The Danes were
also happy, although they could not understand it so well. He
preached about the lost coin and implored the congregation to
attend church regularly and gather around me so that we could
work together in love. I opened and closed the service with prayer
and a short address to the congregation. Pastor Anderson and I
did not agree about everything, but it is good that we avoid the
frequent American practices of denouncing each other as heretics
or trying to cause schisms. Despite our varying viewpoints, we
regard each other as brothers, so I was especially grateful for his
visit and his message to the congregation. . . .

I told you in my last letter that a Danish church was to be
organized in Neenah. Together with another man from here I
went there on 7 September. Pastor Adam Dan was also present
and preached on Sunday. The next day we held a meeting, at
which I was elected secretary. A church was organized with the
name "Our Savior's Danish Lutheran Church of Neenah and
Vicinity." Its goal is to be tied as closely as possible to the mother
church. The congregation elected me pastor. I shall visit Neenah
one Sunday each month and possibly one weekday, as well. Some
of us met to collect donations for the mission among the Danes in
this country and to see whether we could publish a periodical. The
congregation in Neenah cannot expect much, because it is so far
away and too small to support a pastor of its own. Even though it
is small, there is hope that it will grow. I live about fifty kilometers
from there by train. The journey is not difficult because I live
very close to the station. I travel through one town and a few
stations, but most of the trip is through the forest until close to
Neenah. Then there is pasture land, which makes the landscape
look like Denmark. The train crosses a bridge over a rather large
lake. The factory town of Menasha is on the other side. Both are

impressive towns that face each other much like Hamburg and
Altona. The surrounding countryside is very attractive. The two
towns are rivals, however, and try to surpass each other.

I was in Neenah again from 4 October until 7 October. On 4
October we had a congregational meeting to discuss church
practices. We decided to adhere fully to Danish customs as well as
to the Danish liturgy. On 6 October I delivered my installation
sermon. We have our worship services in a Norwegian church,
and the people saw the rare sight of a pastor wearing a robe and
fluted ruff collar pronouncing absolution by laying on hands. On
previous occasions I had not worn a robe, and in the Norwegian
church the laying on of hands is not done when pronouncing
absolution. They pronounce the forgiving of sins to all at one
time. We also performed an infant baptism.

That evening I held a meeting at a private home. There is a
great deal of agitation in Neenah, much of it in an Adventist
direction. . . .

In my last letter I reported that we were going to build a
church, but we were fooled. The church in which I was ordained
was offered to us, and, believing it was better to buy a sanctuary
than to build one ourselves, we negotiated with that Scottish
Presbyterian congregation. We agreed that, subtracting what the
town had given for the construction of the building, a fair price
would be seventeen hundred dollars. We could not get the deed,
however, before the Presbyterian congregation had met. We had a
worship service in it the next Sunday anyway. Afterward an
Irishman who belonged to that congregation came in and, angrily
informing us that the building was not yet officially sold, took the
key. When his fellow Presbyterians heard about the incident,
however, they became angry at him and said that since the key
had been turned over to us the building was in our hands. We
had no choice but to send a policeman to get the key from the
Irishman. At first he resisted giving it up, but later he delivered it
and paid the expenses. Since that time the Presbyterian congregation has met and rejected the sale. They agreed to let us
continue to use the property but not to own it. We were sorry to
hear that, because it was too late in the year to begin construction,
and now we will have to stay home all winter. We have not lost

our courage, though, and are collecting money and making
preparations so that we can begin work as early as possible in the
spring. . . .

*A.L.J. Søholm (1844–1928) described his ministry scurrying about Danish
Lutheran congregations in New York and New Jersey.* (Source: *Meddelelser*,
VII [May 1874], pp. 106–09.)

Perth Amboy, New Jersey
7 January 1874

We have come to the end of the beautiful days of Christmas.
For me it was a joy to see the affection with which our countrymen kept the season in this land where holidays are neglected.
All of the Danes prepared for it, and only a few who are
deeply mired in sin or are wild fanatics misused Christmas by
working on it. We had worship services on Christmas Eve and the
next afternoon, and both times the church was full. At noon on
Christmas I went to Oxford, and in the evening, as night was
approaching, reached my destination. Some Danes met me at the
station and took me to the church, where we had a worship
service at 7:30 P.M. A large number of our countrymen attended, as
well as some Swedes. There was another service on St. Stephen's
Day, because almost everybody wanted to celebrate Christmas
for two days. I also performed a marriage ceremony, as I had
done on Christmas here in Perth Amboy. After visiting some
members of the congregation who were sick, I took the evening
train in a heavy snowfall to Dover, where some Lutherans
and Methodists had gathered to hear the Christmas message. Early
the next morning (Saturday), I took the train to New York to visit
Castle Garden, but found only a few Danes there. At 6 P.M. I left
New York in the snow and went to Troy, Albany, Green Island,
and Lansingburg, four almost adjacent communities on the
Hudson River. Since I took an express train, I arrived there at
midnight. I would have had to spend the night at the station, but
it was closed. I did not know my way around there and a policeman told me that the address where I wanted to go was out
in one of the suburbs. An American came by, however, and said

he was going out that way. I followed him through a very heavy
snowfall across the immense bridge that spans the Hudson to
Green Island. There I met another courteous policeman who
helped me and showed me the way to the man I wanted to visit. It
was very late at night, and I was happy to get a few hours' sleep.
By telling about this insignificant little trip at night, I am only
trying to show that it is not as dangerous to travel in America as
some adventurers describe it in horror-filled stories. The next
morning, the Sunday between Christmas and New Year, there was
a lot of snow on the ground. The worship service had been
scheduled for 10 A.M. in a Presbyterian Sunday school in
Lansingburg, but since we had to wait until the trolleys were
running from Green Island many of the other Danes and I did
not arrive there until about 11 A.M. Despite the bad weather, quite
a few men and women attended. After the service there was a
meeting at 4 P.M. I was invited to a home in Lansingburg, but also
had time to visit several other Danes. At 4 P.M. the building was
full of men and women. Twenty took part in communion. More
wanted to do so, but since I had only a small amount of altar
bread, the others had to wait until next time. After the service the
wish was expressed that I come once a month, and I promised I
would. Almost all of the Danes are from the Haderslev area,
although there are some from Flensburg. In Lansingburg there
are fifteen or sixteen families in addition to all the families and
young people in neighboring towns. There are few places where I
have been more warmly received than here. Some of the people
had not heard a sermon in Danish for years. . . .

Monday morning I went back to New York and visited Castle
Garden. I reached Perth Amboy that evening and was glad to
have a few days to rest at my little home before the end of the
year. It was not really rest, however, because I had to prepare my
sermons for New Year's Eve and New Year's Day.

The congregation in Oxford is gaining inner strength and
solidarity. At Christmas it added thirteen members. Here in Perth
Amboy there is more resistance, but our little congregation
received six new members at Christmas. It is now evident that the
weapons the Norwegians used to hinder the Danish mission here
were inadequate, so they are being more careful. One faithful man
told me that the Sunday after Christmas a Norwegian pastor

preached a sermon in which he accused our countrymen of being Grundtvigians. We must remember that the Norwegians define "Grundtvigian" broadly, making even Vilhelm Beck one of them.[3] In short, they think the entire Church of Denmark is Grundtvigian. . . . His own friends had to admit that was going too far, however. . . . The Norwegian pastor has not visited me yet. We never see each other except when our paths cross on trips. We are not hostile toward each other, but occasionally there are arguments between our parishioners.

A.L.J. Søholm

J. A. Heiberg (1848–1936) reported on the growing pains of two young Lutheran congregations in Chicago. (Source: *Meddelelser,* X [March 1875], pp. 156–57.)

Chicago
11 January 1875

I believe I told you before that I have begun to preach to the Danes on the South Side. The Danish-Norwegian who was the pastor down there, Mr. Wiese, disappeared without a trace a little before Christmas. The congregation had dwindled during his ministry and the Norwegian Synod was tired of paying the man. The congregation was unable to support him. After the worship service last Sunday I organized a Danish congregation named "St. Stephen's Church." It has about twenty contributing members whose goal is to gather as many Danes as possible for the Kingdom of God—and there are a large number of Danes here— and to build a church and call a pastor from Denmark. I shall send you the constitution. You may think this is a modest beginning, but we began with only twenty-three here on the West Side and have succeeded well, praise God. I shall continue to minister to the church on alternate Sundays. We use an English Baptist church for our worship services. A Danish Baptist attends

---

3. Vilhelm Beck of Copenhagen, who headed the Inner Mission Society in Denmark, was actually an outspoken pietistic opponent of the Grundtvigians.

frequently and has tried to cause trouble by holding a worship service every other Sunday at the same time as we do, 4:30 P.M. His first attempt was a bit of a failure, however, because nobody came.

We are surrounded by enemies and insincere friends, and in general the Danes of Chicago are indifferent about the important things in life. My patience is often put to the test. I wish I could report that the time is ripe to send another Danish pastor to Chicago. We certainly need another so that we could fight back-to-back. But I believe he would have to be an ordained man from Denmark. For various reasons he is needed more here than elsewhere.

I can report that my own congregation is growing a bit externally, and with God's help internally as well. Growth is slow, but that is always the case. Only the Lord can examine hearts and really know. At Christmas the church was absolutely full. Dark memories press hearts into church at that time of year. Our singing is being done more and more by the congregation. We have a faithful little choir that sings out and teaches the congregation the tunes of the hymns. We have resurrected the old Epiphany festival in Chicago, and that evening I held a worship service and sent the offering ($6.60) to the "Heathen Mission." I am very pleased with our church council. Little by little we have gotten the congregation's "best men" involved, and they are sincerely and willingly helping to carry the work of the church. All of our accounts were in good shape at the end of the year. We had a cash balance of one hundred fifty dollars after all the expenses were paid, but we also have a debt of seventeen hundred dollars.

The weather turned bitter cold after 1 January. The last few days it has even been thirty degrees below zero, and it has been a bit difficult to get it really warm inside the church. It is built differently from the solid Danish churches back home.

L. M. Gydesen (1827–90) found his pietistic Lutheran congregation in Omaha intolerant in certain cultural respects. (Source: Meddelelser, n.s. II [November 1881], pp. 30–34.]

Having worked for two years here in Omaha and farther out in Nebraska, I feel I should report on my activities. . . . It seemed to me, and still seems so, that Omaha is of great significance for our missionary work. . . . I found a large number of Danes here, but the church was no longer the center of their lives. Interest had declined while the Norwegian Synod and the Conference[4] served them. They were more interested in their clubs, the Danish Society and the Veterans' Brotherhood. Life focused on them and there were conflicts between them, pitting brother against brother. After thinking about this night and day for three weeks, I visited each of these societies and asserted that the church is above them and is the place for gathering everything that comes from truth. I explained that we could unite to our mutual benefit. I must say that I have asked for help several times, never in vain. This step, which was not taken rashly, met resistance at first, expecially among those Danes who had been in the Conference and who believe "it is a sin to read newspapers." They thought I should condemn the societies.

There used to be a dramatic society here in Omaha that had shorter productions once or twice each winter. During the period when the congregation belonged to the Conference the dramatic society had a benefit for the church, which resulted in an organ worth one hundred dollars. Last winter it decided, without my knowledge, to do it again, because the church needed painting and equipment. Some of our pastors protested, however, and several articles critical of us appeared in Omaha. I did not reply to them, except in private letters.

Then the congregation decided to cover the church debt by having its usual bazaar. The debt had grown in recent years and had to be paid off, or else the creditors would take the property. The bazaar was held in successive years, and now the church does not have any debts. But it, too, met with resistance, and it came

4. The Norwegian Synod, founded in the early 1850s, was the most traditional, high-church Lutheran denomination among Norwegian immigrants. The Conference, founded in 1870, included both pietistic Norwegians and Danes until 1884, when the latter withdrew to form their own synod.

from a group that I had not expected to protest. It hurt me greatly, and still does. I suppose these problems exist in all American and Danish-American churches, but I cannot understand why I, as the pastor of an independent congregation, should have to deal with them. It is the duty of the congregation to raise funds, and when this is done within the bounds of morality and respectability, I should not have to make any excuses.

Another matter with which I have had to deal is the question of who can become a member of the congregation. I bring this up here not only because it affects Omaha, but also because it is a current issue in our young denomination. If it is not solved in one way or another, it can have consequences for the future of the denomination. It was discussed, but not solved, at one of our conventions.

Finally, I have to request the committee to send as soon as possible a pastor who can serve three settlements: Rock Creek, Bennett, and Trundville. I have asked about this before. I get requests to come from all directions, and I have to work past my breaking point to satisfy all of the demands. If we could get a man to take up the work southwest of here, and after a while another to work to the north and in Washington and Dakota Counties, we could get by for a while. But the settlements are growing fast and it will not be many years before they all need pastors. I know that the farmers want their clergymen to serve as schoolteachers, as well, and would like to hear the committee's position on this.

Here in Omaha we have begun to discuss having a school. I hope we can make progress on this soon, but hard times pass slowly, so I am not optimistic about it. If I stay in Omaha, we will get a school sooner or later. I can postpone my hopes, but never give them up. . . .

L. M. Gydesen

Hans Jørgen Pedersen (1851–1905), president of the Danish folk high school at Elk Horn, Iowa, lamented widespread irreligiosity and materialism. (Source: Meddelelser, n.s. III, pp. 40–42.)

Elk Horn, Iowa
March 1882

We are often requested to tell friends in Denmark about our
work, our struggle, and our progress. That is certainly reasonable,
but friends should not judge us too harshly if we cannot fulfill the
request very well. It is not easy to relate one's own activities, and
there is the danger of being misunderstood. If I describe objective
facts about missionary activity, you might read too much into them
because you are not acquainted at firsthand with the real conditions. You might conclude from the acute need for pastors
that all of the Danes here are spiritually alive. The large number
of church buildings and the size of the offerings might lead you to
believe that Christian fellowship is very strong here. So you can
understand my reluctance to write. I cannot understand why the
good people back home believe that church life must be so strong
over here. It is a simple fact that 90 percent of those who left
Denmark were not influenced much by Christianity. Only in the
most recent years have I met some who were spiritually alive
before they emigrated. Most immigrants are peasants in the truest
sense of the word. Oppressed by the poverty that weighed heavily
on them at home, their burden was suddenly lightened. Not only
can they easily earn a living here; they even have a little left over.
Under these conditions many are inclined to kneel before Mam-
mon as he appears in this rich American society.

Their memories of Denmark are far from brilliant—rather dark,
in fact. They constrast "poor" Denmark with "rich" America. The
result is not difficult to guess. Is there any real reason to expect it
to be otherwise?

In terms of religion the situation is quite different. Newcomers
are amazed by the number of "sects" here and all the turmoil they
cause. Things were different back home, where nobody ever
discussed spiritual matters outside church and where people
attended only on holidays and family events. To many of you this
may seem to be a backhanded slap, but I assure you that I have
met hundreds of immigrants who claim that spiritual life in
Denmark was quite foreign to them.

The majority of our parishioners are such people. Only in the
most recent years have we added a few from congregations in

Denmark that were spiritually alive. Most of them feel an affinity with the Inner Mission[5] and are very wary of "the Danish church," which they correctly label "Grundtvigian." Little by little they overcome this fear and often become our most active members. Very few Danes of "high church" persuasion come to America.

It may sound that it is difficult to "gather" congregations among such people, and that is certainly the case if one keeps one's outmoded concept of the church. But it is not at all difficult to gather people who want to support a pastor and build a church. Our people have brought along from Denmark respect for the clergy and the church. They believe it is wrong not to have their children baptized. They are used to doing so and say that it "can never do any harm."

A visit by the pastor to the sickbed or deathbed is greatly appreciated, and many place high value on "getting a Christian burial." Among the many members of the church, each of whom had his own reason for joining, there is an especially active little flock in each congregation. They know what they are looking for and they help advance our missionary work before the throne of grace. Thank God for them. Through their activity and their prayers we get the grace to persevere. They keep us afloat when we are about to sink. . . .

H. J. Pedersen

Thorvald Lyngby (1856–1914) of the Danish Evangelical Lutheran Church analyzed the competition afforded by non-Lutheran denominations in Racine, Wisconsin, a community with a large Danish population. (Source: Kolding Folkeblad, 22 December 1882.)

. . . Racine has about a score of churches, I don't know exactly how many. Among the most beautiful is our Danish Emmaus Church. The cost of building it six years ago was nine thousand dollars. Since the state does not support worship, the congregation had to bear the entire expense. Unfortunately, there is a heavy debt of four thousand dollars weighing on us. The congregation numbers about 160 registered, contributing members. That is

5. The Inner Mission was a pietistic, revivalistic organization within the state church.

nothing compared to the number of Danes in Racine. The Norwegian Lutheran church here includes both Norwegians and Danes, as does our congregation. There are also two Danish Baptist churches, each with its own pastor, and a Norwegian or Scandinavian Methodist church. These sects are defensive; they work vigorously—and cunningly—to get members. Large numbers of our countrymen allow themselves to be caught and torn away from our church as soon as they come here. They are prey for the false, deceiving leaders of the sects and their equally ambitious followers.

What can the reason be for this regrettable state of affairs? I find two reasons. First, a lot of our dear countrymen leave home not knowing much about real Christianity. Most of them don't know what either the Lutheran or Baptist tradition really is. The Baptist faith, with its rejection of infant baptism, appeals to the natural mind. Those who are not already grounded in love to something else can easily be lured into the first sect that offers some noise that is mistakenly assumed to be spirituality and Christianity. This relates to what I believe is the second reason, namely that the state church back home is unsatisfactory. The pastors are royal officials, and the individual Christian sees the state church not only as an institution through which he can get his religious needs fulfilled, but also as a secular force. But spiritual needs and force cannot be harmonized, and people cannot believe that the state, with its worldly power and legislation, has anything to do with matters of the heart. Hence, in many places they don't attend public worship services. This gradually leads to complete indifference to religion. People grow cold to the Lutheran state church and fall into the arms of all kinds of mendacious sects. I don't see the answer in separating church and state, however; it must be something else. If we first foster inner life, the outward forms will naturally follow. Faith does not whimper, but says "where there is no way, I shall make a way."

Peter Christian Trandberg (1832–1896), a Lutheran revivalist from the Baltic island of Bornholm, withdrew from the state church before emigrating in 1882. Although he remained a Lutheran, he often attacked the irreligiosity of Danish immigrants and the Grundtvigian tendencies of many of their pastors. Trandberg taught at a Congregationalist seminary in Chicago from 1884 until 1890. (Source: *Skandinaven,* 3 June 1885.)

What reasonable and well-informed Christian would deny that the Lord has raised up and preserved a living, faithful flock even in the state churches? Even though God's Israel has lived in exile for more than fifteen hundred years (since the days of Constantine the Great), and in many respects has been bound and inhibited by worldly powers, the sun of righteousness has nevertheless sent its benevolent beams and healing power down upon the saints, and the source of life has let healing streams flow out to them. The inclusive churches have allowed these rays of grace and streams of life to pour out upon people who are not directly in their midst. The light and life of salvation have also come through the state churches to the Scandinavians in North America. We should all appreciate that and thank God.

But on the other hand, we should not overlook the faults of the state churches or inclusive churches. Sins, great sins and abomination—their sins will endure until the appointed time will render justice for their trespasses. And just as salvation, life, and blessings have come to Scandinavians in the New World from the faithful in the old country, so has also the impure and corrupt spirit and leaven of the state church been brought to our people in this land.

So many Scandinavian Lutheran pastors are infected with this spirit that it is difficult to know what to think of them. Since they preach Christian truths, for the most part, one should hope they are believers. Yet it cannot be denied that they so noticeably lack the fire and power of the Holy Spirit, as well as its fervor, warmth, and enthusiasm, that their preaching usually has no impact on the infidel masses here. Their sermons are foggy and unclear, lack luster, and are uninspiring. They fail to draw a distinct line between the way of life and the way of death. Hence, they usually have little influence on the people. All of God's children have reason to cry about this. Perhaps there is one true Christian among every hundred immigrants in the United States. A few of these have been converted in one way or another after arriving here. There may be two, three, four, or five believing, spiritually alive Christians among every hundred members of the so-called Scandinavian Lutheran churches in this country, not to mention the thousands and thousands who have turned their backs to God, the church, and Christianity. What we need here is a glowing word of revivalism and salvation among these dead or slumbering masses. If the Lord extended the lives of these priests so that they could preach for one hundred years, perhaps not a single soul would be brought to life and salvation through their preaching, even in those places where there may be hearts and ears receptive to the truth.

An immigrant from Fyn found a spiritual home among Methodists in New England. (Source: *Dansk Kristelig Talsmand,* 15 March 1884.)

Norwich, Connecticut
25 December 1884

It is Christmas, and my thoughts turn to Denmark. With sad joy I remember my childhood home where my parents, brothers, and friends live. I am alone in this foreign country. Alone! "Am I with you, or don't I mean anything to you?" That is what a gentle and friendly voice says. I recognize the voice; it is the voice of Jesus, my Lord and God. He is with me and means more to me than all the world. He is my Savior and hope of salvation. May He forgive me for saying "alone." That was only an old habit from the time before I knew Jesus.

Three and a half years ago I left Denmark to seek my fortune in the far West. Almost everything went well for me, but something was missing. Then, fourteen months ago, I went to a Methodist church with some friends. Later I attended often. I heard sermons about peace and salvation and an invitation to come to Jesus and drink the water of life freely, and to come just as we were. I felt that if I had to wait until I became better, I would never come to Jesus. On New Year's Eve, 1883–84, I said farewell to the world and all its pleasures and chose Jesus.

I went to a class meeting and asked for intercessory prayers. They were willing to pray for me. Their hearty "God bless you, brother" and friendly way of talking to me, together with my own struggle in prayer, gave me evidence within a few weeks that my sins had been forgiven through faith in Jesus Christ, our Lord. Is it so surprising that a short time later I asked to be admitted to your church? It is so surprising that I wanted to work for Jesus, who saved my soul from perdition, and that I chose the congregation in which I had been converted and whose pastor and members I had come to love like brothers and sisters, just as they had loved me?

If I have lost friends for the sake of Jesus, then He, true to His promises, has replaced them a hundredfold. May His name be praised forever. Dear countrymen, give your hearts to Jesus, just as you are. He will do everything.

> Rasmus Pedersen
> from Stubberup on Hindsholm

A Methodist missionary in Oregon described life in the Pacific Northwest. (Source: *Kristelig Talsmand,* 25 November 1892.)

> Portland, Oregon
> 26 September 1892

It might interest the reader of *Kristelig Talsmand* to hear how we are doing out here on the Pacific Coast.

As far as the climate is concerned, I suppose it can be compared with southern France or northern Italy. Here in Portland, 160 kilometers from the sea, we seldom if ever see snow. Once in a while a little falls, but it melts in a short time. During the winter months we get a lot of rain, but it is not so cold that roses fail to blossom all winter. It is warm in the summer, of course, but we do not have the stifling heat that plagues the Midwest. The terrible thunderstorms that cause so much damage in the East are also completely unknown here. Many Norwegians and Danes live here on the coast; there are probably fifty thousand of our people spread around the towns and countryside of Washington and Oregon. The soil is generally fertile, but since most of it is heavily forested, it takes a long time and a lot of work to clear the land for agriculture.

Regarding spiritual matters, we now have congregations in all of the larger towns as well as several out in the Scandinavian settlements. As you know, our mission out here is only a few years old, but God has blessed our work and it has borne fruit. Twenty-three preachers attended our recent conference; only three were absent. They work in six states. You can see that our mission field is large. We hope that the Lord of the harvest will send more workers to His vineyard here. Our brothers began this year with a prayer that it would be a blessed twelve months, and with His help it will be.

Let me conclude by wishing God's best blessings on you as well as on all of the other brothers and congregations in Denmark. We know that you are interested in our work here in the "far West," and we hope to hear that you are doing well in Denmark.

Yours in Christ,

Egert M. Stangeland

Burrel Smith helped organize the Methodist church at Perth Amboy, New Jersey, in 1874. After spending the 1880s in Wisconsin, he returned to that congregation. (Source: *Kristelig Talsmand,* 8 April 1892.)

Some time has passed since I sent my last letter to my beloved native land and to *Kristelig Talsmand.* I request the editor to receive these lines. I find it interesting to read the newspaper and see the progress our denomination is making in beautiful little Denmark. May God be with it always, and may He lead His work to victory! After the unfortunate fire in the church in Holstebro, I see that a much larger and more attractive building has been erected. It was a joy to read about the ceremonious dedication that took place a while ago. May the house of God always be used to the glory of the Lord and for the conversion and salvation of many souls. I often read in the columns of *Kristelig Talsmand* that there is strife and dissension, resistance and persecution, even from people who call themselves Christians; but these things only confirm the words of Paul that "they who would live divinely in Jesus Christ shall be persecuted."

Here in America we have to drink from the same cup, served us by our countrymen who, in the name of religion, despise us believers and ridicule life in Christ. The Methodist teaching of God's perfecting grace has from the beginning been despised by those who call themselves Christians but are insincere in their faith. Wesley's diary testifies abundantly to this. But it also testifies to the spiritual victory in the struggle against the forces of darkness and the worldly lords who ruled England during that dismal period. The powerful conversion of thousands of souls from darkness to light and from Satan's power to God's, their glorious testimony and the saving grace of Jesus, together with their holy behavior during life and triumph in death, are evidence of our church's spirituality. The Lord alone deserves credit for the victory of Methodism in all countries. . . .

After an absence of eleven years, I have returned from the West to the friendly city of Perth Amboy where, almost twenty years ago, I first preached in a little schoolhouse that we used until we were able to build our present sanctuary. I must say that I feel quite at home among brothers and sisters here. Quite a few of the original members still live here. Others have gone elsewhere in America, and some have gone to their eternal rest. My wife and I have been given a friendly reception by all our friends here, both old and new. May the Lord bless all of us and reward our united effort with the conversion of many souls! Please pray for us and visit us.

Perth Amboy, whose population has doubled since I was here before, is only thirty kilometers from New York, and a round-trip ticket costs only forty cents. It is a good town for workers. There are many different kinds of factories and other places of work, and the average daily wage is as good as anywhere. Spiritually Perth Amboy is, with a few exceptions, the same as Denmark. The town is well located on the bay that leads into New York, and is not far from the Atlantic Ocean. The climate is mild, and Perth Amboy does not have the severe winters of the West, where many settlers have to endure a lot of hardship because of lack of fuel and suitable housing. If any of our friends in Denmark wish to emigrate to America, I believe that with a good conscience I can recommend this place as much as any other.

In my thoughts I often visit the congregations back home. I still have some old acquaintances here and there. Best regards to all of my known and unknown friends. God bless the superintendent, the editor, and all of the preachers. God bless Denmark!

Burrel Smith

Carl Eltzholtz, a prominent Methodist minister and temperance advocate,
emigrated in 1887. He found Chicago a promising field for evangelizing
Scandinavians. (Source: *Dansk Kristelig Talsmand,* 15 September 1887.)

I ended my last letter with our arrival in New York. When the
ship anchored at the pier, Pastor Hansen came on board to
welcome us. He received us with great friendliness and was very
helpful with our belongings during the long inspection by the
customs authorities. When that was finished, we followed Brother
Hansen to his pleasant home, where we were received with
considerable friendliness. On Saturday, 11 June, we paid a visit to
the *Mission Rooms,* where Dr. Reid (one of the leaders of our
mission board) gave us a hearty welcome. The next day I
preached twice in the Norwegian Methodist church in Brooklyn.
In the morning a lot of people attended and the Lord was with
us. It was a great joy to meet some of my spiritual children here.
On Monday we went back to *Mission Rooms* to discuss western
Europe with the mission board. The next day we drove across the
remarkable Brooklyn Bridge and walked back. It was under
construction when we left America about nine years ago. This
bridge is truly one of the wonders of the world. In the afternoon
we visited Greenwood Cemetery, which is so famous for beautiful
and costly monuments. In the evening I gave a temperance lecture
in the Norwegian Methodist church in Brooklyn. Wednesday
morning we left New York on the New York Central Railroad
and, after a very tiring journey, arrived in Chicago Thursday
evening about 6 o'clock. It was terribly hot. The heat and dust
made the trip difficult. Since I'm writing about the journey from
New York to Chicago, I can't fail to mention the trip along the
Hudson River. The landscape that unfolds before the traveler's
eyes for a very long stretch is especially beautiful. We also crossed
the big suspension bridge spanning the fearsome abyss at the
world-famous Niagara Falls.

Upon arriving in Chicago, we went to Pastor Treider's pleasant
home, where we immediately felt heartily welcome. We also met
Brother O. Jacobsen, pastor of Maplewood Norwegian Methodist
Church. On Friday we felt somewhat recovered from the long
journey. Thanks be to God for graciously leading us so far. It is

indeed refreshing for the body and soul of a traveler to find friends—as we did in New York and Chicago—who are willing to open their hearts and homes. I have not adjusted my watch since we left Copenhagen. Unless it is fooling me, it is 10:34 in the evening in Copenhagen, but only 4:34 in the afternoon here in Chicago—we have come so far west. On Sunday, 19 June, I preached in the morning at the Maplewood church and in the evening at the church on West Indiana Street. Attendance was good at both churches. In both places I had the joy of meeting many good friends from previous times. The joy was mutual.

Just to show you how much influence the Danish-Norwegian Methodist Church has on the people in Chicago, I'll mention that we presently have five congregations in the Chicago area belonging to the Danish-Norwegian Conference. I believe there are just as many Swedish Methodist churches in the area. . . .

Carl F. Eltzholtz

In a letter to a colleague N. Hansen Nyrop praised religious egalitarianism and commented on Danish Methodists' spiritual and material progress in South Dakota. (Source: *Kristelig Talsmand,* 22 June 1894.)

Sioux Falls, South Dakota
22 May 1894

Dear Pastor Thaarup,

. . . Yes, religion is a force in this country, and its considerable influence is largely due to freedom in the area of religion. We don't have a state church tying people to a national creed. The churches in America are more independent and not tied to the beliefs of the majority. In the churches there aren't any rented pews where the big capitalists sit alongside the high officials. All of the seats are available to the beggars and the president himself. A millionaire can sit beside a worker without blushing with embarrassment. Once in one of the Danish state churches I saw a poorly dressed woman sit where a local gentleman usually sat. When he came in a bit later and saw the woman, he chased her out. The poor woman hurried out of the church as though some supernatural being had punished her, but it was only a gentleman.

The apostle did not mean that rich people should be able to buy the best seats in church; he wrote: "My brethren, show no partiality as you hold the faith of our Lord Jesus Christ, the Lord of glory. For if a man with gold rings and in fine clothing comes into your assembly, and a poor man in shabby clothing also comes in, and you pay attention to the one who wears the fine clothing, and say, 'Have a seat here, please,' while you say to the poor man, 'Stand there,' or, 'Sit at my feet,' have you not made distinctions among yourselves, and become judges with evil thoughts?" (James 2:1–4) In the eastern part of the United States this unfortunate practice has been adopted in a few places, but we will pray to the Lord to keep the Methodist Church uncorrupted in this respect.

We Methodists are the most respected denomination in America. In Denmark there are Lutheran churches everywhere, but here our church buildings can be seen in the towns as well as in the country. As a result, we're not called "heretics" or "fanatics." Once in a while we meet a Lutheran immigrant who, with his pipe in his pocket and a straw in his mouth, tries to convince us that he belongs to the only true church while we Methodists are thieves and robbers. In Sioux Falls, which belongs to the district to which the conference in Chicago assigned me, there are three Methodist churches.

This town has a rather attractive location on the banks of the Sioux River close to a large waterfall. That is why Sioux Falls is so named. The town has about twelve thousand inhabitants, nineteen churches, four universities, and residences for three bishops.

Our work among the Scandinavians here began two years ago, but due to various hindrances has proceeded slowly. Last winter we had several good meetings, though, as a result of which many souls were saved and some were admitted to the church on probation.

The center of my own activity is Viborg, a small town originally named Danville but rechristened Viborg after Viborg, Denmark, because so many Danes live there. We have a congregation of seventy members there, as well as a sanctuary and a parsonage. The buildings are not suitable, however, so we plan to build new ones this summer. The foundations have already been laid, and we will get to work next week. We hope that within a few months

Viborg will boast two new buildings and that many souls will find salvation under the roof of our church.

A large number of our members are farmers. An American farmer owns as much land as a squire in Denmark, but since the land is not expensive our farmers are not rich. Most of the people in the area of Viborg are Danes who came to Dakota ten or twelve years ago, bought land, and built their first homes by digging cellars in the ground and covering them with sod roofs. At that time there wasn't a building to be seen, only the immense prairie. It was impossible to imagine that people lived underground. Huge swarms of grasshoppers plagued Dakota in those days, darkening the sun and the sky. The farmers often lost everything they had sown because the grasshoppers ate the crops right down to the soil. Many of the families were poor when they came here and lived for several years without any comforts. Their only food was corn, and they made coffee from rye that they had to drink without cream or sugar. Now most of the people in this area are quite prosperous. The sod huts have given way to attractive houses. Flat wild prairies have been transformed into waving fields of grain. Pieces of land once bought for two hundred dollars are now valued at five thousand dollars.

Most of the farmers have organs in their homes, and their children are trained in music. The children are educated in rural schoolhouses. Many go to school until they are twenty, so they get a good education.

Our Viborg congregation has two additional part-time preachers and two Sunday schools. We worked hard for the Lord last winter and saw the Lord lead sinners to the foot of the cross and set free those who were captives to sin. In the hope that brothers and sisters in Denmark will be with us in their prayers, I conclude this letter and send my greetings to all the readers of *Talsmand*, especially those whom I know.

N. Hansen Nyrop

The Baptist minister in Racine, Wisconsin, reported that his congregation was active and that the Lutherans attacked his ministry. (Source: *Den danske Evangelist*, May 1869.)

Racine, Wisconsin
1 April 1869

. . . I began my ministry in this congregation in September of last year. My family remained in Chicago, where I had spent five years preaching the gospel in addition to my secular work. On 1 January I was ordained with prayer and the laying on of hands by the elders. Beforehand, however, some of the brothers examined me to determine my qualifications for the position. Niels Nielsen from Chicago, L. Petersen from Raymond, and Jens Henriksen from Freeborn County, Minnesota, attended my ordination, as did two American ministers, Rawly and Wiinyard [sic], a Negro minister from Racine.

After the worship service we had a Christian feast that lasted until 4 A.M. That night we had the joy of hearing many glorious and encouraging speeches. One brother spoke about obeying God's commandment regarding baptism. He said it was an offense to God whenever a converted person disobeyed the Lord's will in such a clear matter. One man, whose wife belonged to our congregation, became so bitter that he walked out of the meeting. Jens Henriksen suggested that we pray for the man. We did so, and our prayers served a dual purpose. One young girl was awakened by our prayers; she is now a beloved sister in our congregation. We hope that the man who walked out will soon be immersed. We see that prayer has a purpose and that the Lord is with us.

Here in Racine there is some agitation among the Scandinavians. Our worship services are well attended, and occasionally the main floor of the church as well as the balcony is overflowing, even though the building holds a considerable number of people. The Lutheran pastor here in town is doing everything he can to keep the people away from the truth, but the harder he tries to stop the truth from spreading the greater progress it makes. The Lord's Word produces glorious fruit. Since 1 January we have had the joy of baptizing eight new members, and many other people are seeking the truth. The congregation currently numbers ninety members. Our Sunday school, directed by Brother Simmers from

Copenhagen, includes between twenty and thirty children. I'm not
sure exactly how many. . . .

H. A. Reichenback

*Laust Jakobsen, a Baptist lay evangelist, prepared himself for church work
in southern Minnesota and adjacent areas of Iowa and Wisconsin. (Source:
Den danske Evangelist, January 1875.)*

LaCrosse, Wisconsin
11 December 1874

. . . I left Denmark on 13 April and reached America on 4
May. Our heavenly Father has in his grace led me and those who
traveled with me though all of the dangers and difficulties so that
we arrived safely at our various destinations.

I am now living in Freeborn County, Minnesota, with my
parents and five brothers and sisters in a large Danish settlement.
We are only a few kilometers from a new chapel that belonged to
a Danish Baptist congregation of about 110 members. All of them
lived in this area. I knew and loved many of them in the old
country. There is also a small Danish congregation in Albert Lea,
not far from here. I knew many of its members in Denmark.

On Sunday, 10 May, I worshiped for the first time in the chapel
of the Clarks Grove congregation. I later handed over my
membership certificate to the minister and that congregation.
Since they already had a minister, I thought I would get some rest
after preaching the gospel strenuously for eight or nine years.

What a joy it was to sit in the pews and listen to the minister, J.
Henriksen, or to my boyhood friend, J. Sørensen! But it was not
long before I, too, was preaching to the congregation once in a
while. I mentioned getting some rest, but did not want to be
unemployed. Before I left Denmark I promised not to become a
farmer in America. If I could not find religious employment
there, I would return to Denmark.

Since I wanted to learn how to read English, and because I
wanted to travel in Iowa and Wisconsin, I asked for permission to

attend the elementary school in our district. Permission was granted, and I went to school with the small children from 11 May until 25 July. In all, I went to school forty-seven and a half days.

I worked a little for my parents at harvest time. I also used those autumn days to teach myself more English, write letters, and visit the homes of other church members. . . .

In many parts of America our countrymen lead peaceful lives and lose some of the disdain that they usually have for us and our Biblical principles in Denmark. It is not unusual for a Danish Baptist preacher to visit a settlement here and have all of the Danes in the area gather to hear him.

Regarding the respectability of Danes in America, that is often because it is very difficult to get intoxicating beverages in many of the areas where they live. Besides, the Danes are so few that they don't have many parties. We Baptists get more respect here because America doesn't have a state church. In some areas the Lutheran pastors visit them only rarely, and they can hardly get their children baptized. In Cedar Falls, however, the Danes have sufficient opportunity to indulge in every kind of sin, and have Lutheran churches in town as well as in the country. A Danish Lutheran pastor ministers to them. As a result, most of them are unwilling to listen to us. Conditions there are about the same as back in Denmark. . . .

Laust Jakobsen

Jakobsen subsequently became the minister of a rural Baptist congregation in Kansas. (Source: Den danske Evangelist, February 1879.)

Jamestown, Cloud County
Kansas
2 January 1879

Dear Brothers and Sisters in the Lord,

God's peace be with you! It has been almost five years since I left you, and it has been a long time since I wrote to you in *Den danske Evangelist*. I shall now break my silence and let you know that last June I finished my service in the Danish-Norwegian missionary organization. The following month I married a woman who was converted and baptized in Chicago immediately after coming to America five years ago.

Shortly after visiting the Danish Baptist congregation in this area, I accepted its unanimous call to become its minister. The members promised to support me to the extent their God-given property allowed. After serious reflection, I accepted the call, but I reserved the right to travel around a bit and preach the gospel in other settlements. I arrived here on 31 July and immediately began work. Shortly thereafter the Lord chose to put my dear wife into the sickbed. Before she had fully recovered, however, I fell sick. It was some kind of liver trouble that lasted for six weeks. After I recovered it came back again and again.

The congregation decided to build a manse last summer, and one brother donated an *acre* of land for it, and that piece of real estate is now my earthly home. Friends and fellow believers bring good, praise the Lord, and I can say that I am happy in my marriage as well as in my new position. The congregation numbers thirty-odd members who are quite spread out. There are also some Danish families that attend our worship services occasionally. There are many Scandinavian settlements around Kansas. Brother George P. Petersen came here while I was sick. He preached some in our church when I was sick or in other areas. He has preached in Danish and English in various settlements.

Because of my illness I have not been able to travel around much. On only two occasions have I visited a settlement thirteen kilometers west of here, and I have gone once each to two other settlements, forty kilometers east and one hundred kilometers west of us. We have our regular worship service every Sunday as well as Sunday school for the children and a Bible class for the adults. In addition, we have a prayer meeting once a week.

Since I came here we have had to bury two members and five children. One other man is dying. I believe our congregation is spiritually stagnant. I wish the Lord would send the Holy Spirit upon us abundantly and let a real revival take place in our midst.

Brothers and sisters, pray for me!

L. Jakobsen

L. Jørgensen, a Baptist minister in Wisconsin, ministered to Union casualties during the Civil War. (Source: Den danske Evangelist, April 1864.)

Raymond, Wisconsin
12 November 1863

. . . In addition to my duties here, I have been called to various places during the past year. The first was to the army at the request of the government. I helped the sick and wounded, especially the Scandinavians, since the government was not in a position to give them sufficient help. At that time there were more than one hundred thousand sick and several thousand wounded after the large battle at Murfreesboro that lasted three or four days. I collected several hundred dollars' worth of shoes, clothes, books, and so on in our congregation and from other sources. I also had about two thousand tracts in English, German, and Danish. I visited about eighteeen hospitals and camps, distributed books and other items, and spoke words of consolation and admonition to healthy, sick, and dying men. All of the horrible scenes I witnessed while staying in hospitals both day and night took their toll on my body and soul. The most heart-rending thing were the cries of the wounded in the dark and stillness of night. When oaths and swearing were added to the cries, it was like hell to my ears. I undertook this trip of twenty-seven hundred kilometers in February and March. Upon returning home I became very sick and was close to death, but the Lord protected me.

My second journey, which covered more than one thousand kilometers, was to Minnesota in June and July with a group to establish a new Danish colony out there, where land is cheaper and it is therefore easier to make a home than here where everything is relatively expensive. I also began the first Danish congregation there.

According to rumors and the newspapers, Indians have attacked Danes in Minnesota. For the sake of those who are concerned about the fate of our brothers and sisters there, I would like to add that none of our fellow believers have been harmed by, or have even seen, hostile Indians.[6] I have seen, spoken with, and traded with many Indians, and all of them have been very friendly. The fact that they revolted last year was entirely the fault of the whites' fraudulant ways of trading, but nobody says anything about that. . . .

L. Jørgensen

A Baptist couple in Nebraska acknowledged American religious freedom but also expressed their alienation. (Source: *Den danske Evangelist,* April 1885.)

Yale, Valley County, Nebraska
12 January 1885

We are well here, thank God, but there are only a few of us and we are foreigners in a land where the people do not understand our message of the grace and love of God. There are only five of us believers in the area and three more about twenty-five kilometers from here. We can gather only once or twice a month.

It would be desirable if there were more of us, but we don't want to convince anyone to come over here. There are more things wrong with America than you in Denmark can imagine. People write home about all the positive things, but most forget to mention everything that is negative. It is not easy to adjust to a foreign country, and no more than back in Denmark is everyone successful here.

If we could take our property back to the old country, we would prefer to be there. Admittedly, we have more freedom to assemble here, in schoolhouses, for example, than in Denmark, and Baptists are not a despised sect here. But when we try to speak about the truth to Danish Lutherans here we discover that they have the same prejudiced view of us as in Denmark. The more we try to imitate our Lord and Savior, the more we feel alienated from the

6. This is almost certainly a reference to the "Sioux Uprising" of 1862 in Minnesota.

so-called Christians. We learn that the way to the Kingdom of God is just as narrow here as in Denmark. . . .

Niels Poulsen Dahl
and wife

The Seventh-day Adventists offered strong competition in some immigrant communities. (Source: *Den danske Evangelist,* February 1873.)

Freeborn County, Minnesota
4 December 1872

Unfortunately, I do not have much to report regarding the growth of the Kingdom of God. There are revivals among the Americans in various places, but among the Danes in Minnesota there is little or no increase in the number of spiritually awakened.

L. Jørgensen, who once contributed to a split in our congregation, has now joined the Seventh-day Adventists. He also preaches to them. If he keeps any Sabbath at all, it is Saturday. John Matteson was here this autumn. A few members of our congregation joined the Adventists, and many Lutherans were baptized. The sincerity of their conversions is questionable, however. The Adventists trap people with the letter of the Law. The most harmful thing about their doctrine is that they console the ungodly in all of their evil by teaching that the soul dies or is annihilated and that the Devil shall be burned up and become ashes or cease to exist. This doctrine, which is a comfortable cushion for the ungodly, has unfortunately made a strong impression on the Danes and other people.

Under the leadership of a Swedish immigrant, John Forsgren, Scandinavian Mormons assembled in Iowa before beginning a carefully organized trek to Utah. (Source: *Skandinaviens Stjerne,* 15 June 1853.)

Keokuk, Iowa
18 May 1853

Dear Brother Hansen,
Today I'm going to sit down and write you a short letter as

Brother Forsgren requested. He went to get our oxen, but we
expect him to be back this evening. We have camped here for
three pleasant weeks. This Mississippi River is on one side of us
and the forest on the other. Many people have already left and
gone west. Our gatherings, songs, and prayers can be heard for
miles. Tents and wagons form streets and avenues, so our camp
looks like an entire town. The most unpleasant thing are the
violent thunderstorms that strike now and then. The air is pure
and there hasn't been any illness among the Saints. Those Danes
who were alive the last time I wrote are still living. Brother
Forsgren has replaced the dead with American Saints. We have
thirty-four wagons and four oxen for each wagon. They cost us so
much, though, that the cows we hoped to get cannot be had.

All of the men in charge of our money have acted fairly. There
are a few dissatisfied people among us, but there will always be a
few of them. They can go wherever they want and grumble until
they are blue in the face.

Any reasonable person can understand that this kind of a
journey will seem unusual to those who are not acquainted with
immigrant life. For the Saints, however, it is easy, because they
have hope, faith, and love, and they know that their difficulties do
not equal the glory that will be revealed to God's people.

I have had the opportunity to become acquainted with the
quality of men I heard about in Denmark: Brother Haight, D.
Spencer, Wheelock, Joseph Young, Orson Pratt, Clawson, and
many others. I can testify that they are messengers sent by the
Lord. If I could preach again in Denmark, I would implore my
countrymen twice as loudly to leave Babylon and come to the land
where all noble souls can gather. I would sacrifice my life and
everything else for the fact that Joseph Smith was sent by God as
a prophet of your salvation in the time that is at hand. I testify
that is true in the name of our almighty Lord, Jesus Christ. Amen.

A plan to break camp the day after tomorrow and head toward
Kanesville. All of the brothers and sisters in New Orleans will be
home this year. Agent Brown expects two more ships from
England, and after they arrive he will come up here. Only three
hundred are coming up from St. Louis; twelve hundred will stay
behind until next year. . . .

C. Christiansen

A missionary who helped Scandinavian proselytes emigrate to Utah described life in a Mormon wagon train. (Source: Skandinaviens Stjerne, 1 October 1861.)

Fort Laramie

19 August 1861

President John Van Cott

Dear Brother,

You probably expected me to write to you from Florence, but it was impossible for me to write because all of my time was taken up with the Saints. I'll never forget Florence, but thank God everything is going well and now we have arrived here. Everyone is looking forward to traveling on to Zion.

When we arrived in Florence, about two hundred of the church's wagons were there to receive the poor. I have the joy of reporting that not a single one of the Danes was left behind. Those who did not have sufficient means traveled on the church's wagons. We had a few deaths, including Sister Olsen from Nørrebro, who was buried in St. Joseph, and a girl, age eighteen, from Vendsyssel as well as a widow, age seventy, from the Aalborg Conference, both of whom were buried on the prairie. Otherwise, health in the company has been good except for the usual problems of adjusting to a different climate. Two couples were married on the prairie. We haven't seen a single buffalo and only a few Indians, who proved to be very friendly. A short distance from Loup Fork eighteen hundred Indians were encamped and planning to wage war against the Sioux. Most of the tribes have gone that way. . . .

At first we had sixty wagons in our company with A. C. Volly as captain. Now we have divided into two companies. Elder Porter is the captain of the second. Olin Hansen is in charge of defending the first company and Phister the second. I serve as chaplain, adviser, and so on. Everything is going well and nobody wants to turn back. All of our cattle and wagons are in good condition. I have six oxen and two cows. My wife churns butter and makes good coffee, and is doing better than ever. All of us are in good health, thank God.

I have many other things to write, but I have to mail this letter

soon. You will hear from me again as soon as I can write. I would
be happy to receive a few lines from you.

N. Wilhelmsen

*Christian Madsen, who had been a Mormon missionary in Denmark, de-
scribed an immigrant trek to Utah and the so-called "Mormon War" with
American troops.* (Source: *Skandinaviens Stjerne,* 15 October 1858.)

Salt Lake City
25 July 1858

Dear Brother Widerborg,

We arrived happy and well on 9 July after traveling across the
prairie for thirty-nine days. The company consisted of about forty
men with forty-seven mules and horses. Brother H. Eldridge was
our captain, and Joseph W. Young was captain of the guard. We
assume that the rest of the company, including Brother Iversen,
left Iowa three weeks after us and that they will arrive here early
in September.

I drove one wagon with four mules across the prairie. Knud
Svendsen from Vendsyssel drove another. Each of these two
wagons accommodated five people, and each constituted a kitchen.
Ædler was our cook, Øman cooked for the second kitchen, and
Poulsen for the third. The entire company consisted of thirteen
wagons and five horsemen. Everyone, both people and animals,
survived the ordeal. All of the Indians we met were friendly. We
kept a strong watch at night and sometimes during the day.

Fourteen of the men are now scattered around the valleys. Some
of us are staying here in the city a while to work during the
harvest. Knud Svendsen and I have worked for Brother Benson
for six days. We've built fences, done gardening and carpentry,
and so on. Tomorrow we're going out to cut grass. I expect to
work on a threshing machine for Brother Little, who is Brother
Orson Pratt's adviser. Then I might get some land in one of the
settlements, get it planted, and work for the Kingdom of God in
accordance with the prophecies and the advice of my brothers.
Brother Erastus Snow and I visited Brigham Young on Sunday, so
I saw and spoke with that glorious and divinely gifted man whose

influence produces peace, joy, life, wisdom, and love!

The American troops are now on their way back to the United States. I don't know what the conditions of the peace treaty are, but Brigham has said that if the United States does not abide by them, there will be trouble. The States have to withdraw from the "Mormon War" without losing face. Because of the mercy of the Lord, they got off without being punished for their injustice. The entire army, including Cumming and others, can thank Brigham Young that they are still alive today. The young lions of Zion were not bloodthirsty, but they were justifiably indignant and wanted to punish this great injustice as a testimony to the world that the Lord had delivered the army into the hands of God's people and that, according to Brigham Young, for a few days a third of our boys were ready to wipe them off the face of the earth.

There are a lot of heathens here these days, especially people who belong to the army. They are orderly and don't disturb the peace or harm anyone. The merchants are unhappy, though, because when the troops leave, the profitable trade will be over. . . .

Christian A. Madsen

O. N. Liljenquist, a tailor from Copenhagen, found life in Utah bountiful and encouraged other Danes to emigrate. (Source: Skandinaviens Stjerne, 15 June 1869.)

Hyrum City, Cache Valley,
Utah
15 April 1869

President Jesse N. Smith
Dear Brother,

It was six years ago when I wrote my last letter to Scandinavia, and I'm sure it was to you.

We have been very busy since last autumn building the railroad. This enterprise has given the local residents several thousand dollars. Recently the Saints in Hyrum have realized that they should pay their immigration debts and contribute something to delivering poor people from Babylon. I am sure that if our more prosperous brothers in Utah were fully aware of the need and misery of their fellow Mormons in Scandinavia, they would contribute more toward liberating them.

The grasshoppers did a lot of damage to the crops last year, but we were nevertheless able to sell a great deal of grain to the railroad agents. We also sold a large amount of timber to the railroad. Last month a branch of our Cooperative Mercantile Institution was opened here. Business is lively and everyone seems to be satisfied with it. The Female Relief Society is making good progress. Its members have planted mulberry trees on a large piece of land here in town and want to produce silk. We have two schools in addition to a Sunday school and an evening school where we practice reading and writing the Deseret Alphabet.[7] A new steam-powered sawmill produced 130,000 board feet of lumber last autumn, and a new shingle machine has also been built. We expect to have our new church building ready this summer if we can get all of the materials for it together.

The health of the community is better than ever, and the Saints are as happy as can be expected. I am happy to report that there is no poverty in town, and the people are united on economic matters. "Civilization" is marching forward, but fortunately it passes through Utah Territory without leaving behind any of the ungodliness that accompanies it. . . . Our struggle against ungodliness is by no means over, but our aim is to denounce all injustice until God's peace and blessing cover the earth.

When I was a missionary in Scandinavia, many people asked me how long it would be until God's judgment fell on the gentiles. Perhaps they asked me so that they could postpone their conversion until the eleventh hour. I want to tell such people how much they are missing by not obeying the gospel the first time they hear it. They could be united with God's people here and receive the blessings and teachings that prepare us for the great day. But they have put off their conversion and will not be endowed with the glory that awaits the humble and the faithful.

To the Saints in Scandinavia I wish to say this: Be courageous, because your deliverance will follow shortly. Your brothers in Zion are concerned about you and are working to help you emigrate.

7. Introduced in 1854, the Deseret Alphabet of 38 phonetic characters was intended to assist immigrants in learning English.

Whether you emigrate this year or next is of little consequence if you are true to your religion and patient in times of trial. The Lord is guiding everything for your benefit, and I pray that His blessing be upon you.

O. N. Liljenquist

A former tailor from Vendsyssel in northern Jutland commented on several aspects of life in Manti, Utah, a community with many Danish immigrants. (Source: Skandinaviens Stjerne, 15 March 1870.)

Manti, San Pete County
Utah Territory
10 February 1870

President Jesse N. Smith
Dear Brother,

This is just a short letter to let you know that my family and I are doing well in the Church of Jesus Christ of Latter-day Saints, with Brigham Young as its president, prophet, and leader.

We built a stone house last summer. It has a livingroom, two bedrooms, a kitchen, a cellar, and an attic. We have also planted several fruit trees, including some mulberry trees, and about fifty kinds of flowers. I am a farmer, gardener, tithes accountant, and postmaster.

The women here in Manti and in other settlements held meetings to protest the Cragin and Cullom bills and all other similar bills.[8] We are in the process of buying our land from the United States. It seems a little strange to buy land that was once purchased from the Indians.

We are happy that the railroad has reached Salt Lake City, and we hope it will be extended southward through the territory, if the United States would just let us live in peace. If not, we will still live according to our religion, come life or death. We are not afraid of them. They can kill the body but God, our eternal Father, controls both body and soul. There are many upright

8. The Cragin Bill of 1867 would have abolished jury trials in polygamy cases. Two years later, the Cullom Bill tried to subject Utah to total federal control. See Mulder, *Homeward to Zion*, p. 289.

Saints here, but also some "bad eggs" who take the easy way to salvation that the Josephites, Godbeites, and Harrisonites offer.[9] The way to the Kingdom of God is narrow, and few remain true until the goal is reached.

Every other Saturday we rejoice in the School of the Prophets in Ephraim. Last year we harvested a lot of wheat and other feed, even though the grasshoppers came. In all likelihood they will be back again this year. The Saints in Ephraim who belong to the School of the Prophets joined with those in Manti to have a Christmas party that about four hundred Saints attended. We had the joy of President Orson Hyde's presence. We have had a mild winter, but there has been some illness, especially mumps, which our daughter Grethe has. . . .

Jens C. A. Weibye

In a letter to his Mormon father-in-law in Denmark, Carl Larsen defended polygamy and commented disparagingly on government officials. (Source: *Skandinaviens Stjerne,* 1 March 1871.)

Salt Lake City
19 January 1871

Elder P. O. Thomassen
Dear Brother,

Thank you for your letter of 20 December. Since returning from my mission in Denmark I have had some amusing experiences, including a few religious ones. I'll try to tell you a little about them. First, the "learned" chaplain of the American Congress, Dr. Newman, challenged our president to a debate on the frequently discussed question, "Does the Bible sanction polygamy?" Brigham Young found it beneath his dignity to defend our principle, but sent Orson Pratt in his stead. The debate lasted three days. The first two Elder Pratt lathered his learned opponent, and the third he shaved him as smooth as an eel. I attended the entire debate. Shortly afterward several American newspapers, both in California and the eastern states,

---

9. The three groups were sects on the periphery of the Church of Jesus Christ of Latter-day Saints.

wrote things like: "The learned Reverend Dr. Newman recently went to 'the city of the Saints' to convince both the prophet and all true Mormons that polygamy is wrong. He wanted to point out verses in the Bible that forbid its practice. Old Brigham did not himself refute Dr. Newman, but sent one of his apostles, Orson Pratt, who did it so impressively that we must tell the learned gentleman from Washington the same thing the Savior told the woman: 'Go and sin no more.'"

Then Rabbi Sneerson, a Jewish clergyman from Jerusalem, delivered a lecture in the old tabernacle about Jewish manners and customs, faith and hope. He and his fellow believers are certain that the God of Israel will gather them to the promised land. Toward the end of his speech he said loudly and clearly, "In Jerusalem there are many Jews who have more than one wife, because the Law of Moses does not forbid it." As you know, I am not a polygamist.

Secretary of State William Seward stopped here while traveling to China. He attended the worship service in the new tabernacle, where Brigham Young preached that day. I don't know what Seward thought of it. Brigham and Captain Hooper helped the decrepit old gentleman back to his coach after the worship service. . . .

At the moment there are a lot of miserable scoundrels here who are changing the laws of both God and men, such as Supreme Court justices, marshalls, generals, and so on. The Devil will have his day. Perhaps the Methodist minister was right when he said at the funeral of our deceased Governor Shaffer: "He has died and gone to heaven; you, my friends United States government officials, and I will not see him any more." Judging by his own words, both he and the officials are going to hell, because if they went to heaven, I suppose they would meet the governor.

I haven't seen your family recently, but I know they are well. I've had to lie in bed for several days, but this evening I got up to write these lines while my wife and Mrs. Madsen, who lives with us, are at the theater to pay tribute to Miss Adams's beneficence work. I twisted my right ankle a while ago and haven't been able to walk, but I hope to be healthy again in a few days.

As you know, I have a good job as assistant bookkeeper for the Walker brothers. I am currently earning one hundred dollars a

month. Our business is lively and indications are that it will get
even better, so I expect to have more work and, hopefully, a
higher salary. . . .

Your son-in-law,
Carl Larsen

*Despite the anti-Mormon literature, which began to flood Denmark in the
1850s, describing the alleged enslavement of women in polygamous Utah, a
female immigrant wrote about the joys of living there.* (Source: *Skandinaviens Stjerne,* 15 January 1858.)

Farmington, Davis County
Utah Territory
24 July 1857

Dear Brothers and Sister,

I could not resist the temptation to write to you, because I know
all of you will be happy to hear from Zion, your home. I long
deeply to hear from you, from little Denmark, and to know whom
the Lord has given the grace to emigrate home this year. I would
also like to know whether any of my friends or acquaintances have
joined the Church. I know that the work of the Lord goes forward
with power every day, and it is a joy to hear the testimony that is
constantly given to the Danish Saints.

I have not yet had the opportunity to give you a description of
this area, the beautiful valleys between the mountains. All of
nature is remarkably beautiful out here. Salt Lake City lies in a
lovely valley surrounded by high mountains that form a wall
around it. The city is not densely built up, like cities in Denmark.
Nevertheless, it holds several thousand inhabitants. The houses are
so far from each other that each one has a garden and a yard.
Many people also have several *acres* of land outside the city. The
streets are wide but unpaved. The sidewalks are made of clay and
are lined with trees, as are the streets. Clear water from the
mountains flows along both sides of the street like streams. It is
fresh and delicious. It is remarkable to look up at the high
mountains, which in many places are covered with forest. People
drive up there to get timber and fuel. The cattle always run loose,
and it is strange to see horses, cows, sheep, and all kinds of cattle

grazing in the mountains. The slopes are very steep in many
places, but they are so accustomed to it that it is nothing for them
to run up and down. This is true not only of the Salt Lake Valley,
but of the other valleys as well. Every city or town is surrounded
by mountains. In some places there are sulphurous mountains,
from which flows boiling water. I traveled past one such place
between Salt Lake City and Farmington.

People here dress quite like the Danes, especially the ladies.
They wear round hats. The men's clothing resembles that of
sailors; in the summer they wear colored shirts of chintz and in
winter of wool. They usually wear coats and have straw hats as
well as gray and brown plush hats. Their military uniform is a
dark blue coat with gold buttons and gold braid, dark trousers
with scarlet piping, a scarlet scarf, and now they have a new kind
of hat made of black felt and silk plush adorned with black
feathers. They are round and go up like a sugar loaf but look
dashing. . . . The Fourth of July was American Independence
Day and was celebrated everywhere in the United States. Here in
Farmington it was celebrated with music and a military parade
through the streets. Today is 24 July, when we remember the
founding of the Church in the desert. The celebration was held in
a forest in the mountains several kilometers from Salt Lake
City. . . .

Marie Louise Lautrup

*An apostate Mormon, disillusioned with the power of the church's hier-
archy, described his change of mind. (Source: Holbæk-Posten, 28 August
1870. This letter initially appeared in Svendborgs Amts Tidende.)*

Omaha
17 May 1870

Dear Father-in-law,

You may be surprised to get a letter from me in this town,
nearly two thousand kilometers from Utah, the so-called "Zion." I
came here with my wife and child two weeks ago, and I'm sure I'll
never go back to my home in Utah. Religion caused me to leave
my beloved Denmark and, along with other simple, betrayed
people, undertake a very difficult and unpleasant journey to a

desert between the mountains in North America. I never appreciated my native country before I arrived in the desert, and
now, as so often in the past, I wish I were back in Denmark. It
would have been easy to return this year had I received a fair
price for the house and land I owned in Utah. But it has practically never been possible to acquire money out there, because
most trade is done by barter. I got only one-fourth of what I paid
for the house, but I don't care very much. The joy of having seen
through the swindling there and getting away from it makes up
for the loss.

I have a good job here as a carpenter and am paid three dollars
a day. I intend to work for a year, if God grants me good health,
save some money, and return to Denmark next year. I love that
country and think of it constantly. Since I can earn a good wage
here, though, I think it would be best to have some money when I
come back.

But let me tell you a little about Utah, because you don't know
how things really are there, even though I wrote to you so often. I
always kept quiet about the evil and abominable things that are
done there. I filled my letters with descriptions of high mountains
and Great Salt Lake as well as various religious reflections. Why
did I do so? Because something akin to the spirit of the papacy
permeates the Mormon establishment in Utah. One is threatened
with hell, eternal damnation, and excommunication. The last of
these means that the individual is ostracized and loses his job
because, according to Mormon doctrine, a backslider should not
have a job. Non-Mormons have no right to employment, and
apostates have even less. We were led to the funeral chapel to
swear an oath that we would submit to death if we ever denied
Mormon doctrines and so on. The constant fear of breaking these
oaths that we had supposedly made to God, and the uncertainty as
to whether all of this really was divine, made me pretend that two
and two were not four. Finally I realized that I was serving the
most repulsive society that I know. In Utah it is taught that unless
a man has more than one wife he is doomed. Because of that, and
out of sheer lust, many become polygamists. Men even marry
women who are mothers and daughters of each other. Cheating
and fraud are more common there than anywhere else because of
the barter system. I could fill ten pages and more with accounts of

dishonesty and immorality in Utah, but time does not allow it. I wanted nothing more than to take care of my wife and child and to have the opportunity to counter the scoundrels who go around in Denmark and deceive the people. I want to expose their real deeds and doctrines. Many, many letters have been written home to Denmark about the real situation in Utah, but converts to Mormonism won't believe them until they arrive in Utah. Then their eyes are opened.

An immigrant from Stenlille, Denmark, who went to Utah but decided against becoming a Mormon expressed his disenchantment in a letter to his family. (Source: Bornholms Tidende, 9 June 1882.)

Mendon, Utah
30 October 1881

I am well, but it is very boring for me here because my religion is not the Mormon religion, and I don't talk much with "the holy Mormons," as they call themselves in Denmark. They're certainly not holy here. In my opinion they're some of the biggest "monsters" the world can hold. They only care about getting money from the people who serve them. Whenever the preacher preaches in this town, they run to him and behave as though they were crazy.

This evening I visited K. Then a Dane and an Englishman came and demanded two and a half dollars. They claimed that the Lord had come down into the temple and said that every person should give half a dollar to build another temple for him. The present temple is good enough for people, but now they were supposed to build a better one for the Lord. The people actually believe such fables. They're mad at me because I don't want to become a Mormon, but I don't care. They accuse me of being a heathen because I don't believe what they say. I don't want to give the men half a dollar, and they can laugh at me if they want to.

One night recently one Mormon stole twenty-five kilograms of butter and two lamb thighs from another Mormon. Whenever anyone has stolen something here, he just asks for forgiveness. Once a man got the whim that he wanted two wives. He stole a

girl and hid her in a cellar for nineteen days. Then he took her to
Salt Lake City and married her. He sneaked her out of town at
night. That's how the "Saints" behave over here. Let us pray to
God that we never fall into such errors and blaspheme the Lord's
Word as the people here do. The Lord has been here on earth,
but he never spoke to Joseph Smith, Brigham Young, John
Taylor, or any of the twelve Mormon apostles or the seventy
scoundrels and foxes who live like parasites on the earnings of the
common people. May God punish them for their deceit and the
lies they tell the people! If the Mormons in Saltoste and Døjringe
knew how things are here, they would not come to Utah, but
rather quit the Mormon church and go back to the Lutheran faith.

The Mormon preachers lie that this is a good place to live and
that the Lord visits them and shows them places that have lain
fallow for many years. John Taylor is their president and god.
They pray to him just as a pastor in Denmark prays to God in
heaven. It's like a graven image to me when I hear that they pray
to a person who lives in Salt Lake City.

If you meet any Mormons, let them read these lines and listen
to what they have to say about such a holy land. You can't believe
what the Mormons write home, because they write nothing but
lies. After I get back to Denmark I'm going to tell the Latter-day
Saints exactly what their religion is. I expect to return home in a
year from the world's capital of lying, and that is just what this
place is.

· X ·

Disillusionment and Defeat

Although the number of Danish immigrants who returned to Denmark permanently was relatively low—as were the numbers of returning Swedes and Norwegians—many expressed varying degrees of disillusionment with their lot in the New World. Some had arrived with unrealistic expectations, having succumbed to the inveigling rhetoric of emigration agents, shipping lines, land companies, and other vested interests that thrived on the flow of immigrants. Others were the victims of natural catastrophes and crop failures that kept them in poverty. Some Danes found claims of American freedoms exaggerated, while to others materialism, the hectic pace of urban life, or the solitude of the prairie proved depressing.

Yet nothing shattered the dreams of immigrants more than the boom-and-bust cycles of the American economy. Usually lacking adequate housing, cash reserves, a firm command of English, or connections with well-established individuals, newly arrived Danes often fell victim to constrictions in the labor market. Those who disembarked immediately before or during the depressions of 1873 and 1893 were especially hard hit. Warnings not to emigrate filled their letters to younger siblings and others who were contemplating following in their wake. Many also wrote to the editors of their hometown newspapers, urging them to caution the townspeople to remain in Denmark. The letters in this chapter reflect the anguish of those and other lean years. It should be emphasized, however, that most Danish immigrants did not despair, despite emotional strains, the instability of the American economy, and other tribulations. The overwhelming majority of their letters were generally optimistic.

Anders Bertelsen, a farmer from Zealand, told a tale of unmitigated woe in the Danish area of Greenville, Michigan. (Source: Holbæk-Posten, 25 August 1870. This letter initially appeared in Sorø Amtstidende.)

Because we arrived here in Michigan in very bad condition and are leading a hard life, I am writing these lines in the hope that

you might be able to help us. There is neither work nor accommodations to be had here, so we are leading miserable lives.
My poor wife and children are crying out of despair. I wish we
had listened to you, brother! People are very poor here, and
it looks like there will be a crop failure. What will become of
us? . . .

We left Copenhagen on Maundy Thursday, sailed to Kristiansand, Norway, and from there to New York. There was a
headwind all the way, and we suffered immensely. Over here we
have reaped only misery and poverty. Our money all went for the
voyage, so now we are destitute in the middle of this wretched
country. There is nothing but forests and sand dunes here. I was
never seasick, but my wife and the children suffered a great deal.
We had to use four different railroads to reach this place and
were herded from one train to the next like animals. The children
were almost trodden underfoot. It was a dangerous voyage, and
what have we gained from it? We have wandered about miserably
here in America and live in a shack with neither a ceiling nor
windows. And since the harvest will be bad, what will happen to us
this winter? Please do what you can to help us! If there is anyone
who will pay our fare back to Denmark we will all be happy to
work. Our daughters are big and can work anywhere as servant
girls. Many tears were shed during the voyage over its difficulties
and because we worried about what was in store for us. America is
not like the descriptions of it; much different, in fact. I wasn't able
to make it farther than here to Greenville before my money ran
out. This is a message of grief, but my pen cannot express how
miserable our condition is.

*Difficulties involving prohibition and the eight-hour working day contrib-
uted to the disillusionment of an anonymous Dane in Omaha. (Source:
Kolding Folkeblad, 24 August 1892.)*

> Omaha, Nebraska
> North America
> 30 July 1892

For many years, probably as long as emigration to the United
States has taken place, Danes have generally believed that the

easiest thing in the world was to get rich in America. Twenty or thirty years ago the most fantastic stories came from here. That was when the gold rush in California and mining in neighboring western states were getting underway. Most will remember these wonderful, strange rumors that reached Denmark, tales of large nuggets found by more or less well-known persons. Then there were the stories about the elegance and luxury that even common laborers enjoyed in America. They were enough to quicken the pulse of even those who were not known for being credulous. They meshed well with the expectations of enjoyment and extravagance among the Danish peasantry in the 1860s, when progress in agriculture had lifted them up to a level where there was bright prospects. But as their incomes rose, so did the desire to acquire all kinds of things. For many, this desire increased faster than incomes, and a catastrophe was inevitable.

There were not many who accepted wholeheartedly the tales about the gold nuggets and so on, but there were a lot of printed and private letters encouraging people to "Come to America!" It has often hurt me to hear those voices, because I know how bitterly disappointed many will be. The purpose of this letter is to counter the feverish efforts to lure friends, relatives, and everyone else to the United States.

Of course, I don't suppose my words will have much effect, but I feel a need to get my countrymen to look objectively at conditions among North American workers. I fear I won't get any rest if I remain silent. I mean this seriously, and believe it is high time to eliminate the last remnant of the myth of America as the promised land. It is time to tell the Danish people that they will have to work for a living over here, just as anywhere else. I want to ask my countrymen back home to consider how well off they are, both spiritually and materially, before they decide to emigrate to America. Stay home, if you have a home; emigrate only if you find it intolerable to be in Denmark. Don't listen to the stories about high wages. They are always expressed in Danish currency and never mention the high prices here. Don't listen to the tales about the freedom-loving Americans; in many respects they are *humbug*. Thousands of people will agree with me that if there is any country where the aristocrats are in power, it is America.

To prove that I am justified in using a harsh word like *humbug*, let me give you a few examples taken from public life. I am thinking about *prohibition*, which forbids the production or sale of alcoholic beverages in Maine, Kansas, Iowa, and North and South Dakota. Then there is the latest news: the eight-hour day law enacted here in Nebraska last summer. It looks beautiful on paper, and both laws were intended to improve social conditions. But the way such laws are enforced is anything but beautiful. Consider prohibition. We need go no further than the small town of Council Bluffs in Iowa, right across the Missouri River. One saloon after the other lines the street, even though the state *legislature* and a referendum approved prohibition seven or eight years ago. At first liquor was sold secretly, but now it is sold openly. Everyone knows that the authorities are being bribed. That is a public secret.

The eight-hour day law was passed by the *legislature* in Lincoln last winter. According to this law nobody is allowed to work more than eight hours a day unless he is paid time and a half for every hour of overtime. (A few kinds of work are excepted.) Although the law was approved by Nebraska's supreme legislative body and went into effect on 1 August 1891, there is not a single place in Omaha (except work given by the city) where people feel obligated to obey it. Several of the large companies called in their workers one by one last July and asked them whether they preferred to work eight or ten hours a day. Partly out of fear that they might be fired, and partly because they feared that a shorter day meant less pay, most decided in favor of ten hours. This plebiscite was dutifully recorded, and now the financial barons plan to present it to the state legislature.

These examples should reveal the difficulties the American administration is experiencing these days. They also show how little is done to preserve the freedom that the American people, led by George Washington, acquired a century ago.

Many people seem to be impressed by the "freedom" and "equality" to keep their hats on when they meet a clergyman or government official, to enter a government office without knocking on the door, or to have permission to walk along the railroad tracks. But their ability to hold on to their rights is literally disappearing from their consciousness.

I shall not delve into purely economic matters. I realize that many Danish-Americans, both in town and in the country, are prospering. That is an undeniable fact. I shall only remark that migration has reached the Pacific Coast, and in the last few years it has turned back eastward. Unemployment is rising alarmingly in the cities, and there are complaints of a labor surplus everywhere. During the past four or five years the usual daily wage here in Omaha has dropped to about fifty cents.

There is one final thing that I have to mention. It takes a lot of spiritual humility to stand against the terrible, blasphemous masses who, like a whirlpool, try to pull in everyone and who have no equals when it comes to immorality. Parents should keep this in mind when their sons and daughters consider emigrating.

Poul Christian Andersen emigrated from the Rold Forest in northern Jutland in 1881. Following a visit to Denmark he told about the hardships of immigrant life. (Source: *Kors og Stjærne,* 15 March 1915. This letter initially appeared in *Den danske Pioneer.*)

Shawano, Wisconsin

Having returned to our home in America, my wife and I would like to thank all of our friends in Denmark for their hospitality and friendliness. Everyone will understand that after an absence of thirty-four years it would have been a great disappointment to see the old country declining, or that it had not lived up to our hopes and expectations. But we found everything just as we had hoped and wished, both in town and in the countryside.

I left my home area of Rold Skov thirty-four years ago and came haphazardly to America. I came to work and earn some money. For many winters I had to leave my wife and children and go to the big forests out west as a lumberjack, and come back when it thawed in the spring. In the summer I worked in the brickyards or took odd jobs. It was not long before I was well acquainted with the country and its conditions. After a few years I rented a farm in northernmost Wisconsin, up near the Indian country. I ran it for a while, my wife helping me faithfully all the while. When I was away working, she took care of all the farm business, which was always considerable. There was a lot to look after.

The year I spent in Denmark I kept track of what was happening, and I must tell anyone who is considering emigrating to America that if he believes he can earn a living more easily over here than in Denmark, he could not be more mistaken. People have to work here, and very hard at that. Without a lot of determination and a pair of strong arms, there is no point in even considering America. And anyone who has these things can unquestionably make just as good a living in Denmark.

It sounds beautiful, and it also looks beautiful, when fur-coated Americans visit Denmark at Christmas and tell about all the material goods they have over here. But they forget to mention all of the hardships they have had to endure. They also fail to mention those who failed completely—those people whom one sees frequently, despairing and helpless in a foreign country where, despite their good intentions, they have not been able to find any work at all.

As long as conditions are bright and times are good in Denmark, as they are now, I would advise in the strongest terms against coming over here.

At the moment a farmhand earns so little that he cannot save anything. If he does not want to save money, but is simply interested in having a good time, he can do that just as well wherever he is, and America has nothing special to offer him, either.

May the Lord keep his protecting hand over the dear old country and its people, and not allow war or other misfortune to befall it.

A Dane in Minnesota claimed that in many respects the highly touted "New Scandinavia" failed to live up to its reputation. (Source: *Holbæk Amts Avis,* 29 May 1885.)

Minneapolis
10 May 1885

Dear Editor,

Since discussing the very bad situation of workers in the United States in my previous letter, my report has been confirmed by a report that the Swedish-Norwegian ambassador in Washington has sent his government. I assume that his dispatch has come to the attention of my countrymen through the Danish press. I only wish to repeat one very interesting point, namely the charitable organization has not used the office in all instances, and that those who are responsible for their own plight seldom apply to charitable societies because they realize that it is useless, and, reveal that during the past three years it has investigated 45,000 families representing 180,000 individuals. Considering that the organization has not used the office in all instances, and that those who are responsible for their own plight seldom apply to charitable societies because they realize that it is useless, and, finally, that in a city like New York there are many other similar organizations, it is clear that the degree of need and misery is enormous. The same conditions can be found everywhere in this country. Therefore, I repeat: Stay home. All that glitters is not gold. To a considerable degree this is the workers' own fault; as long as they use their political rights against their own interests they cannot expect better conditions. I wish the dissatisfied could be put ashore in New York with five dollars in their pockets. That would cure them.

Before I emigrated to America I received a description of Minnesota from the agent of the Bremen Line in Copenhagen. Everything was described in glowing terms. Among other things, the climate was supposed to be extraordinarily pleasant. The truth is that Minnesota has completely tropical summers and Siberian winters. That is hardly "pleasant" for people who come from a temperate climate. Furthermore, the soil was allegedly extremely fertile, rich in humus atop a layer of marl. I have not been in all parts of Minnesota, but judging from what I have seen and heard the soil is usually fifteen to thirty centimeters deep, not especially rich, and has a layer of red sand under it. The grain that comes to Minneapolis from various areas of Minnesota would not be salable in Denmark. Moreover, the death rate in Minnesota, compared with that of the eastern states and Europe, supposedly proves that the climate here is extremely healthy. Some statistical tables were appended to prove that the death rate in Minnesota is significantly lower than elsewhere. It is completely justifiable to question the veracity of these reports. They are put out by railroad companies who have a vested interest in seeing the state populated. But even if the statistics are correct, they fail to prove anything. In a young state like Minnesota, where most of the people are immigrants, people in the prime of life, and where there are relatively few children or old people, mortality statistics naturally differ from those in the older eastern states, not to mention Europe.

If I have tried to counter the American propaganda, which is sent to Scandinavia by the ton, I in no way wish to deny that there is good, fertile land in the United States. That is a fact that cannot be denied. Do not believe, though, that our farmers are living under happy conditions. In many areas land that lies anywhere near a town or railroad station is just as expensive as in Denmark. Farther away from the towns, where the land is reasonably priced, farm produce is almost unmarketable. Even close to the railroads shipping is difficult. The farmers are subject to the tyranny of the railroad companies. Along the railroads the companies have built large elevators where the farmers can sell their grain, but they get a shamefully low price, which the railroads determine. No businessman dares to compete, because if he does he realizes that the railroad companies would demand such a high fee for transporting the produce that marketing it would be impossible.

Settlers in America are slaves of the railroad magnates. Nevertheless, a man can occasionally become rich, but only if circumstances are right. For example, if a railroad junction is built close to a man's property, and the resulting station grows into a town, he and all of the others in the vicinity instantly become millionaires.

An epidemic of Asian cholera is predicted to come to America this summer. As is well known, this unwelcome guest appears where conditions are least sanitary. If this prediction comes true, then prospects are not so bright for us in Minneapolis. I have never seen such horrible filth as in this city. Thousands of loads of manure and household trash are piled up in the yards, and some even in the streets. If a person has to remove some of it due to lack of space, he simply throws it into the Mississippi River, which provides the city's drinking water. The bodies of dead dogs and cats lie in the streets by the hundreds. Well-informed people claim the city has a health commission, but apparently the commission does not clamp down on peaceful citizens.

The Norwegians here are preparing to celebrate Norway's

Constitution Day on 17 May. They are divided into two camps.
Yesterday I spoke with a Norwegian who was extremely irritated
that one group had turned its festival arrangements over to the
"Danish" actor Waldemar Dahlbom. He was not satisfied with the
other group's festival committee, either. It was sufficiently
Norwegian, but it insisted on the "spirit of Wergeland,"[1] and he
thought that was demanding too much.

It is well known that the Americans do a great deal of
advertising. One method that is hardly known in Denmark is
rather common here. That which is supposed to be brought to the
attention of the public is painted on a large piece of canvas in
large letters of every possible color. This is then stretched across a
large wagon drawn by four horses decorated with countless
multicolored ribbons. A band of about fifteen or twenty musicians
sits in the wagon and plays while the wagon is driven slowly up
and down the streets of the entire city. On one side of the coach
an individual throws out small printed announcements. It must be
a rather expensive way of advertising.

I shall conclude with a joke taken from an American newspaper:

President Cleveland (to his private secretary): Have you been drinking
    this morning?
No Sir!
Is there a distillery here in the neighborhood?
Not as far as I know.
Then where is that repulsive odor coming from?
I don't know, unless it is from that Chicago alderman who is waiting
    in the next room and wishes to speak with you.
All right, but ask him to go over to Georgetown and speak with me
    on the telephone!

Peter Sørensen

1. The writer is referring to the prominent nineteenth-century Norwegian poet
Henrik Wergeland, who urged his countrymen to cast off the cultural hegemony that
Denmark exercised over Norway even after ceding it politically to Sweden in 1814.
It was largely due to his prompting that Norwegians began to celebrate the Seven-
teenth of May as Constitution Day.

An anonymous Dane in Chicago became discouraged in his efforts to help fellow immigrants find employment in the Windy City. (Source: Jyllands-posten, 5 July 1882.)

Chicago
14 June 1882

I will not befriend any emigration agents by doing this, but I shall try to give a brief description of conditions here. A frequent question in Scandinavia is: "Should I go to America?" If all who ask it would allow me to answer, I would definitely say "No."

The author of these lines has been a correspondent for *Jyllandsposten* for three years and has absolutely nothing to gain by misrepresenting the facts.

The reason is simple: There is no demand for labor. The emigration agents will tell those who desire to leave that I do not know anything about conditions here, or that if I do my information applies only to a single part of the country. But my letters to *Jyllandsposten* will dismiss such arguments, as they have been written in many different states from the Gulf of Mexico to the Canadian border. Besides, I have nothing to gain by persuading people to remain in Denmark.

There is only one class of people who are presently needed here and who shall continue to be needed—people with money who want to buy land, or people with a little money who want to get land free. But even homesteaders need some money, for one cannot claim land, build a house, not even a wooden one, and live until one has reaped the first harvest, without some cash.

Recently I have gone around with immigrants, not once but several times, and tried to help them find work. What kind of luck have we had? Everyone says they do not need anybody. Even cabinetmakers, who are usually in short supply, cannot find employment. A cabinetmaker has to go down one step and say that he will be satisfied to work as a carpenter, but there does not seem to be any demand for carpenters, either. Let me add that American carpenters need tools, and many who come over here cannot begin to work because they do not have enough money to buy tools.

If a cabinetmaker cannot find work in his own field and has tried without success to get a carpentry job, he begins to despair and says, "No, now I'll have to sweep the streets." But he discovers that others thought of that first and the streetsweeping jobs have been taken. If he finds work he discovers that the high wages disappear and that the attractive figure of two dollars a day is now a thing of the past.

The most intelligent thing to do is to wait until one has a little more than the cost of the voyage before one comes to America. It is fantastic to go to New York and see Central Park and the Obelisk. It is *grand* to see Niagara Falls crash down on the rocks, and, finally, it is fun to see *The Cable Railroad* in Chicago, where the trams run along the streets without steam, horses, or other visible means of power. But it is terribly boring if at the end of the voyage one does not find the employment that one hs relied on to get the basic necessities. It must be a miserable feeling to sit atop a green trunk in a foreign country and wait for a job. In recent times I have seen many people sitting like that, and I can assure you that it is anything but a happy sight. Even if one can help an immigrant find work and give him a little money, there are still many left who get more experience than food during their days in America.

The purpose of these lines is simply to warn people not to come here merely to make a living. Everyone needs enough money to support himself until he can find employment. I would be pleased, and it would benefit many people, if other newspapers would print this letter and thereby let their readers know that at the moment it is difficult to find work in America.

Near the end of the Civil War H. Døllner, the Danish consul in New York, advised Danish military officers not to expect positions as mercenaries in the Union army. (Source: *Berlingske Tidende*, 1 February 1865.)

Royal Danish Consulate
New York
10 January 1865

Many Danes come to New York without financial means or a knowledge of English. Among them are officers of the Danish army, who expect to find the same positions they had at home. Since many trained young men have served in the American army for several years, it does not not need foreign officers at present. Common soldiers will undoubtedly be accepted for some time and will receive good pay; efficient soldiers, who can write and speak English, can expect promotions. Skilled craftsmen and workers who can understand English can quickly find remunerative employment. But I warn my countrymen against coming here without funds or bringing their families before they are assured of work. Upon arrival here, Danish immigrants must beware of swindlers. Often they come to the consulate after they have gotten themselves into difficulty or fallen into the hands of swindlers who have sold them as soldiers. Then the consul can no longer help them. We recommend Poul Schou of 70 New Chamber Street as the honest and respectable proprietor of a boarding house. Room and board cost approximately one *rigsdaler* per day.

A Dane in Indiana listed several reasons for not emigrating to America. (Source: *Vendsyssel Tidende,* 23 June 1882).

16 May 1882

Dear Friends,

I have traveled around the United States a great deal and become acquainted with conditions here. Because I see that emigration from Denmark is growing, I am sending you these lines and advising you not to believe all the false accounts you hear about America, which are one cause of that large emigration. Real estate brokers and their lackeys, the agents, describe everything in such an attractive way when they travel around Denmark. You cannot even believe your best friends, because they are unreliable. Admittedly, land can be had here at a good price— and free in some places—but it is situated far from places of employment and trade. In this area the poor man and his family have to live in a sod house, and the family breadwinner must seek employment elsewhere, separated from his wife and children. Even if he can make a daily wage of four or six crowns in the summer he cannot really thrive, because it is impossible to find work in many places during the winter. Such a person has to put up with this situation for a long time before he gains any degree of financial independence. Everything is very expensive, and in many regions there is a little security for one's life and property. People who find themselves in such a situation wish they had never seen America and wish they could return home, but do not have enough money to do so. Yes, if people only knew what the poor immigrant has to endure, they would certainly stay home in dear old Denmark. For those people who have enough money to buy land in areas that are inhabited and not far from the railroad stations, life is more comfortable, but in those areas land is just as expensive as in Denmark. Furthermore, the climate is unhealthy in most regions, and even the water is bad. The best soil has too much water. There are stretches of land hundreds of kilometers long that are under water and cannot be drained because they are flat. Consequently, those who have money are better off in Denmark. Young people can earn good money in the summer. Laborers get eighty crowns a month plus board, but they are unemployed in the winter and use up their savings. Skilled tradesmen receive a good daily wage, eight to twelve crowns, but have to pay fourteen or sixteen crowns a week for food and seldom have work in the winter. I have spoken with many Danes who have lived in America for years without managing to save anything. They could just as well have remained in Denmark. In many places people live like heathens. If a child is born he is neither baptized nor taught anything about his soul. If a person becomes ill he falls victim to quacks who pretend to be doctors. Anyone can be a doctor in this country, and these butchers often make the patient more sick rather than cure him. If a person dies, he is buried like an animal, the only difference being the coffin.

I will therefore advise every Danish man and women to stay in peaceful Denmark. However, if this good advice cannot lower America fever, and it spreads to epidemic proportions and infects the healthy body of Danish society, only experience will show that the false voices that call from the land of Columbus are not telling the truth. Those who feel they absolutely must try their luck in America should book passage on one of the good Danish ships of the Thingvalla Line. All Scandinavians are satisfied with the way they are treated on that line. The food is much better than on

German and English ships. Unlike their competitors, the Danish ships do not take more passengers than they can accommodate comfortably, and emigrants can be sure that their luggage will not be mishandled.

Best regards for a happy future.

P. C. Pedersen
Transesville Post Office
Pulaski County
Indiana, America

A former sergeant in the Copenhagen police department who settled in Missouri described the United States as a land of hypocrisy and fraud. (Source: Bornholms Avis, 9 August 1870).

Newspapers often carry articles proclaiming the advantages of emigrating to America—the good life that awaits the newcomer, the ease of earning a fortune, the so-called "freedom" and "equality," and so on. Very seldom does one find a different description of the matter or a warning to the blind individuals who, for the most part, are heading for disaster in the New World. Hence, I would like to give a short description of conditions in America, and I sincerely hope that my countrymen will ponder my words seriously.

As far as I know, none of my friends or relatives in Denmark want to emigrate, and I certainly have nothing to gain from preventing my countrymen from doing so. It hurts, though, to see all of the adversity and misery that immigrants suffer here, and I regard it as my duty as a human and a compatriot to do my best to present the conditions here in a correct light. I have been in America for four years and see no prospect of seeing my greatest wish fulfilled—to live in dear old Denmark once again. Rather than focusing on myself, however, I simply wish to enlighten my countrymen that it is to their great advantage to remain at home in their fatherland.

I will pass over the difficulties of the Atlantic crossing, because those hardships are nothing compared to the troubles that begin after the immigrant has landed in New York. He is constantly regarded as a potential victim by criminals and cheaters who try to separate him from every coin he owns and, if he has none, he is referred to a so-called "immigrant society," which merely tries to steer him out of the large cities, where as many as twenty thousand hapless immigrants are unemployed and hungry. Most of them are compelled to sell the clothes they brought along at an absurdly low price in order to keep body and soul together.

Even after the immigrant has managed to get away from the city, in most cases he is still unable to find remunerative employment and must be content to work for room and board. After he has finally learned a little of the language, he might be fortunate enough to find a job paying twelve to sixteen dollars a month, unless his health has succumbed to the fever that is everywhere.

He must put up with being looked upon condescendingly by the Americans, most of whom assume that all immigrants are convicts who were ne'er-do-wells in the old country. He soon discovers that the celebrated "freedom" and "equality" of America exist only in theory. In Denmark we are accustomed to order in all things, but that is not the case here. What order can there be in a country where everyone wants to rule and where every official, from the senators right down to the sheriff or policeman, is a crook? Every day the newspapers carry a story about this senator or that representative being indicted for fraud or bribery.

And what about "religion"? How is it treated here? In this country there are droves of people who wander about calling themselves clergymen, but in reality they are people who are too lazy to work and who therefore choose to live by the sweat of the common man's brow. These "clergymen" are constantly bickering with one another, and no abomination is so bad that one of them would resist committing it to reach his goal. Swearing, lying, and giving false testimony are normal behavior for them. If you want proof of this, simply read any of the Scandinavian-American newspapers and you will discover that I am not exaggerating at all, or wait until you arrive here and you will see the truth of this.

I am well acquainted with conditions here and speak from experience, and I must advise in the strongest terms anyone who can remain in Denmark not to emigrate to America. If someone wants to come anyway, he must have enough money to buy a piece of land. That is the best and probably the only safe thing to do, but above everything keep this warning in mind and in the course of time you will discover to your regret that you acted unwisely by not following my advice.

There is one more important thing that I must mention, namely the climate, which is not like the climate in Denmark. The summer is especially unbearable. For quite some time the temperature here has been thirty or thirty-two degrees Celsius, and it is impossible for anyone who is not accustomed to such heat to work for long in the sun.

Another evil that plagues this country, particularly the rural areas, are people who call themselves "doctors" or "attorneys." Anyone can practice medicine without passing an examination or being subjected to any kind of control. These quacks have killed a large number of people, but the authorities have not done anything to change the system. The attorneys are almost as bad; they do not take your life, but they steal all of your worldly possessions.

Put all these things together and compare them with conditions back in Denmark. Judge for yourself how advisable it is to come to America! Don't believe anyone who writes to you and claims that things are going well for him in America. I know many people who have written to their families back home, telling them that they were prospering here. After those friends and relatives had been lured to America, they discovered that "prosperity" meant not having enough clothes to keep themselves warm, and that their friend or relative who had preceded them was only after their money, clothing, and labor. In no case can you believe emigration agents or others who travel around Denmark seducing young people into coming to America, for those scoundrels profit from collecting as many emigrants as possible.

Consult experienced and honest people, and you will discover that in almost all instances they will advise you against emigrating.

In conclusion I will remark that not everyone who comes to America is in bad straits, but I do not believe I am exaggerating when I maintain that only one out of one hundred is truly happy, and only ten out of one hundred eke out even a marginal existence. The others either meet disaster or lead miserable lives. Isolated and shunned in a foreign country, with tears in their eyes, they look back to the fatherland where they had friends, relatives, and other sympathetic people.

E. H. Bylov
Rolla, Missouri
5 July 1870

Index

The contents of the immigrant letters as well as the Preface, the Introduction, and the introductions to the individual chapters and letters are comprehensively indexed. Special emphasis has been placed on the names of the writers, the provenance of the letters, and the most important topics mentioned in these documents. Readers desiring information about the relationship of Danish immigrants to specific subjects, such as Indians or the Homestead Act, are advised to consult both the appropriate entry in the index and the chapter or chapters in which the particular subject might be most likely to occur. The thematic format of the entire compilation is intended to facilitate such searching.

3ₒω   ک
1ₒω
m